# 'DEATH OF A SALESMAN' IN BEIJING

**Arthur Miller** was born in New York City in 1915. After graduating from the University of Michigan, he began work with the Federal Theatre Project. His first Broadway hit was *All My Sons*, closely followed by *Death of a Salesman, The Crucible* and *A View from the Bridge*. His other writing include *Focus*, a novel; *The Misfits*, first published as a short story, then as a cinema novel; *In Russia, In the Country, Chinese Encounters* (all in collaboration with his wife, photographer Inge Morath) and '*Salesman' in Beijing*, non-fiction; and his autobiography, *Timebends*, published in 1987. Among his other plays are: *Incident At Vichy, The Creation of the World and Other Business, The American Clock, The Last Yankee, Resurrection Blues* and *Finishing the Picture*. His novella, *Plain Girl*, was published in 1995 and his second collection of short stories, *Presence*, in 2007. He died in February 2005 aged eighty-nine.

**Dr Claire Conceison** is a director, translator, and scholar based at Duke University and MIT. Her teaching and scholarship focus on theater in China, play translation, Asian American theater, and sport as performance. She is the author of *Significant Other: Staging the American in China* (2004) and co-author with Ying Ruocheng (1929–2003) of his autobiography *Voices Carry: Behind Bars and Backstage during China's Revolution and Reform* (2009).

*By the same author*

*Plays*
After the Fall
All My Sons
The American Clock
The Archbishop's Ceiling
Broken Glass
The Creation of the World and Other Business
The Crucible
Danger: Memory!
Death of a Salesman
An Enemy of the People (*adapted from Ibsen*)
Finishing the Picture
The Golden Years
Incident at Vichy
The Last Yankee
The Man Who Had All the Luck
A Memory of Two Mondays
Mr Peters' Connections
The Price
Resurrection Blues
The Ride Down Mount Morgan
Two-Way Mirror
Up From Paradise (*musical*)
A View from the Bridge

*Screenplays*
The Crucible
Everybody Wins
The Misfits
Playing for Time

*Fiction*
Focus
I Don't Need You Any More
Jane's Blanket (*for children*)
Plain Girl
Presence: Stories

*Non-fiction*
*The Crucible* in History and Other Essays
Echoes Down the Corridor: Collected Essays 1944–2000
On Politics and the Art of Acting
'*Salesman*' in Beijing
Situation Normal
The Theatre Essays of Arthur Miller

*With Inge Morath*
Chinese Encounters
In Russia
In the Country

*Autobiography*
Timebends

# 'DEATH OF A SALESMAN' IN BEIJING

## ARTHUR MILLER

Photographs by Inge Morath

Introduction by Claire Conceison

Bloomsbury Methuen Drama
An imprint of Bloomsbury Publishing Plc

BLOOMSBURY
LONDON · OXFORD · NEW YORK · NEW DELHI · SYDNEY

**Bloomsbury Methuen Drama**
An imprint of Bloomsbury Publishing Plc

Imprint previously known as Methuen Drama

| 50 Bedford Square | 1385 Broadway |
| London | New York |
| WC1B 3DP | NY 10018 |
| UK | USA |

**www.bloomsbury.com**

**BLOOMSBURY, METHUEN DRAMA and the Diana logo are trademarks of Bloomsbury Publishing Plc**

Originally published as *'Salesman' in Beijing* in 1984 in hardback and subsequently in paperback by Methuen London Ltd.

Reissued in 1991 and 2005 by Methuen Drama

First published as *'Death of a Salesman' in Beijing* in 2015 by Bloomsbury Methuen Drama
This paperback edition first published 2017

Copyright © 1983, 1984, 1991, 2005, 2015 Arthur Miller

Preface copyright © 1991 Arthur Miller

Photographs copyright © 1983, 1984 Inge Morath/The Inge Morath Foundation/Magnum Photos

Introduction copyright © 2015 Bloomsbury Methuen Drama

This paperback edition first published 2017

All rights reserved.

Arthur Miller has asserted his right under the Copyright, Designs and Patents Act, 1988, to be identified as author of this work.

All rights reserved. No part of this publication may be reproduced or transmitted in any form or by any means, electronic or mechanical, including photocopying, recording, or any information storage or retrieval system, without prior permission in writing from the publishers.

No responsibility for loss caused to any individual or organization acting on or refraining from action as a result of the material in this publication can be accepted by Bloomsbury or the author.

**British Library Cataloguing-in-Publication Data**
A catalogue record for this book is available from the British Library.

ISBN: HB: 978-1-4725-9208-8
PB: 978-1-4725-9204-0
ePDF: 978-1-4725-9205-7
ePub: 978-1-4725-9206-4

Cover design by Louise Dugdale and Eleanor Rose
Cover image: Arthur Miller (centre) and Ying Ruocheng (right) examine a set model for the 1983 Beijing production of *Death of a Salesman* while Inge Morath (left) observes and photographs.
Photo by Su Dexin. Courtesy of Beijing People's Art Theatre

Typeset by RefineCatch Limited, Bungay, Suffolk

To find out more about our authors and books visit www.bloomsbury.com
Here you will find extracts, author interviews, details of forthcoming events and the option to sign up for our newsletters.

# CONTENTS

Introduction by Claire Conceison, 2015   viii
Preface to the 1991 edition by Arthur Miller, 1991   xxxiii
How it happened by Arthur Miller   xxxvi
Acknowledgments   xxxix
List of images   xli

*'Death of a Salesman'* in Beijing   1

# INTRODUCTION

BY CLAIRE CONCEISON, 2015

## Acknowledgments

For their kind assistance in China with archival materials, photographs, and interviews, I thank Liu Zhixin and Sun Huizhu (William Sun) of the Shanghai Theatre Academy; Nick Rongjun Yu, Lei Guohua, and Xie Jingying at Shanghai Dramatic Arts Centre; Wang Xiaoying at the National Theatre of China; Yang Lixin, Yang Le, Pu Cunxin, Mi Tiezeng, Li Shilong, Li Liuyi, Zhang Minyi, and Liu Zhangchun of the Beijing People's Art Theatre; and Mechele Leon of the University of Kansas. My gratitude to Arthur Miller and Ying Ruocheng, a decade after their passing, remains profound.

## Introduction

In their book *Chinese Encounters*, Arthur Miller and his wife, photographer Inge Morath, provide a textual and visual account of their maiden voyage to China in 1978. Miller begins the text that accompanies Morath's photographs with an illustrative anecdote about his cultural re-encounter, upon his return to the United States, with something formerly considered mundane and meaningless—two neglected pencil sharpeners perched on his desk:

> If a visiting foreigner—let us say a Chinese—were ever to notice them, he might well wonder why they were there since people always apply a logic abroad which they would never dream of using at

home. . . . The moral, as I see it, is that no one can think he knows a country until he can easily separate its merely idiosyncratic absurdities from its real contradictions. We do not 'know' China when we still notice and are even startled by things no Chinese pays the slightest attention to. But the ability to be surprised is a virtue in a photographer, especially if like Inge Morath her eye can be caught while her mind is informed with knowledge of the Chinese language and a long familiarity with China's arts.

Morath and Miller 1979: 7

Unpacking Miller's seemingly common-sense observation is trickier than meets the eye: the dialectic he identifies calls for a simultaneous perspective from both within and outside a culture; self-reflexivity on the part of the transient foreigner; and the ability to discern the absurd from the real, as well as the noteworthy from the irrelevant. His statement asks us to examine how we "know" another nation, another culture, another history—and it acknowledges that the artist "knows" these things—literally, *sees* things—differently.

Miller's observation about his wife's sensitivity as a photographer can be compared to the same sensitivity in the playwright, the actor, the translator. Isn't it precisely the gift of such artists to draw our attention to the two pencil sharpeners facing each other on the desk in such a way that we discover—in that which we had formerly overlooked—a profound truth about ourselves and our existence? If so, what do we make of Miller's observation about cultural difference, and about being startled by those things to which the native citizen pays no attention? What is the distinction between the tourist's ignorant gaze and the artist's keen eye? How did Arthur Miller's 1983 experience directing *Death of a Salesman* in Beijing turn a fresh gaze on theater-making in mainland China? And how does our revisiting that production now, during the centennial year of Miller's birth, shed new light on his perception and understanding of China at the time, as well as his impact and legacy then, now, and in the future?

Arthur Miller arrived in China long before he and his wife Inge Morath actually visited in 1978. His early plays first became available in English in Beijing at the same time they became available in the United States, in American literature collections at elite institutions like Tsinghua University, a college with a mix of Chinese and foreign faculty offering instruction in both Chinese and English.[1] It was at Tsinghua that Ying Ruocheng, an undergraduate student from a privileged Manchu family, first read the play *Death of a Salesman* at a librarian's recommendation in December 1949, less than a year after the play had premiered in the US on Broadway and only a few months after the establishment of the People's Republic of China by the Chinese Communist Party. In his autobiography, Ying recalls that he had never heard of the play or its playwright before, but that his first encounter with *Salesman* was transformative:

> I took it away, and started reading it, and I finished it that same night. I was so drawn to the play, but immediately thought it would be impossible to produce at that time in China [. . .] But it left a very deep impression on me. I was the president of the student drama club [and] I dreamed of staging three plays in particular: *The Corn is Green*, *Major Barbara*, and *Death of a Salesman*.[2]

Ying would graduate from Tsinghua the following year and become a founding member of the Beijing People's Art Theatre, China's premiere theatre company. In 1983, he would fulfill his dream of staging *Salesman*, in a landmark cross-cultural collaboration with its playwright, Arthur Miller, that established a deep bond between the two men, as detailed in Miller's diary here. Miller mentions Ying Ruocheng on the first page of the original edition of this book, the last page of this book, and almost every page in between, and Ying's image is featured on the cover of every version of the book that has been published and in many of the photographs inside. The production of *Death of a Salesman* in Beijing was truly a partnership, one quite unique in the history of intercultural theater collaborations. In addition to the many other valuable insights in this book, it is the record of a great friendship between two of the most formidable artists and intellectuals of the twentieth century in their respective countries (see Figure I.1).

---

[1] Tsinghua University was originally established in 1911 as a preparatory school for Chinese students embarking on studies in the United States through the Boxer Indemnity Scholarship Program, a fund created by President Theodore Roosevelt from the excess of the Qing government's payment of indemnity after being defeated in the Boxer Rebellion.
[2] *The Corn is Green* was produced at Tsinghua University before Ying Ruocheng graduated in 1950 (his future wife, Wu Shiliang played the lead role opposite him), and Ying collaborated with Miller to stage *Death of a Salesman* in 1983. He directed *Major Barbara* at the same theater company in 1991. See Ying and Conceison 2009: 122–4.

# INTRODUCTION

**Figure I.1** Ying Ruocheng and Arthur Miller during rehearsal for *Death of a Salesman* at Beijing People's Art Theatre in 1983 (photograph by Su Dexin, courtesy of Beijing People's Art Theatre).

The pair first met when Miller came to Beijing on his aforementioned visit with Morath in 1978, hosted by the US–China Peoples Friendship Association (USCPFA), while Ying was in the midst of preparing for a forthcoming visiting appointment at the University of Missouri at Kansas City (UMKC).[3] China was just beginning to open after the Cultural Revolution (1966–1976) and Ying was shocked that the American playwright he had so admired for the past thirty years was actually in town. He and Beijing People's Art Theatre president, the renowned playwright Cao Yu, introduced Miller to writers and artists during his 1978 visit so he could learn about their sufferings during the recent decade of political turmoil. Based on those revelations, Miller suggested, two years later, that the best play for a potential collaboration in China would be his 1953 hit *The Crucible*. He felt its depiction of the historical Salem witch hunt (standing in for the McCarthy-era purges) provided an

---

[3] As a visiting artist/professor at UMKC in 1982, Ying Ruocheng directed his translation and adaptation of Ba Jin's novel *Family* (*Jia*) with a cast of college students; this production was videotaped and aired repeatedly on national television in China after Ying Ruocheng's return, enthusiastically received by critics and the public.

ideal metaphor for the targeting of Chinese intellectuals who endured endless campaigns during the Cultural Revolution.

As Ying recalls, these initial conversations with Miller took place in 1980 when he and Cao Yu visited the United States to arrange for a touring production of the play *Teahouse* from their theater company (a tour that never materialized),[4] and continued in 1982 while Ying was a visiting professor at UMKC:

> [Arthur] suggested *The Crucible* because he had heard so much about persecution during his visit in 1978—laments of intellectuals who were wrongly accused during the Cultural Revolution and so forth. I had to convince him to choose another play [. . .] I wouldn't allow my unfulfilled dream of staging *Death of a Salesman* to be shattered, so I tried my best to convince Arthur that just a story of persecution like *The Crucible* wasn't enough anymore. The whole trauma in China had gone much deeper than just the persecution of intellectuals anyway. There would not have been any particular danger in producing *The Crucible* in the early 1980s, contrary to Miller's perception. Such tales were common—in fact, they were the fashion at the time. It was the period of *shanghen wenxue* (scar literature), with so many works of literature exposing the persecutions suffered during the Cultural Revolution, so in that respect *The Crucible* would not have been something new—whereas *Death of a Salesman* was truly a breath of fresh air, especially because of the way it was staged.[5]

The first production of one of Arthur Miller's plays in China would indeed be *The Crucible*, staged at the Shanghai People's Art Theatre in 1981,

---

[4] This 1980 visit with Cao Yu to the United States was Ying Ruocheng's first travel abroad to the West (at the age of 51). At the time that Ying met Miller in 1978 in Beijing, he had never traveled outside of China. Arthur Miller is mistaken when he claims in his preface to '*Salesman' in Beijing* that Ying had "some personal experience in the United States" when they first met. The touring production of *Teahouse* that Cao and Ying tried to promote on their visit to the US in 1980 never materialized—though the play toured to Europe, Japan, and Taiwan during Ying's lifetime (with him in the role of Pockmark Liu), it never reached the United States. It was not until 2005 that *Teahouse* finally toured to the US (with a different, younger cast than its original version), two years after Ying Ruocheng had died. It was Ying's translation that was used for the surtitles in English at performances, and the production marked the first time a spoken drama by a professional Chinese theater company had ever been performed in the United States. Ying's translation of *Teahouse* has been published by China Translation and Publishing Corporation (1999) and in Chen (2010).
[5] Ying and Conceison 2009: 160.

directed by one of China's greatest directors of the twentieth century, Huang Zuolin (1906–1994). Miller met Huang during his first trip to China in 1978. Though fluent in English and well acquainted with British and European dramatists, Huang was previously unaware of Miller's plays or his stature as a playwright in the United States. He prepared for meeting Miller by reading an article about him that had been published in a Chinese journal, written by Mei Shaowu, the son of famed Beijing opera actor Mei Lanfang. After meeting Miller in person and discussing his plays, Huang decided to stage *The Crucible* at Miller's recommendation, and he commissioned Mei Shaowu to translate the script.[6] Not surprisingly, Huang Zuolin's production included deliberate allusions to the Cultural Revolution that echoed the "scar literature" discourse of the day. Critically well received, it ran for fifty-two performances (see Figure I.2).[7]

**Figure I.2** The first staging of an Arthur Miller play in China: *The Crucible* (renamed *The Witches of Salem*) at Shanghai People's Art Theatre in 1981, directed by Huang Zuolin. In this scene, a confession of witchcraft is forced from Tituba. "Realistic makeup" was used to depict Tituba's Barbados ethnicity and the Anglo identity of other characters (photograph by Jiang Jie'an, courtesy of Shanghai Dramatic Arts Centre).

---

[6] See Ou Rong and Qian Zhaoming 2013.
[7] Han Dexing 2014: 74. In order to attract audiences, Mei Shaowu changed the title to "The Witches of Salem" (*Salamu nüwu*), the title under which the play is still produced in China today.

Two years later, *Death of a Salesman* was chosen for the Miller collaboration in Beijing over both *The Crucible* and *All My Sons* because it introduced newer and more challenging aspects of modern theatre to Chinese artists and audiences who had been deprived of such fresh forms during the Cultural Revolution. The structuring of time in the play, the development of character, the tension between inner psychology and outward action, between fantasy and memory, and the formal blending of realism and expressionism—all of these are described by scholars of Chinese theater as breakthroughs on the Chinese stage for which Miller and his play are credited.[8] As Ying Ruocheng elaborates:

> [A]t the time that Miller wrote the play he was rather keen on trying out new forms. For instance, the walls didn't exist for the people in the play anymore, especially for the central character, Willy Loman. Willy could walk through any wall. He could communicate with whomever he was in the mood to. And Arthur created the necessary ambience for such things to be believable, to be credible. People were shocked—especially Chinese audiences, who were not accustomed to this kind of surrealistic style . . . (160–1)

Ying Ruocheng was a strong advocate for staging *Salesman*, both because of the impact it had had on him in his youth and because he felt it was the most representative of Miller's works as the play that had jumpstarted his formidable career. Miller, who had originally preferred *The Crucible* or *All My Sons*, agreed to *Salesman*, insisting that Ying both play Willy Loman and do a new translation of the play.[9] Ying Ruocheng's script became a renowned case study in Chinese–English drama translation.[10] Completing the task in only six weeks in preparation for Miller's arrival, Ying's 1983 version differed from the existing 1979–1980 translation by Chen Liangting because he maintained Miller's linguistic style, but infused the dialogue with colloquial Beijing speech and local flavor, one of the hallmarks of Beijing People's Art Theatre plays by local Beijing playwrights.[11] While the language spoken by the

---

[8] Han Dexing 2014: 76.
[9] Ying and Conceison 2009: 161.
[10] Deng Di 2008: 149–51.
[11] Wu Ge 2006: 54.

**INTRODUCTION** xv

Lomans emerged from the *hutongs* (lanes) of Beijing, their utterances were still situated in a Brooklyn, New York context.

This cultural hybridity would become an important aspect of the play in its rehearsal process, audience reception, and enduring critical legacy. As Miller discusses throughout his diary, and Brenda Murphy analyzes in her survey of several international stagings of *Death of a Salesman*, a central question of the Beijing production was defining the location of the action as well as the nationality and ethnicity of the Lomans. In employing Beijing dialect and slang in his approximation of Miller's colloquial New York English, Ying Ruocheng attempted to replicate "language that would have been spoken in a crowded Chinese city at the end of the 1940s," while preserving all references to places like Yonkers and Brooklyn. Ying asserts that "the best result is when the play is performed and, after five minutes, the audience forgets about the actors' appearance and ethnicity and buys into the belief that they're watching Americans." According to Ying, as Miller journeyed through the rehearsal process, he began to see the cast as a second-generation Chinese family in Brooklyn.[12]

Mi Tiezeng, the actor who played Happy in the Beijing production, recalls that Miller continuously encouraged him not to imitate a foreigner, but told him to "act yourself" (*yan ni ziji*).[13] Playing an American onstage for the first time, Li Shilong as Biff wanted to please the distinguished guest director, though he had never heard of him before and had never read his plays. Li's strongest memory—one shared by every member of the cast I have interviewed (including Ying Ruocheng and Zhu Xu, who played Charley)—is of Miller timing every scene of each rehearsal with a stopwatch. Miller insisted that the pace of the play be precisely the same as the Broadway production of his original English version. Li admits that at first he found this bizarre, but gradually he came to realize that this constraint placed on the actors prompted a transformation that shifted from external to internal: when actors had to speed up their lines, it resulted in less overacting and more "natural" delivery of dialogue with clearer motivations. Miller explained to the actors that the play was written for everyone, not just Americans, and that mothers, fathers, sons, and brothers are similar all over the world. "He told us to act like a

---

[12] Ying and Conceison 2009: 162–3.
[13] Interview with Mi Tiezeng at Beijing People's Art Theatre, July 3, 2014.

Chinese mother, father and son," Li recalls.[14] Miller describes the result of this process as "creating something not quite American or Chinese, but a pure style springing from the heart of the play itself—the play as a non-national event, that is, a human circumstance" and concludes that the actors became "Lomans-as-Chinese-looking-people [placing] them in some country of the mind . . . not in any earthly geography."[15] Li and others emphasize that this new approach to Chinese actors playing foreigners became the model that subsequent productions of Western plays at the Beijing People's Art Theatre followed (Figure I.3).

Introducing a new stage aesthetic to China, just as it had in the United States when it premiered in 1949, Miller's production of *Death of*

**Figure I.3** Willy, Biff, and Happy (Ying Ruocheng, Li Shilong, and Mi Tiezeng) in the 1983 production of *Death of a Salesman* at Beijing People's Art Theatre, directed by Arthur Miller (photograph by Su Dexin, courtesy of Beijing People's Art Theatre).

---

[14] Interview with Li Shilong at Beijing People's Art Theatre, January 2, 2015.
[15] Miller 1983: 155, 172, cited in Murphy 1995: 123.

*a Salesman* in Beijing in 1983 challenged (and ultimately rejected) the conventional practice of using "realistic makeup" (*xianshi huazhuang*) in the form of facial pigment, wigs, and nose and chin prosthetics for Chinese actors playing foreign roles. In reimagining the Loman family as a Chinese American family living in Brooklyn, whether or not that was a reality local audiences could grasp, the production evoked culturally integrated reception: the unfamiliar story of the plight of a New York salesman, set in a particularly American domestic and national idiom, portrayed through the bodies, faces, and linguistic expression of Chinese actors who remained, for the most part, "Chinese." A frequently discussed legacy of Miller's direction of *Salesman* in Beijing is this departure from the conventional Chinese practice of using costumes, makeup, and mannerisms to convey a "real" foreigner (though of course that reality is highly imagined, resulting in an effect similar to the "yellowface" adopted in American films of an earlier era, such as *The Good Earth*, in which Western actors portray Chinese characters). As Chinese scholars William Sun and Wu Ge have both pointed out, Miller was resistant to adopting the entrenched Chinese tradition of realistic makeup attempting racial verisimilitude onstage because of American political associations with disparaging simulation of racial identity in performance forms such as minstrelsy. Sun and Wu assert that this resistance reveals a lack of familiarity or deep understanding of the history and effects of these practices in China.[16]

The "wig incident" (*jiafa shijian*), as it has come to be known, is one of the most often cited events of the entire production process of the mounting of *Death of a Salesman* at the Beijing People's Art Theatre. Miller describes the event in great detail in his account and Ying notes its significance, as do all cast members I have interviewed, as well as published scholarship about the production in both Chinese and English.[17] In his diary entries from April 25–29, Miller recounts his struggle to convince the costume, makeup, and wig staff at the theater—

---

[16] For more on the issue of cross-ethnic casting in China, including case studies of plays from 1987 to 2002, see Conceison, *Significant Other: Staging the American in China* (2004). See also Sun's full discussion of the issue in his essays "Power and Problems of Performance across Ethnic Lines" (2000) and "Arthur Miller: A Dramatist Full of Paradox" (2005).

[17] Miller 1984: 179–207, 233 (esp. 181–6); Ying and Conceison 2009: 163–4; Murphy 1995: 122–4; Wu 2006: 54–5; Sun 2000: 91–2; Sun 2005.

appealing to Ying Ruocheng as the linguistic and cultural bridge between them—to abandon their plans to wig and make up the entire cast to look like foreigners. This causes not only a substantial loss of face for the hardworking staff, but also leaves them (and some of the actors) bewildered. As Brenda Murphy points out, "Chinese actors felt naked on stage without heavy make-up and wigs."[18] While Miller was sensitive to these ramifications, he stood his ground, identifying the central conflict as the actors "want[ing] to imitate Americans, to play-act people they are not, when what I want is exactly who and what they really are."[19]

This telling moment, of course, strikes at the heart of fundamental questions of both artistic practice in the theater (playing "the Other" on stage) and of cross-cultural perceptions off stage. While for Miller, the actors donning wigs in rehearsal conjured blackface minstrelsy and Hollywood excess, and made them "weirdly unidentifiable, not only as individuals, but as humans," for the cast members themselves it was a tool long used in their acting training to play foreign roles.[20] The earliest modern Western dramas in China at the dawn of the twentieth century employed a more presentational style of acting, but as Wu Ge illuminates, once Stanislavski's techniques were introduced in China via Soviet experts in the 1950s, the relationship between actor and character shifted from "I play" to "I am," making actors more—not less—dependent on makeup and wigs to achieve this transformation.[21] In short, while Miller regarded actors approximating the physical appearance of foreigners as off-putting and alienating due to his own aesthetic training

---

[18] Murphy 1995: 122.
[19] Miller 1984: 182.
[20] Miller 1984: 182.
[21] The origin of Chinese *huaju* (spoken drama) is traced to a stage adaptation of *Uncle Tom's Cabin* created and performed by overseas Chinese students in Tokyo in 1907. Shortly thereafter, spoken drama troupes were formed in cities like Shanghai and Beijing, and Western plays such as Ibsen's *A Doll's House* and Wilde's *Lady Windermere's Fan* were staged alongside plays in the new Western form written by Chinese dramatists like Tian Han and Cao Yu. This "Westward gaze" in the theater began as part of a larger cultural shift (marked by the New Culture and May Fourth Movements) toward the vernacular in literature and toward adopting Western models to address China's social issues. It is important to note that Western-style drama was deliberately imported to China by pioneering Chinese intellectuals and not disseminated by foreign colonizers as was the case in many non-Western societies. Thus, Chinese spoken drama has a long history as a "Sinified" cultural form used for domestic purposes, as well as a long history of adapting new trends via the temporary visits of foreigners who came to China as collaborators or performers.

and socio-political circumstances, Chinese actors found the absence of these markers off-putting and alienating on the same basis: Chinese actors *feel* more like foreigners when they do not *look* physically Chinese. Miller's authority as the director, as author of the play, and as a real foreigner trumped the comfort and conventions of the cast and artistic staff of the theater, with Ying Ruocheng as the conduit for each side to comprehend the perspective of the other. A compelling question remains whether this lasting legacy of how foreigners have been portrayed at the Beijing People's Art Theatre from 1983 up until the present reflects the liberation of isolated Chinese artists, as Miller interpreted it, or the vestiges of neo-imperialism that shape Chinese practices according to Western models. Participants, audiences and scholars of the production debate the ultimate cultural meaning of this shift, but all acknowledge that the practice of Chinese actors playing foreigners on stage was forever changed by Miller's visit to China.[22]

Arthur Miller's influence in China emanating from *Death of a Salesman* in 1983 goes far beyond removing wigs and makeup. In the wake of the production, several new Chinese plays that adopted some of its hybrid realist-expressionist techniques found their way to the stage, most notably Jin Yun's *Uncle Doggie's Nirvana* (1986), which imitated elements of *Salesman*'s structure, character, and even plot: the main character is a peasant struggling to keep his land who throws himself in front of a fire at the end of the play, hinting at suicide.[23] In terms of the long-term influence of the actual collaboration with Miller on his actors and the impact of the live performance on audiences, cast members fondly recall the director's supportive, caring manner toward actors, and they speak of working with Miller as one of the most enriching and satisfying experiences of their careers. They also describe the deep impression that seeing the production left on individual audience members, including a Peking

---

[22] For more on this and an overview of the Ying-Miller collaboration and its impact on Chinese theater, see Ou and Qian, 2013.

[23] *Uncle Doggie's Nirvana* (*Gou'er ye niepan*) is widely regarded as the most significant Chinese play of the 1980s. Directed by Lin Zhaohua, it won the National Best Play Award in 1986. Ying Ruocheng directed his own English translation of the play at Virginia Commonwealth University in 1993, the same year he directed *Death of a Salesman* at the College of William and Mary (about which he notes, "I must admit that when I was directing *Salesman*, it felt rather odd at times to be explaining to American actors how Americans behave" (184)).

University professor who was so moved by the play that he walked all the way back to the campus reflecting on it afterwards (a distance of 11 miles).[24] In her survey of international productions of *Salesman* beginning with the first European production in Vienna in 1950, Murphy notes that the "universal indicator of a successful production" of the play is an opening night audience with tears in their eyes sitting frozen in "awed silence" for a prolonged period and then erupting in a crescendo of applause.[25] This was indeed the reaction in Beijing in 1983. As Miller recalls in his final diary entry on May 7:

> [T]he audience's [reaction was] passionate. At the end they would never stop applauding. Nobody left. When he was taking his bows, I thought I saw a tremendously serious victory on Ying Ruocheng's face. The gamble had paid off, the Chinese audience had understood *Salesman* and was showing its pride in the company. The row of Americans were cheering, Milton Gordon's eyes were still red and wet, Ambassador Hummel was pounding his palms together, and I thought Chinese and Americans alike were trying to assure each other of the durability of both countries' affection.[26]

Ying Ruocheng's account of the reaction of the opening night audience concurs with Miller's:

> As the curtain came down, there was absolute silence for what seemed to us [actors in the wings] like a long time. [. . .] And then, all of a sudden, I don't know who started it, but it came like an avalanche: the applause came forth and it didn't end. Everyone was cheering. I was relieved and excited—all of that effort had not been in vain . . . the audience rushed forward to the edge of the stage, shouting and pointing.[27]

The performance would be repeated more than fifty times and then tour to Hong Kong and Singapore. A year after the production, when Ying

---

[24] This is Li Shilong's recollection. He also recalls that foreigners in the audience gathered outside the theater and shouted the characters' names (i.e. "Biff! Biff!") as the actors departed from the theater on their bicycles to return home.
[25] Murphy 1995: 107. Murphy notes that on opening night in Vienna, there were twenty-two curtain calls.
[26] Miller : 251–2.
[27] Ying and Conceison 2009: 167. Ying describes the entire 1983 collaboration with Miller on pp. 157–69.

introduced Miller as an honoree at the Kennedy Center Awards in Washington, DC, he recalled the opening night curtain call in a similarly powerful way that echoed Miller's interpretation of the audience's reaction as a temporary but efficacious bonding of the two nations from which most of the spectators hailed (see Figure I.4):

> There was a long pause—and then the applause burst forth. And in the audience were a number of Americans and most of them did not understand a word of Chinese, yet they were even moved. You could see the tears streaming down their faces. And I saw the future of mankind—that we can communicate—not only intellectually, but emotionally. What we proved was that as far apart as the Chinese and the Americans are geographically and historically and in so many other ways, we are one humanity. We laugh at the same jokes; we cry the same tears; and we all love Arthur Miller.[28]

The translator of 'Salesman' in Beijing into Chinese, Wang Xiaoying, remembers hearing repeated radio broadcasts of the 1983 production of Death of a Salesman in her home (which was near Beijing People's Art Theatre) when she was in elementary school, and later, as a student at Peking University, she saw a Chinese television broadcast of the production of Ba Jin's Family that Ying Ruocheng translated, adapted, and directed at University of Missouri-Kansas City in 1982. It was not until Wang's translation of 'Salesman' in Beijing was published in 2010 that Miller's account became available and accessible to the Chinese-reading public, though Ying Ruocheng purchased copies of the English version of the book in the US and brought them back to all the staff at Beijing People's Art Theatre who had been involved in the production.[29]

Even before the 1980s, but especially since, Miller has been securely positioned in the top trio of American playwrights in China, alongside Eugene O'Neill and Tennessee Williams. These are the three US playwrights whose plays are assigned to students in universities and theater academies, and that virtually every theater artist in China

---

[28] Ying and Conceison 2009: 157. The other 1984 Kennedy Center awardees besides Arthur Miller were Lena Horne, Danny Kaye, Gian Carlo Menotti, and Isaac Stern. Incidentally, Elia Kazan (the director of the original 1949 Broadway production of Death of a Salesman) was an awardee the preceding year.

[29] Miller 2010: 26–4.

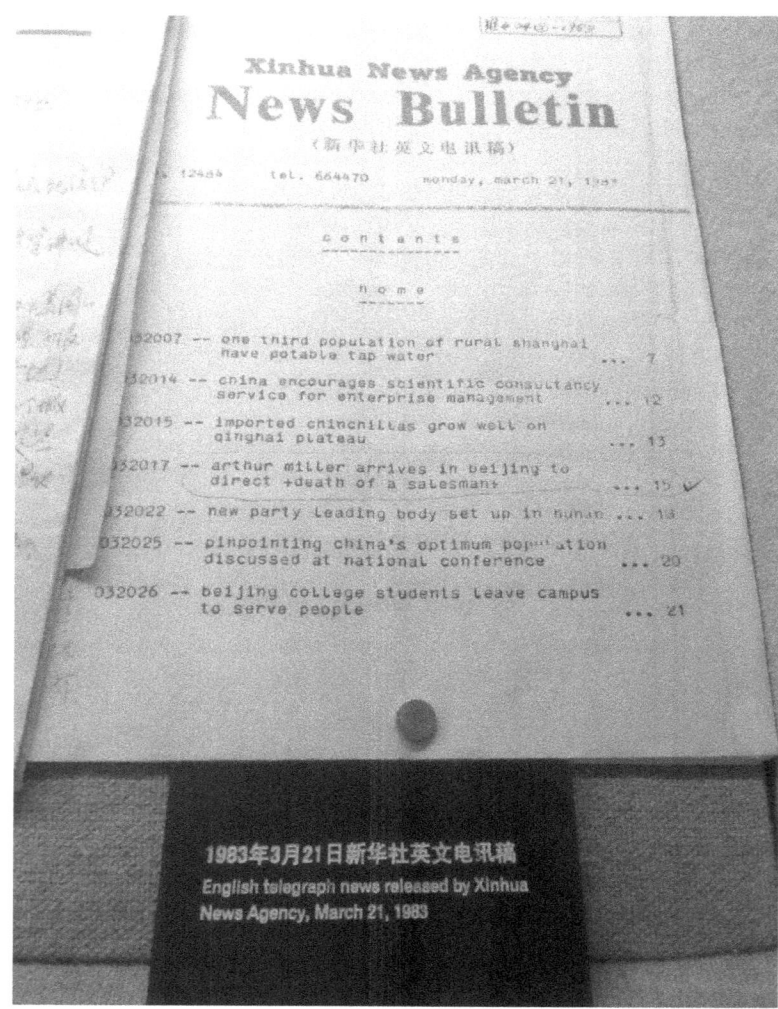

**Figure I.4** Xinhua News Agency News Bulletin from March 21, 1983, listing the major news events of that day in China, including Arthur Miller's arrival in Beijing (Beijing People's Art Theatre Museum exhibit on *Death of a Salesman*, courtesy of Beijing People's Art Theatre).

# INTRODUCTION

knows.[30] Several Chinese books, dozens of doctoral dissertations, and hundreds of journal articles have been published about Miller and his plays. While research on O'Neill and Williams encompasses the full range of their works and careers, emphasis in Miller scholarship tends to be on *The Crucible* and *Death of a Salesman* to the exclusion of many of his other plays, and the focus is on conventional material such as thematic questions and artistic innovations, rather than application of new theories or discoveries.[31] The most noteworthy aspect of this conventional approach to Miller—absent from scholarship on O'Neill and Williams, since they never collaborated with artists in China on productions of their own plays—is the ground-breaking cross-cultural encounter Miller initiated in China when he directed *Death of a Salesman* in Beijing and his enduring record of that experience in this book (Figure I.5).

**Figure I.5** Ying Ruocheng, Inge Morath, and Arthur Miller at a press conference in 1983 (photograph by Su Dexin, courtesy of Beijing People's Art Theatre).

---

[30] The position of O'Neill, Williams, and Miller (in that order) as the best known and most respected American playwrights in China is declared in published books and articles in China, as well as interviews I conducted and casual conversations I had with actors, directors, designers, and theater educators. Edward Albee is usually mentioned as a somewhat distant fourth. In the US, this same group of playwrights is considered the top four of twentieth-century playwrights (see, for instance, Gussow 2002: 7).
[31] Zhao Yongjian 2014: 55.

Miller meticulously describes his personal and artistic journey in his diary, which was first published in 1984, reprinted in 1991, republished upon his death in 2005, and now is republished again in this edition in honor of the centenary of his birth. Along with this new introduction, photographs from the Beijing People's Art Theatre archives that have not appeared in previous editions are included here, in addition to photographs of other professional stage productions of Miller's plays in China from 1981 to 2015 at the National Theatre of China, the Shanghai People's Art Theatre, and the Shanghai Dramatic Arts Centre. All were significant in their dissemination of Miller's dramaturgy in China, and all were directed by prominent Chinese directors and featured famous Chinese actors (see Appendix).

The first of these productions, as previously stated, was *The Crucible* (renamed *The Witches of Salem*), staged at the Shanghai People's Art Theatre in 1981, directed by Huang Zuolin and starring a young Xi Meijuan as Abigail Williams. Huang is unique in global theater history as an individual who promoted in a single country both Stanislavski's realist acting techniques *and* Brecht's epic theater approach in opposition to Stanislavski. Huang famously combined these two theories with Mei Lanfang's Beijing opera principles in a distinctly Chinese aesthetic labeled "*xieyi*".[32] For his staging of *The Crucible* using the script translated by Mei Lanfang's son Mei Shaowu, Huang juxtaposed a symbolist set design (featuring a large cross) with an immersive realist acting approach. Actors learned about the history of witches in seventeenth-century European Puritan society and considered the inner psychology of their characters, though the play's socio-political metaphor was clearly about the Cultural Revolution. In 2006, the Shanghai Dramatic Arts Centre restaged *The Witches of Salem* to commemorate the centenary of Huang Zuolin's birth, inviting his grandson Zheng Dasheng to direct the new production. Zheng used a very different style than his grandfather, creating a play-within-a-play aesthetic in which actors (including star couple Lü Liang and Song Yining, and veteran actor Xu Chengxian who had appeared in the 1981 version) wore contemporary clothing and remained on the periphery

---

[32] For more on Huang Zuolin's concept of *xieyi*, see Conceison 2004: 69–71 and 250–1, and 2011: 319.

watching the action during scenes in which they did not appear. One critic referred to the production as a refreshing take on a classic play in an era of "cultural fast food" (*wenhua kuaishi*).[33]

In addition to these two professional stagings of *The Crucible* in Shanghai, Beijing-based director Wang Xiaoying mounted an award-winning production of the play in 2002. Keeping the 1981 title *Witches of Salem*, Wang created an expressionist aesthetic that featured set pieces such as towering abstract wooden forms and huge white masks, and oversized rope nooses that suddenly flew down to hang above the audience at a climactic moment. Wang explained that he wanted to apply a "small theater concept" to a large proscenium space, and so he deliberately constructed an oppressive atmosphere encroaching on the audience from all directions, surrounding them on four sides and even from above. The acting style he developed was in scale with the visual elements—grand and emotional, at times histrionic. Such melodramatic impulses had been distasteful to Arthur Miller and are in direct contrast to the aesthetic he carefully crafted for his 1983 production of *Death of a Salesman* at Beijing People's Art Theatre, but continue to appeal to mainstream Chinese audiences today. Wang Xiaoying's 2002 version of *Witches of Salem* won numerous accolades, including three Plum Blossom Awards for its leading actors Zhang Qiuge, Wang Weiguo, and Wang Xiaomei.[34] It was revived in 2015 for the centennial of Miller's birth (see Figure I.6).

Arthur Miller's staging of *Death of a Salesman* was the only production of the play in China for nearly thirty years, until another director at Beijing People's Art Theatre, Li Liuyi, mounted a new and very different version in 2012 for the sixtieth anniversary of the theater company. He localized and contemporized the story without changing the script, steering the actors' interpretations toward evoking a trendy current-day Chinese vibe, rather than a 1950s foreign feel. In creating this hyper-modern sensibility, ironically, Li and the actors drew on traditional *xiqu* (Chinese opera) elements, by staging the play in the vast space of the Capital Theatre using only minimal physical elements, most notably invoking the *xiqu* convention of "one table and two chairs."[35] As both director and set designer, Li Liuyi employed minimalism, with only a few chairs,

---

[33] Han Dexing 2014: 75.
[34] Han Dexing 2014: 74–5.
[35] For more on this aesthetic, see Conceison 2011: 319.

**Figure I.6** The 2015 revival of the National Theatre of China's 2002 production of *The Crucible* (entitled *The Witches of Salem*) directed by Wang Xiaoying (photograph by Li Yan, courtesy of photographer Li Yan).

a table, a bench, a Juliet balcony protruding from an enormous back wall, a cluster of tree branches, the iconic refrigerator, and numerous white spheres of varying sizes scattered on the floor. Lighting effects cast looming shadows to create an expressionist, nearly-futuristic environment with a universal feel. The expressionist style production was highly regarded by critics and moderately appealing to mainstream audiences, running for a respectable twenty-two performances in Beijing People's Art Theatre's largest proscenium venue (see Figure I.7).

The first Sino-American cross-cultural production of an Arthur Miller play since his own project in 1983 came in 2011–2012, with the paradigm reversed when director Lei Guohua from the Shanghai Dramatic Arts Centre journeyed to the University of Kansas as a visiting artist. Lei first taught workshops for a few months in Lawrence, Kansas in 2009 and 2010 and then she returned to campus the following year to direct *All My Sons* with a cast of university students. She linked her choice of the play directly to Miller's lasting legacy among theater artists in China and even revealed that her theater company in Shanghai had harbored hopes that Miller would return to China for an encore project:

> In 1983, Miller traveled to China to direct *Death of a Salesman* at the Beijing People's Art Theatre in Beijing. The play was a smashing success and deeply touched the Chinese people. In 2004, my theatre and I planned to invite Miller to return to China for a production of *All My Sons*. Unfortunately, he left the world forever before this was possible, but his work and soul have never left us.[36]

Employing a Brechtian style, Lei added a narrator that directly addressed the audience, and she incorporated film projections as a way to highlight the lead character's mental state. She also drew parallels between the story of lives sacrificed for the sake of business in Miller's play to recent events in China, such as the 2008 tainted milk scandal.[37] Under the

---

[36] Press release for the November 2011 production of *All My Sons* directed by Lei Guohua, produced by University Theatre, University of Kansas.
[37] In July 2008, milk and baby formula containing the banned chemical melamine (added to boost protein content) caused the severe illness of hundreds of thousands of babies in China (including six fatalities). Public admission of the crisis by authorities was delayed until after the Beijing Olympic Games in August. Eventually, several individuals held responsible were prosecuted and imprisoned (two were executed).

**Figure I.7** The 2012 production of *Death of a Salesman* at Beijing People's Art Theatre, directed and designed by Li Liuyi (photographs by Li Chunguang, courtesy of Beijing People's Art Theatre).

co-direction of Lei Guohua and University of Kansas University Theatre Artistic Director Mechele Leon, the group of students from Kansas traveled to China one year later where the production was remounted as part of the 2012 Shanghai Contemporary Theatre Festival, produced by Nick Rongjun Yu at the Shanghai Dramatic Arts Centre.[38] Thus the production is unique on many fronts: a professional Chinese director worked with American college students to perform an American play in English; a college production developed in the US traveled to China for an encore performance in a vastly different cultural context; and Miller's play *All My Sons* premiered in China more than thirty years after it was first considered for production in Beijing. In March 2015, the Hong Kong Federation of Drama Societies produced the first professional Chinese production of *All My Sons*, directed by Luther Fung and starring veteran actor Chung King-fai.

While Wang Xiaoying's 2002 production of *The Witches of Salem* was revived in Beijing for the Miller centenary in 2015, the Shanghai Dramatic Arts Centre decided to mark the occasion by inviting the first American director to stage a Miller play with Chinese actors since Arthur Miller himself. David Esbjornson, an experienced director of Miller's work at leading theaters in the United States (*The Ride Down Mount Morgan* in 1998, the world premiere of *Resurrection Blues* in 2002, and *All My Sons* in 2010), was chosen to bring a team of designers to Shanghai to create a new version of *Death of a Salesman*. The production was to be part of a series of Sino-Western collaborations hosted by SDAC—the previous two years saw co-productions of Moliere's *School for Wives* with a French director and *Uncle Vanya* with a Russian director. Unfortunately, preparations for the centenary *Salesman* production were halted when the lead actor cast to play Willy Loman had to withdraw for medical reasons. SDAC Deputy General Manager Nick Rongjun Yu (who is also China's most prolific and most produced living playwright) has been developing collaborations with Western directors since 2000 in projects that Miller and Ying hardly could have imagined when they pioneered such efforts in 1983.

The partnership between Arthur Miller and Ying Ruocheng that culminated in both this diary and the groundbreaking stage production it recounts was unique in the history of theater. The success that Miller and Ying achieved in the 1983 Beijing production of *Death of a Salesman* was a victory reached after many months of struggle, discussion, compromise, collaboration, and trial-and-error. Miller's documentation of that process

---

[38] Information on the University of Kansas/SDAC production of *All My Sons* is from email correspondence with Mechele Leon on January 24, 2015.

in 'Salesman' in Beijing is one of the most valuable accounts of intercultural theater exchange collaboration that has ever been recorded. Ying Ruocheng was that rare Chinese citizen with the capacity to translate not only language, but also cultural difference. His participation, along with Miller's curiosity and spirit of adventure—and a brilliant play—made the Beijing production the success it became and the landmark it remains. It also launched a lifelong friendship between these two great men of the theater. One man, Arthur Miller, was a Jew raised in Brooklyn, who began writing plays as a student at the University of Michigan and continued to create new and significant works until his death in 2005. He was one of a rare breed of American public intellectuals who explored in his art the depths of the individual human conscience. The other man, Ying Ruocheng, spent his youth in missionary schools in China, speaking fluent English and reading foreign classics. Shortly after his collaboration with Arthur Miller, he rose to become China's vice minister of culture. His knowledge of Western language and culture, along with his training as a professional actor, director, and translator, afforded him the common virtue of "the ability to be surprised" that Miller identified in Inge Morath for similar reasons. As I collaborated with Ying on his autobiography from June 2001 through his death in December 2003, I discovered that he had not only an incredible memory for detail, but also a remarkable ability to draw attention to "pencil sharpeners on desks" and the life-lessons they can teach us. And if there ever was an American playwright and a play in the American canon that accomplished this same feat, it was Arthur Miller and Death of a Salesman. Willy Loman is the human embodiment of the neglected pencil sharpener, emptied of symbolic meaning until he buys a life insurance policy and crashes his car . . . or, rather, until he is written into the pages of the American psyche—and, later, brought to life on the Chinese stage—by Arthur Miller.

Arthur Miller had generously agreed to pen the foreword to Ying Ruocheng's autobiography, though he passed away before he was able to fulfill that promise. The invitation to write this introduction allows me to return that gracious favor to Mr. Miller, whose support during my collaboration with Mr. Ying and affection for his dear friend were an inspiration.[39]

---

[39] I extend my gratitude as well to Mr. Miller's assistant Julia Bolus for many years of kind communication, and to Miller's late wife Inge and his daughter Rebecca.

# Appendix: Public productions of Arthur Miller's plays in China (PRC)

| Sept 1981 | The Crucible | Shanghai People's Art Theatre | Huang Zuolin |
| --- | --- | --- | --- |
| May 1983 | Death of a Salesman | Beijing People's Art Theatre* | Arthur Miller |
| 1988 | The Crucible | Central Academy of Drama, Beijing | Yin Guochun |
| 2000–2001 | The Crucible | Shanghai Theatre Academy | Zhou Ke |
| May 2002 | The Crucible | National Theatre of China | Wang Xiaoying |
| Sept 2006 | The Crucible | Shanghai Dramatic Arts Centre | Zheng Dasheng |
| Mar 2012 | Death of a Salesman | Beijing People's Art Theatre | Li Liuyi |
| Nov 2012 | All My Sons | Shanghai Contemporary Theatre Festival** | Lei Guohua |
| Jan 2015 | The Crucible (revival) | National Theatre of China | Wang Xiaoying |
| Mar 2015 | All My Sons | HK Federation of Drama Societies | Luther Fung |

* Toured to Hong Kong and Singapore in 1985 and 1986 and revived occasionally thereafter as part of BPAT repertoire.
** Performed in English by student actors from the University of Kansas.

# Bibliography

Chen, Xiaomei, ed. *Columbia Anthology of Modern Chinese Drama*, Columbia University Press, 2010.

Chen Yingxian, "Arthur Miller's Significance in Contemporary Chinese Theatre" (*Ase Mile dui dangdai Zhongguo xiju de yiyi*) in *Sichuan Drama*, vol. 6, 2006: 19–21.

Conceison, Claire. *Significant Other: Staging the American in China*. Honolulu: University of Hawai'i Press, 2004.

Conceison, Claire. "Staging the West in China." *Insight* (publication of the University of Michigan Museum of Art). January 2008.

Conceison, Claire. "Behind the Play: The World and Works of Nick Rongjun Yu." *Theatre Journal*, vol. 63, no. 3, October 2011: 311–21.

Deng Di, "Ying Ruocheng's Influence on the Chinese Drama Translation Theory." *Hundred Schools in Art*, vol. 2, 2008: 149–51.
Gussow, Mel. *Conversations with Miller*. New York: Applause, 2002.
Han Dexing, "Arthur Miller in China" (*Ase Mile zai Zhongguo*) in *Theatre Arts*, vol. 2, 2014: 69–77.
Li Liuyi. Interview with author. Beijing People's Art Theatre. January 3, 2015.
Li Shilong. Taped interview with author. Beijing People's Art Theatre. January 2, 2015.
Miller, Arthur. *Death of a Salesman* (Text and Criticism). Edited by Gerald Weales. London: Penguin Books, 1996 (reprint of Viking Press 1967 edition).
Miller, Arthur. *"Salesman" in Beijing*. New York: Viking Press, 1984.
Miller, Arthur. *"Salesman" in Beijing*. London: Methuen, 2005.
Miller, Arthur. *Arthur Miller Diary: "Salesman" in Beijing* (*Ase Mile shouji: "tuixiaoyuan" zai Beijing*). Chinese version of *"Salesman" in Beijing*. Translated by Wang Xiaoying. Beijing: New Star Press, 2010.
Mi Tiezeng. Taped interview with author. Beijing People's Art Theatre. July 3, 2014.
Morath, Inge and Arthur Miller. *Chinese Encounters.* New York: Farrar Straus and Giroux, 1979.
Murphy, Brenda. *Miller: Death of a Salesman*. Cambridge: Cambridge University Press, 1995.
New York Times, The. "Arthur Miller 1915–2005" (Obituary and links to other resources in *The New York Times* online, accessed 25 March 2015): http://www.nytimes.com/ref/theater/newsandfeatures/MILLER-REF.html
Ou Rong and Qian Zhaoming. "'Death of a Salesman' in Beijing Revisited." *The Arthur Miller Journal*, vol. 8, no. 2, Fall 2013: 57–76.
Sun Huizhu (William Hui-zhu Sun). "Power and Problems of Performance across Ethnic Lines" in *TDR: The Drama Review*, Winter 2000: 86–95.
Sun Huizhu (William Hui-zhu Sun). "Arthur Miller: A Dramatist Full of Paradox" (*Ase Mile: chongman beilun de xiju dashi*) in *Culture Review*, vol. 2, 2005.
Wu Ge. "Ying Ruocheng, Arthur Miller—The Two 'Salesmen' of Sino-American Theatre Exchange" (*Ying Ruocheng, Ase Mile—Zhongmei xiju jiaoliu de liang ge 'tuixiaoyuan'*) in *Chinese Theatre*, vol. 7, 2006: 52–5.
Ying Ruocheng, trans. *Ying Ruocheng mingju yisi* (Ying Ruocheng Famous Play Translation Collection [8 volumes]. *Teahouse* by Lao She. Beijing: China Foreign Translation Publishing Corporation, 1999.
Ying Ruocheng, trans. (Revised by Claire Conceison.) *Teahouse* by Lao She in Xiaomei Chen, ed. *Columbia Anthology of Modern Chinese Drama*, Columbia University Press, 2010.
Ying Ruocheng and Claire Conceison. *Voices Carry: Behind Bars and Backstage during China's Revolution and Reform.* Lanham, MD: Rowman and Littlefield, 2009.
Zhao Yongjian, "Review, Reflection, Outlook—Arthur Miller Research in China" (*Huigu, fansi, zhanwang—Ase Mile yanjiu zai Zhongguo*) in *Dramatic Literature*, vol. 7, 2014: 49–56.

# PREFACE TO THE 1991 EDITION

## BY ARTHUR MILLER

Writing a book was the last thought in my mind when I went to China in 1984 to direct a Chinese cast in *Death of A Salesman* at the Beijing People's Art Theatre. There were too many uncertainties to allow for writing anything. Would I manage to communicate with Chinese actors, only one of whom understood English? Would the audience make any sense of the play, whose form, like the society it spoke of, was utterly strange to them? Indeed, one director of the theatre declared on reading the play after rehearsals had begun that "it is impossible to act this thing." And in truth several of the actors would later confess that they could make nothing of it in the beginning.

But it soon turned out that the moon is the moon and actors are actors, the same everywhere. However, what indeed was often very different was their etiquette, what I came to think of as the signals by which Chinese communicate, as well as the assumptions they conventionally make about each other. They are obviously more formal with one another and more deferential to anyone who is older, but—at least in Communist China—the interesting difference was that they rather assumed that anyone expressing a view must be in conformity with whatever social organization he was part of. For instance, it took a lot of persuading for them to believe that Biff, in so stubbornly opposing Willy's belief in money-making, was not speaking for an organization but for himself out of his own experience. More, it was hard for them to imagine that any man would be able to take off and simply float from job to job purely on his own volition. Chinese are attached to society and are directed by it in ways difficult for Westerners to imagine. It was also painfully embarrassing for the actor playing Happy to continue talking to his brother once the latter had closed his eyes and announced that he was going to sleep—this was simply too impolite, and not only for the character but the actor himself.

But beneath these questions of etiquette I found the same basic emotions as we have, the love and pity and false hopes and the rest. The Chinese audience proved this similarity in its reactions to the play whose popularity was such that after a run of many months and much touring through China, as well as television broadcasts, it has recently been mounted again in Beijing with the original cast with two substitutions.

Of course what the Chinese audience makes of this play is another story and no doubt differs from person to person. One woman, an early viewer of our rehearsals, shook her head and referring to Willy said to my wife, Inge Morath—"He's just like my mother." Another, a young man interviewed on CBS TV as he left the lobby of the theatre, thought that Willy's philosophy was absolutely correct. "We all want to be number one man, the boss, this is natural and very good. Biff is wrong." And so Biff would seem to be in post Cultural Revolution China which had just emerged from a period of brutal social levelling, a time when it was immoral for any individual to seek distinction of any kind. (Even keeping goldfish or a pet bird was condemned as perverse anti-social individualism.) To Chinese, Biff sounded a lot like a Red Guard in his refusal to try to excel and personally succeed as Willy was demanding.

This unintended book essentially formed itself partly as the result of the rehearsal schedule. The Chinese rehearse from eight to noon, then break until seven in the evening and work till ten. The hiatus is used for food-shopping and napping. In fear of finding myself separated by language from the day-to-day development of the production, I had brought along a small tape recorder to pick up what I had said during rehearsals, as well as what Ying Ruochang was saying to me. He was Willy, the play's translator, and a fluent English speaker through whom I communicated to the cast. In the afternoons with nothing to do I listened to the morning's transactions, most of which, complicated and onrushing as they were, I had already begun to forget, and typed them out in rough form. What I soon began to realize, now that I could look back even a few days, was that we were all feeling our way rather tentatively into a sort of new and undiscovered country where none of us had been before—they in their imaginary Willy Loman-America and I in a Chinese Brooklyn.

Of course this was all years before the Tiananmen catastrophe, a time, shortly after the end of the Cultural Revolution, when hopes were growing that China had really stepped out on to the road of widening liberties and governmental self-restraint. It seemed impossible, at least to me, that they could ever revert to the violent suppressions of the recent past which they now knew had cost China more than a generation of development. And there seemed a great and growing confidence that a more rational and liberal future was opening up, so much so that they would not even hear of reprisals against those who had persecuted them. No vendetta, the past was the past, they had no need to humiliate former enemies, even those responsible for the deaths and tortures of teachers, writers, artists and workers. I admired their temperance and their resolve to demonstrate tolerance and liberality in order to begin the moderation of civic behavior. Our stage manager, as a matter of fact, had been a militant Red Guard fanatic, one of those who had made the lives of many of the cast miserable in the recent Cultural Revolution period. Worse yet, he was still being a nuisance, rushing at me and jabbing his finger at his watch at the very instant rehearsal time had run out, cutting off a scene or veritably a sentence in order to force conformity with the rules. But now they could smile rather than tremble at his officious antics, and for them this was a big difference. I don't suppose they are smiling any more at such ridiculously meddlesome and often dangerous people.

But China is immortal and will go on winding its way across history, sometimes the world's wise teacher, sometimes its stubbornly ignorant and recalcitrant pupil. This production of *Salesman* happened by sheer chance to occur when the wave of hope was on a steep rise in China. This record of it may be one of a very few candid glimpses inside the minds of quite ordinary Chinese who were actors also in the larger tragedy of our time.

February 1991<br>Roxbury

# HOW IT HAPPENED

## BY ARTHUR MILLER

One in four human beings is Chinese. This can be an awkward circumstance when, for example, one speaks of one of the "world's greatest" writers or actors or painters, and he or she is utterly unknown to the Chinese. And since the greats of Chinese culture are nearly equally unknown outside China's borders, the isolation of this great people seems as incredible as the parochialism of both sides.

As a consequence of the cultural quarantine placed on all foreign works and influences in China during the Cultural Revolution and for more than a decade, the theater artists and audiences were aware only of the forms of Chekhov, Gorky, Tolstoy, Ibsen, and their Chinese imitators, and these only because of the Sino-Soviet connection of the early 1950s. In the 1960s, under the terrible reign of Jiang Qing, Mao's wife and a former actress, only eight "Permissible Plays" were allowed to be shown, and these were more like political demonstrations than imaginative works about the realities of human beings.

During a visit to China in 1978 I met Cao Yu, head of the Beijing People's Art Theatre, and Ying Ruocheng, a director as well as one of that theatre's leading actors, both of them with some personal experience in the United States and eager to begin opening their country to the post-World War II international repertoire. But this was easier said than done; neither they nor anyone else knew whether and how much the Chinese audience could understand Western plays after so many years of such complete isolation. There was also a question about the Chinese actor, trained in an unrealistic style that was at its worst melodramatic and intolerably overemphatic compared with understated Western acting—which, of course, developed out of the far more realistic playwriting of Europe and America, and out of a very different cultural tradition.

Ying Ruocheng had read widely in Western literature, descended as he was from a line of scholars, and Cao Yu had spent a year in America in the 1930s and had fallen in love with O'Neill's work. He had written several seminal plays in the years immediately preceding the Liberation in 1949 that reflect O'Neill's sense of the doom of a poisoned spirit in society. Some of these plays are once again very popular in China. Both men had suffered greatly from the persecutions under the Cultural Revolution and were, in 1978, with the ouster of the so-called Gang of Four, eager to reach out to the West for a new beginning. Their ultimate object, however, was to investigate Western playwriting in order to begin the search for new contemporary Chinese theatrical forms and acting styles.

Arriving in 1978 as a tourist, I soon realized that the writers, directors, and actors I was meeting were trying to tell me something that, in my naiveté and disinformed state, I only gradually caught on to: almost without exception they had only recently emerged from long terms in either prison or exile, and some had lost wives and friends during the previous decade. Cao, then in his early seventies, had been pulled out of his position as the head of the Beijing People's Art Theatre and was turned into its gatekeeper, and Ying had spent years raising rice. Like the other artists I was meeting, they knew nothing of me or of any other American playwright after O'Neill, or, for that matter, of Europeans much after Gorky.

In the next two years, Cao and Ying made a trip to the United States together and Ying played, among other movie roles, the Kublai Khan part in the American television production of *Marco Polo,* and between them they would form a notion of the works their isolation had deprived them of knowing. It is interesting that in 1979 they were talking about doing a production of *All My Sons,* but with the passing of another year and a half they changed their minds and wanted *Death of a Salesman.* In that short period they had come to realize that with China's near opening to the West the audience might conceivably have become sophisticated enough to follow *Salesman,* whose style was entirely innovative for them. Besides, by the early 1980s a small but significant number of new Chinese plays had been written and performed in a style much like that of *All My Sons,* which observes the structure of the classic realist play and would thus have little to teach them about new forms.

What still remained in great doubt was whether they could mount *Salesman* without outside help, and this finally led them to insist I come to China to direct it. Naturally, I was astonished at the idea at first—how could one hope to direct a cast without being able to talk to them? Worse yet, because it was more than thirty years since China had known even a rudimentary commercial civilization, how could I hope to create on stage the realities of a kind of life that had no existence in Chinese memories? I delayed a decision.

But as months passed, the challenge swelled in my mind. For one thing, no foreign director had ever attempted to mount a new play in China with Chinese actors. The old China hands I consulted were no encouragement, *Salesman* to them being the quintessentially American play. Still, it had had no problem being understood in every other culture. Meantime, *The Crucible* was staged in Shanghai and news reports spoke of audiences moved to tears by the memories that the tale evoked of their own sufferings during the Cultural Revolution. Still, I warned myself, the realities of *Salesman* are, or seemed then to be, far more culture-bound. Willy Loman had sprung out of a world of business ambition, a society infected with the success fever; China was more than ninety percent peasant and most living Chinese had been taught proletarian socialist values, the very antithesis of those Willy strives for. The whole effort might end in calamity.

I finally backed into a decision to attempt the production when Professor Chou Wen Chung, head of the U.S.–China Arts Exchange, an independently financed private group at Columbia University, convinced me that it could be done. Born in China, but an American of many years' standing, Chou insisted that the Chinese would indeed understand Willy, and his enthusiasm, added to the hopes of Ying Ruocheng and Cao Yu, made the whole project seem worthwhile.

This book is based on the log I kept each afternoon in the spring of 1983 between the morning rehearsals, from nine to noon, and the evening sessions, from seven to ten. I have left intact the telltale marks of initial naiveté, the misunderstandings and errors of judgment through which I passed in the two months of exhilarating, hard work, and the experience of seeing China along a unique line of vision.

# ACKNOWLEDGMENTS

The production of *Death of a Salesman* in China under my direction was made possible by the Chinese Theatre Association and, from the American side, the U.S.–China Arts Exchange. To both, much thanks.

A. M.

# LIST OF IMAGES

| | | |
|---|---|---|
| 1 | Ying Ruocheng | 13 |
| 2 | Charley and Willy rehearse the casino game scene, with the cast watching and Miller directing | 28 |
| 3 | Zhu Lin, as Linda | 37 |
| 4 | A rehearsal of the restaurant scene | 53 |
| 5 | Biff | 55 |
| 6 | Bernard | 60 |
| 7 | Ying Ruocheng, in wig and costume as Willy, with the wigger whose hairdo was copied for him | 63 |
| 8 | The new Happy | 73 |
| 9 | Rehearsing the fight scene | 90 |
| 10 | Uncle Ben | 108 |
| 11 | Charley | 123 |
| 12 | Willy and the Woman from Boston | 128 |
| 13 | Miss Forsythe | 147 |
| 14 | Letta, in costume, with red tulip | 148 |
| 15 | Uncle Ben and Letta trying on Western-style wigs | 156 |
| 16 | Rehearsal scenes | 162 |
| 17 | The director assesses the costumes | 168 |
| 18 | Rehearsal scenes | 172 |
| 19 | Willy Loman | 199 |
| 20 | The Requiem scene | 199 |
| 21 | Opening night | 213 |

# 'DEATH OF A SALESMAN' IN BEIJING

*March 21, 1983*

Today I met the cast for the first time. Since we arrived only last night, Ying Ruocheng decided, wisely, that I must schedule only a morning session for today. And the truth is I am slain not only by a fearsome jet lag but by not having slept at all last night with the pollution coming in through the open windows of our hotel. Like Prague, Beijing burns soft coal and cooks on charcoal; thus the air is haloed with dust and shoes are never clean. But here they also have sand blowing in from the Gobi desert. Bronchitis is the common ailment. I had almost forgotten how poor they are and as grayly dressed as their city. I have already begun to feel the Chinese urgency about improving the country's economy—there's so much they need, the more so when they know very well that other countries do not lack as they do for life's good things.

The actors did not seem any more tense than an American cast on the first day, but it is still hard to judge their feelings. One has only their controlled expressions to go by; I am like a deaf man searching their eyes for emotions, which finally I cannot read. I realize as I write now that I am still jetnumbed; the frontal lobes die a little after twenty-four hours in air. I am convinced we leave parts of our souls above the clouds.

Anyway, I did address them in a rather formal conference room from the end of a long table lined with two rows of armchairs. I had not retained one of their names although we had all shaken hands at the airport yesterday, but that seems weeks ago and far away. The Linda is especially moving to contemplate. She has a tragic handsomeness and an intelligence in her large brown eyes that speak of suffering and humor, and I notice that she is the first to laugh and to understand Mrs. Shen, my interpreter, a young woman in her late twenties who is dressed in the matronly style of the 1940s, including a large red beret.

I am continuing this at 4:45 A.M., unable to sleep for worry and the slugging my brain has taken by the trip here. I have never experienced such a narcotizing effect before.

Our room is too small, but they promise to change it soon. At least we are not in one of the large hotels, which are the same all over the world and tend to lean on me and make me endlessly thirsty with their processed air. The air in here is lousy, but it's air.

When I sat facing the cast yesterday, along with half a dozen crew, the set designer and lighting man and their assistants, and saw a dozen notebooks with pens poised to take down my remarks, my heart sank, for I had nothing whatever to say. I realized they must expect me to philosophize about the play, the way Harold Clurman used to do, but I dread dropping wrong hints that will mislead them later on.

One of the questions I asked — sensing that they were too respectful of "the Foreign Expert" to open up at this early stage — was whether there was anything in the play that stood out as related to Chinese habits, practices, or beliefs, figuring I would start from some common ground if in fact it existed.

There was a dead silence.

Is it that they do not expect a director to ask but to tell them what to think and do? I don't know. But the ploy certainly got me nowhere. They even seemed embarrassed. Were they? Ying Ruocheng then explained that they had been reading the play together for several days and were still forming ideas about it in their minds. In short, I concluded, they did not understand it.

Well, I am here on the other side of the world, made prisoner by my own curiosity, so I may as well relax and see what happens. Luckily there is a diversion amid the awkwardness — Ying announces that they have erected a mock-up of the set in the rehearsal room down the hall and that I can look at it if I wish. I leap at the excuse to break up the logjam, and we all troop out of the conference room and go into the rehearsal space. This is actually a large stage with walls of brown sound-deadening panels, ceiling at least forty feet high, and a long row of armchairs facing the actors across an orchestra pit covered over with boards, some of them broken and splintery. The mock-up, made of flats from other sets and tacked-together pieces of canvas and wood, is the mirror image of the original Broadway set, with the bedroom on stage left instead of right, and so forth. This makes no difference, but I do not understand why the designer thinks, as Ying Ruocheng interprets him, that by reversing everything "it will bring the set closer to the audience." I am too exhausted to pursue this reasoning. The designer, like everyone, men and women, in cast and crew, wears the standard blue denim-like jacket buttoned up to the neck, ballooning trousers, and a cap. The poverty of this theatre and China is all about me. I refuse to be discouraged. Perhaps their acting will be more fundamental than pampered actors can manage.

The corridors we walk through are hardly lit, due to the electrical shortage, and the gloom is pervasive. There is also a smell of toilet, excepting behind closed doors in the conference and rehearsal rooms. The hallways and rooms are a sort of bile color and have not been painted in many years.

The mock-up, nevertheless, is a wonderful boost to my morale, especially considering that it is a few feet wider and deeper than the original, which was built to fit the much less ample stage of the Morosco Theatre. It is like a Hooverville shack of the 1930s, with stretched-out rags of various faded hues, worn platforms, pieces of stairs from other productions.

I note the presence of a large cardboard box against the right wall, and Ying informs me—interpreting the designer—that this will be the refrigerator. The assistants now produce two chairs and a mahogany table that must once have belonged to a matched set; the chairs have serpentine lines and would not likely be found in an American kitchen. But I withhold this fact, rather than disappoint at this early stage the designer and his prideful staff as well as the actors, who are in a little crowd hopefully watching for my reaction. Perhaps this looks to *them* like an American kitchen, and maybe I ought to leave it at that. This raises a certain philosophical quandary that so far I have not been able to resolve: Exactly where is this play supposed to be taking place? In China? America? Where? I think I shall wait to comment on the furniture until I can decide this question.

Meanwhile, I note with a certain satisfaction that the refrigerator, along with the table and two chairs, will be the only object in the kitchen. The style that I urged on Ying Ruocheng in New York has been established and accepted, apparently. He had wanted a real American kitchen to satisfy the audience's curiosity.

We now sit down in a group, with Shen, Ying, and me facing the actors, who occupy a row of chairs along the wall facing the set. Still in the thrall of my jet-numbed brain, I must swear to myself not to say anything I will regret, for as I look from one face to the next it is clear that they are avid for leadership and direction from the ultimate authority, the man who wrote the play.

I have not "prepared" a production approach; it would have been fruitless to try, when I could not even imagine my cast or how they might react to anything. I have to trust my instincts. I find myself talking about what is really on my mind at this point, the physical and cultural locale of the play. First off, I recall a couple of plays about Westerners that we saw on our last visit to China, in 1978, and how appalling it was to see actors made up with chalk-white faces and heavily "rounded" eyes, walking with heavy, almost loutish gait as they think Europeans and especially Russians do, and worst of all, wearing flaxen or very red-haired wigs that to us seemed to turn them into Halloween spooks. "The first thing I want to discuss with you," I begin, "is the problem of how to act like Americans. The answer is very simple and I urge upon you to try as hard as you can to believe what I say—you must not attempt to act like Americans at all."

The laughter is somewhere between confused disbelief and nervous curiosity. "The way to make this play most American is to make it most Chinese. The alternative is what?—you will try to imitate films you have seen, correct?" They nod and laugh. "But those films are already imitations, so you will be imitating an imitation. Or maybe you will try to observe how I behave and imitate me. But this play cannot work at all—it can easily be a disaster—if it is approached in a spirit of cultural mimicry. I can tell you now that one of my main motives in coming here is to try to show that there is only one humanity. That our cultures and languages set up confusing sets of signals and these prevent us from communicating and sharing one another's thoughts and sensations, but that at the deeper levels where this play lives we are joined in a unity that is perhaps biological. I am not an anthropologist and I can't predict what we will prove through this production; but nothing at all will come of it unless you are emotionally true to your characters and the story. If you are, I am betting that the cultural surface will somehow take care of itself, although I can't be sure at this point what it will appear to be.

"Now, then, to be specific, there will be no wigs—"

A loud burst of laughter that I am not sure I understand, but I join in anyway. I am not even sure they believe I am serious. I glance at Ying beside me, who seems to be looking slightly uneasy, and I see now that they are watching him for a sign of my real intention. But nothing comes from Ying. He is resolutely refusing to intervene.

All this is taking place on the forestage in front of the lowest platform of the set, the kitchen floor, and it suddenly occurs to me that the set is going to be very distant from the audience, unless I am wrongly interpreting the white marks on the floor that indicate the bounds of the real stage in the theatre. I am also growing convinced that the stairway up to the boys' room is in a different location than it was in the original, which worked so beautifully. My brain having given way to fatigue, I now indulge myself and carefully walk the set with the designer. He had one milky eye and patchy whiskers and a yellow-toothed grin the shape of a quarter moon. He is cocky, laughs a lot, and is evading my questions. Under the heading Treat Them Like Equals, I stop moving and ask him to tell me whether in fact he has changed the location of the stairs, which, in his version, makes no architectural sense and would actually be outside the Lomans' house. He agrees with me without an argument, laughing along with an assistant, while the whole cast looks on. Everybody is in on everything, apparently. The next item is the location of the fridge, which he has placed where all the action would be centered on its white surface, so I have him move it to the extreme right. And so on.

It reminds me of Jo Mielziner's description of how he designed the set and how much the play had to be revised to fit it. Jo was a genius and I believe this was his greatest set, but I take his remark as a compliment to the play, which, it seems, caused everyone involved in that first production to claim credit for everything. In fact, as poetically evocative as his set was, its basic design—three rooms on as many levels—was indeed my original concept set out in my stage directions, which called for three platforms. Nevertheless, thirty-five years later I still get letters from drama departments asking what revisions I made to fit the set. And here again in China another designer, this time confronted by a finished design that solved all the problems, has to add his creativity and move an interior staircase outdoors, quite probably in order to leave his mark on it. Well, indifference would be a lot worse.

There are quite a few other revisions on which I insist, all of which he agrees to; at the right I change a latticework arbor going offstage at a crazy oblique angle to a straight-line arch, and I shift the position of the boys' beds on the second floor. But these are details. The main accomplishment of these rather incoherent first few hours is my happening to mention to Ying that when, as Willy, he steps over the wall-line of the kitchen onto the forestage he is entering his own mind. This news seems to surprise and fire him up, and he immediately tells it to the designer, who stops grinning. In fact, the three or four actors who have heard Ying's interpreting of this remark seem also to be struck. I had thought the text made this clear, and the fact that it did not means I have my work cut out for me in demonstrating to them the form of the play, which is the materialization of Willy's mental processes. But I am ready and eager, if I can get my brain functioning again.

Ying Ruocheng had, wisely, prevailed on me not to try to work today, having made the trans-Pacific trip himself a few times. So again we assort ourselves on the long row of chairs and feel each other out. Once more I press the question of their relationship to the play, and the young actor who is cast as Happy, the Lomans' second son, raises his hand. This schoolroom gesture seems at this point to indicate a certain timorousness, which I can only hope is temporary. Shen interprets carefully, even falteringly, but I am already spoiled by Ying's instantaneous and colloquial renderings, and I warn myself to be patient with her. The young actor is saying, "One thing about the play that is very Chinese is the way Willy tries to make his sons successful. The Chinese father always wants his sons to be 'dragons.'"

There is a ripple of laughter.

"You mean he wants them to compete and excel over others?"

"Oh yes!"

I had not expected this to emerge so soon, not in China. There is another China here than the one I glimpsed five years ago and the one I have read about. In those societies the leveling dogma could never have been so openly contradicted, nor would it have been greeted with free laughter. However, in that laughter I sense a recognition of the newness of the change—and I am not yet sure if the laughter is also nervous, as though a moral rule had been nudged. In the cross talk that follows, the other actors reinforce Happy's observation from their own experiences, but while they come up with no new information, I understand that they are trying to tell me that they do relate to the play, that it is not too exotic for them. Thus we are drawn a little more together; I appreciate their effort and try to indicate it to them.

Now a midge of a young woman appears with costume sketches, gouache drawings that are remarkably good. On my complimenting her, Ying repeats with a wry laugh, in which all join, that the Costume Department is best at doing 1940s clothes since that was the last era that Western plays were done in China, everything having closed down on them afterward; but now I realize this means the Revolution itself, not merely the Cultural Revolution of the mid-1960s. Thus, the thread of continuity I am picking up with this production was broken precisely when *Death of a Salesman* was written, 1949, a coincidence that seems fateful now, and strange.

The appearance of the sketches draws every member of the cast crowding around, as this kind of occasion does in any country. And somehow the costumes, purposefully ordinary in American terms, excepting for Ben's Western outfit and Charley's knickers, make the actors' own uniform blue trousers and jackets seem so poor once again. And I wonder what they have all been doing in their lives since 1949—the catastrophes, the hours of triumph, the threats to life and career, the sheer *living* they have managed to get through. I must learn about them. Many of them seem too underweight.

The decor of this rehearsal room is also something to ponder in its basic military brownness fit for a barracks. The whole building, actually designed by a Chinese architect in the 1950s during the period of alliance with the Soviet Union, is a featureless block of brown stucco with obligatory Roman pediments here and there, and gives off the breath of the cemetery vault, like English boys' schools, and causes one to reflect on the ugliness of most theatres in the world, including Broadway's. The only lovely ones are some of Europe's baroque structures, like those in Prague, for example, or the Bolshoi in Moscow, or—above all—the Josefstadt in Vienna, which did not forget the idea of *play* in favor of institutionalized, authoritarian real estate.

We were mostly milling about today, observing one another from the two opposite sides of the world, but I learn that during the Cultural Revolution some six hundred young militants were housed in this and another rehearsal room, year after year. The toilets must have been in marvelous shape with such a mob. How did they rehearse here? I must find out more.

Inge and I have a small hotel room, with an even smaller one for Rebecca, who will return home after two weeks to continue school. She is in heaven here because there are so many babies on the streets.

She has decided that almost all of them are the same age, about ten months. In the States that would imply an electricity blackout nineteen months ago, but the homes here are pretty dark all the time. But things are said to be improving, with eggs finally off the rationing list, for example. However, I see milk being sold on the street to old people and to young parents for their infants, and each customer presents a ration ticket that the attendant checks off. The "store" is simply a three-by-six-foot platform mounted on a tricycle stationed on the corner of the *hutong,* or neighborhood lane, the attendant always wearing a white bag on his hair, as food workers, among others, usually do.

Inge has it right, I think—to her it looks like a country after a great war, and she lived through the war inside Germany. And I recall France and Italy in the late 1940s, with everything in short supply, everyone a little hungry, a little desperate for something with a bit of color to put on, and the buses worn out and people in courtyards or on the streets wiring things together, soldering things that had fallen apart. I recall how in Foggia, in a very good apartment, there was a single twenty-watt bulb in the living room and that was it. Beijing is dark at night. But it seems also quite safe. I must ask about this. I have seen no sign of police, day or night.

But things are not entirely idyllic; on the day of our arrival the town was erupting with street propaganda—teams of young people with loudspeakers on street corners and big posters asking the people to behave politely in public, to obey traffic rules and not jaywalk, not to litter the streets, and to cut out the spitting. If they could cut down on the soot falling through the air it would help even more.

There seems to be no grass in Beijing, only plots of beige loess, which apparently will not hold water. (I would later learn that they have uprooted a lot of grass to get rid of mosquitoes. I am not sure if the trade-off works.) There is much tree planting going on, and along the road in from the airport hundreds of acres of nursery containing sophora mainly, but a few other quick-growing species I could not identify, there being no leaves yet. An immense number of apartment-block buildings, some of them completed and occupied, has filled up whole neighborhoods that were open land five years ago.

Seated next to me in the car coming from the airport, Ying had said, "Those are the apartment houses Willy hates, right?" He still lives in an old house whose rooms face a small courtyard, and all his friends who live in the new buildings envy him. It reminds me of Brooklyn in the 1920s, and the Bronx, too. One of the reasons my family left Harlem for Flatbush was my longing for the countrified neighborhood out there where my cousins lived and, I thought, had a wonderful time outdoors. I am tenuously wondering if the play will seem as strange to Chinese as everyone thinks. Beijing now has a typically American combination of one-story houses with six-story apartments stuck in the midst of them. Willy's feeling crowded—will that identify the moment of social evolution as similar to their own?

Which raises the question whether the 1980s are the Chinese 1920s. The current post-Mao political line seems to come down to something like the pre-Flaubert expansion in France under Louis Philippe, whose slogan was "Enrich yourselves!" One cannot help wondering why the Chinese could not have accomplished more by this time, and the answer seems partly their stupefying ideology, which has crippled their natural ingenuity, stunned them. They themselves seem to feel something similar now; they are apparently no longer interested in being angry at Jiang Qing, Mao's wife and heiress, and the Gang of Four who led them backward, and simply want to get on with modernizing the country. They claim to have accomplished more in these last four years than in the past twenty-five. Is this indeed the takeoff?

I wondered aloud to Ying, after he remarked how Willy would hate these new apartment buildings and how much his friends envied his courtyard, whether "the next generation is going to start leaving the apartment houses to find some little old courtyard to remodel." He laughed and hoped this hope for China, knowing the gentrification of old neighborhoods has happened in London, San Francisco, New York, and other cities. Why not in China? But there are still economic light-years to travel here.

When I told the cast that if this production managed to touch the Chinese heart and mind, perhaps it could help to prove that there is one humanity, I had the sense that I had unwittingly ventured into ideology, such was their silence. Either that, or they simply did not understand what I was driving at. Chinese are as self-defensive about their ethnic uniqueness as anyone else, if not more so, and "one humanity" may sound like something less than a compliment. This is the springtime of their nationalism and people at that stage are not interested in being told they are like everybody else. But I let myself talk more than I should have, I'm afraid. We shall see.

In any case, they were openly gratified to hear that there was great interest in this production in the United States and much curiosity to see whether this quintessentially American play can reach the Chinese.

The difficulties begin. Ying is now afraid that place names in the play, with the exceptions of New York and Boston, which received large Chinese emigration in past years, will be meaningless to the audience — places like Hartford, Waterbury, and Providence. Or, for that matter, New England itself. Already twice now he has muttered that we shall have to find some way around this but at the same time remain faithful to the script. He says he has even repeated my sentence structure, but I have no way of knowing, at least not as yet.

He is also worried about the playing time of the show; he had the actors read it twice before my arrival and it ran four hours. This, I told him, was ludicrous, it cannot possibly run that long. And for the first time he confided a near-complaint, that the actors' speech rate is very slow. "Well, we are going to hurry them up," I said, and he brightened immediately. "Is this something they do in other shows, or just this one?"

"No, I think it's generally true — we don't speak as fast as you."

"But *could* you?"

"Well, yes. I think we could," but he lacked certainty.

"They won't object if I press them on?"

"I don't think so. Just say it's all too slow."

"I sure as hell will."

"We played recordings of the Lee Cobb performance and they were a bit scared by the speed of the scenes. They don't see how they can keep a pace like that."

"But is the normal Chinese rate slower than English?"

"You know, I'm not all that sure."

And so we have our first cultural problem, but I have little doubt in my mind how it is going to be resolved — I do not think, in my ignorance, that linguistic rhythm is divorced from inner motivation and the urgency of the story, and if they have those, they are going to move at the right pace.

The time has come to open the cardboard box I brought from the States with the football, helmet, and shoulder guards. Actors love

Ying Ruocheng.

distractions, and we now collect another little crowd of them as I help Biff into the helmet and place the shoulder guards on him. He has an open, charming smile, looks Mongolian to me, very dark skin and a tall, straight horseman's body. He is about mid-thirties, with a rather pear-shaped lower face expanding out around the jaw hinges. Still, he is handsome. There is some fooling around in the helmet and shoulder guards, which ends with us all seated again and talking about salesmen.

"Actually," Ying begins, "I think they will know what a salesman is." Why has he changed his mind?

Biff, sitting in an armchair in the helmet and shoulder guards, says, "The city is full of salesmen now, they're all up and down the streets."

"But that's different from the traveling salesman, isn't it?" I ask.

There is a silence. They seem themselves to be trying to understand their own city in a new light. The actor who will play Charley speaks, a tall, thin man, one of the best-known actors in China, who is on television a lot and recently starred on stage in the title role of *Ah Q,* based on the beloved Lu Xun's story; he is about fifty but looks younger and has the gentlest of voices. I cannot really place him as the gruff, ignorant, and peasantlike Charley, Willy's best friend, but he does have the personal warmth the part needs and perhaps we can build on that. He and Ying are the "senior members" of the company, along with Zhu Lin, our Linda, who is in her late fifties. "I think," he says, "that the people are learning about the West very quickly now. I don't think we have any *traveling* salesmen, but there are many privately owned small shops now—"

"And they give much better service," Ying adds, wryly. The laughter at this is significantly charged—no step can apparently be taken without political implications. What I find so interesting is that they, along with me, are trying to figure out where the country is at this moment. Ying originally, in New York, had said there were no salesmen in China, suggesting that the audience would have a hard time understanding the play, but that was more true then than it is now, less than a year later, and so he has had to change his mind. It seems more and more likely, to me, that public receptiveness to this play is as much an unknown to them as it is to me.

Zhu Lin—Linda—interrupts: "We have no insurance in this country." Ying has now moved in to interpret in Shen's stead; with him beside me I forget altogether that I am not understanding the Chinese instantaneously; he is but a breath behind the speaker, with not a single hesitation. Zhu Lin, I have been given to understand, is one of China's biggest stars, a surprise since she has no airs, nothing theatrical about her at all. She is wearing the standard outfit, blue buttoned-up cotton jacket and trousers. Her black hair lightly streaked with gray is bobbed to her nape. A deeply serious if not mournful face that can instantly change to a laughing one. She turns to Ying for his confirmation. "I am not sure about the insurance being understood. Especially about him dying for it." And then she turns to me. "Will they pay even though he kills himself?"

"Very likely. It is hard to prove it is not a car accident, after all."

And so we have our second cultural problem. But my faith seems not to have been disturbed, although I do not know why not. I think if they play from the heart it will go over. But I am still suffering jet lag, I remind myself.

"In every other language the word for 'I' is one syllable, except in Japanese." Ying and I are having the remains of our tea as the company dribbles out of the rehearsal hall to the wide paved alleyway beside the theatre where they will mount their bikes and ride off into the night. Inge has been photographing discreetly all afternoon and has already bonded the women in the cast to her by her fluency in Chinese, with which she can begin to satisfy their curiosity about her as a Western woman. In the streets it is she whom men and women follow with their gazes; she is usually carrying cameras and we both wear bush jackets of the same cut, and this de-emphasis on sexual difference, so much like their own, may be what intrigues them. Of course they haven't seen her dressed up yet. Compared with the scene four years ago, the streets now are ablaze with color, the women having found ways to make new clothes as distant as possible from the drab uniforms of the Mao era.

Ying Ruocheng does not conceal his feelings about the Japanese—feelings shared by many Chinese who are less free to announce them. His father was the president of Beijing University—indeed, his grandfather had founded it in the 1890s—and the Japanese were particularly brutal toward him. Ying loses no opportunity to say that much of Japanese culture is derivative of the Chinese, but that with their postwar wealth and alliance with the United States and trade with

Europe they have done a public relations job of unheard-of scope and persuasiveness. With the bonsai, the gardens, architecture, the calligraphy, and theatre, Japan is a small mirror reflecting some corner of vast Mother China's achievements, but poor China has no press agents and was so busy fending off foreign invaders in the past centuries, as well as fighting her own civil wars, that the world has no concept of her contribution as compared with that of the Japanese.

I am reminded of my flying partner on the trip over, a Japanese executive seated beside me on the New York–Tokyo leg of the flight, who, on learning I was headed for China, began talking about the Chinese, with whom he had done some business in the past. Like so many Japanese he was gratified that I seemed to be enjoying the Japanese lunch that we were eating at the moment. "Japanese food," he said, "is very basic, very simple. Our whole culture has that emphasis, in fact. Chinese food is much more suave, with all sorts of strange sauces and odd combinations."

I asked how he found the Chinese to deal with in business. I could see the Caution sign come to a glow, but he decided to take a small step toward candor anyway. "They are very often hard to deal with."

"How do you mean?"

"It is difficult to follow their complicated thinking. They can be extremely indirect, you know . . ."

I looked into this Japanese face from which I was hearing the ancient story of the Mysterious East. "You mean they are slippery?"

"Very often, yes. But of course they have been doing business longer than anybody else and these are very old habits."

"How do you size up their chances now?"

"They are much better organized than under the old regime, of course. But socialism does not provide a high living standard, not anywhere. They are very, very poor. They will have to make great changes, I think."

My first day finished, I am full of hope. I have always gotten on with Chinese and these actors are no exception; I feel related. But my brain is too numb to think. I hope I have not made a fool of myself. In my daze, however, I am already able to give thanks to Cao Yu for the use of his car and driver, who evidently is ours for the duration. Cao Yu, in his mid-seventies now, is recuperating in Shanghai from a serious operation and has sent his apologies for not having been here to greet us. I glimpse—only a glimpse yet—that he and Ying Ruocheng must have a lot riding on this production. More even than I do. I am not able yet to define what that may be, but I know it is there.

## March 22

Arriving at the rehearsal hall at exactly 9:00 A.M., I find Ying Ruocheng, Liu Housheng, General Secretary of the Chinese Dramatists Association, and an ebullient, strong, laughing woman of fifty whose name is Zhou Baoyou—Joe, for short—who is filled with bursting good health from her forty-five-minute bike ride to her office, which she does every morning, winter and summer.

She is the Mrs. Trouble of China's entertainment industry, solving everybody's transportation problems, health and food difficulties, getting them airport and railroad tickets, and in general making foreigners believe they are safe in the laps of the gods. (As I would learn later, she is the daughter of a banker who decided to cast his and his family's lot with the Revolution; she studied English in a Christian school; her enjoyment of life springs in part from the post-Cultural Revolution liberty, which she loves, and in part from her children's success—her son is studying music in the United States and her daughter studies in China. Above all, she wants, she says, "to contribute something," and feels this production will be the best thing she has ever had a chance to help into life.)

Liu Housheng is her boss, a diffident man with short-cropped gray hair, wearing a particularly much-laundered Mao jacket and a gentle, rather humorous look. I take him to be—from his position—a Communist Party member and probably its representative to me, for he has a certain amount of power, I am sure, at the apex of the Dramatists Association. But at the moment I have no interest in pursuing the submerged world of political controls in my eagerness to have my first readings of the play today.

Joe's news is that we must decide what to do about some twenty-two foreign television and print correspondents—and many more than that from Chinese media—who want to interview me about the production. I have already in hand about a dozen requests routed through the Association. Joe, thank God, has kept my telephone number secret but doesn't know for how long this will be possible. After much back and forth it is clear the Chinese have been caught up in the publicity hunger and want me to honor all the requests—a faint surprise, since I had somehow assumed that media pressure would inflame their phobias about being used. Instead it has amplified mine and pleases them no end. This is a very different China. It is funny to hear them talking Chinese among themselves with "CBS, ABC, NBC" thrown in. I finally decide that I will give the journalists interviews independently provided they're kept short. This is not going to work, of course, but has to be tried, I guess.

By ten we have all assembled, the whole cast seated around an ample room in armchairs, scripts in their hands. There is a moment of dread as Linda says the first line—"Weelee!"—from the bedroom, having heard him enter the house. The first surprise is how easy it is for me to follow the scene in my Penguin paperback. It is a triumph of Ying's translation—even the rhythms seem the same, the flows to the peaks and the slopes toward the silences. In a few minutes it is obvious that Zhu Lin and he will easily seem related, husband and wife, and of this particular class. I cannot believe they have come this far in a few rehearsal days. Ying hardly looks at the script, and she only a little more often. What am I going to do with six weeks of rehearsal time!

Zhu Lin is an actress of awesome experience in classic Chinese as well as modern plays—"a heavyweight," in Ying's words. She already knows she must keep Willy from wandering too close to the edge, affects a happiness with his positive moments, insinuates the truth when he cannot bear hearing it, always reaching a hand out as to a child who cannot walk without falling down. I can detect no trace of the declamatory style in either of them, something I had feared and still do. On the contrary, seated side by side in chairs, they create the Lomans' bedroom. Ying has a kind of absolute control that brings Olivier to mind—he simply does what is called for, easily, directly, effortlessly. But a few of his shifts of temper are repetitious and we shall work on those. The shape of the first scene does not yet exist, but the main thing is almost palpable—the truth of where the Lomans are with each other as a couple. The reading approaches a read performance in that they already possess consistent attitudes and are not merely groping. What gratifies me is the absence of the distance I had supposed would separate them from the feelings in the roles, but whatever is lacking, it is never intimacy with their own feelings. Or so it seems. If they were merely posing, imitating "American," I don't think I could follow every speech as easily as I do.

With the reading over I ask the cast to tell me what, in their roles, if anything, they feel alien to. "What are you called on to do that a Chinese would not do?" There is a silence. Then the actor playing Happy says (in Ying's translation), "I can't imagine a Chinese continuing to talk to his brother once he says, as Biff does, that he is going to sleep."

Ying clarifies: "He is talking not so much about impoliteness as that a Chinese would not feel such pressure to continue talking once his listener has said he is going to sleep."

"Then an American, you mean, feels the need to speak more urgently?"

"Exactly, yes. An American feels he must say what he has to say no matter what. Whereas a Chinese would feel that to continue would be ineffectual."

"Is this politesse?"

"No, not really. It is probably a recognition of the limits. Once the limits are reached, that is all that can be done."

I feel there is some hidden relationship to this analysis in a question the actor playing Charley asks a few minutes later. Today he is wearing a sweater in two shades of gray and looks more elegant. "I don't understand why Charley is so kind to Willy," he says.

"He feels pity for him, perhaps."

"Ah." He nods. I don't think he is really convinced.

"Maybe there are people like this, who feel for others and try to help if they can."

"Yes," he says, still weighing the possibility. I like him — an actor who has to make his information work and asks a solid question.

"They are old friends, you know."

"Yes, I know." There is a pause, and then he says, "I don't think any man would be so good to another in China." The others show no reaction.

This reminds me of the problem we had in casting the part in the original production. Kazan had reached out into what seemed the totally wrong direction for Howard Smith, a shouting comic who had been in vaudeville for years before becoming a minor star in farces, where he played the standard bewildered father of teenage girls. *Dear Ruth* was his big current success. Howard had never been near a serious play and had no desire to be, when comedies ran so much longer. He was a stout, gruff, tall man with sparse blond hair and a loud, rather common baritone voice. He read the play and refused the part, surely the best he had ever been offered in his life. Kazan, Bloomgarden, and friends of his all tried to change his mind but to no avail. "That play is *terrible*," he'd say. "Who's going to want to see something that sad?"

Finally, in desperation, a meeting was fixed with him and me alone in Bloomgarden's office. I had learned from Kazan what his objection was, but pretending ignorance I asked him to tell me why he was so against the play. "The poor man, for God's sake; the rotten things his sons say to him. And his boss. Everybody's so down on him. It's just awful!"

"Except Charley," I said. I could see his eyes change. He stopped moving. "Charley gives Willy good advice, lends him money, always makes time for him during office hours. . . . Charley really tries, Howard."

He sat there staring. Finally he said, "I'll think about it." That night he accepted the role. His instincts were as right for it as his personality: a hardheaded, realistic, decent man; slightly dense, perhaps, but filled with human warmth. A mature actor, he was instantly credible, no matter what he did or said.

We had been rehearsing for more than two weeks, the play was fully blocked, and while Arthur Kennedy, Lee Cobb, Mildred Dunnock, Cameron Mitchell had all had their turns asking Kazan or me what something meant, Howard Smith had never asked a single question. He was especially glorious in the card-game scene, where Willy is beginning to talk both to Charley and to his vision of his brother Ben, who has materialized at his elbow as he plays. Charley is of course totally unaware that Willy is addressing a wraith as well as himself, and from his viewpoint Willy is making less and less sense. Howard Smith managed this mystification with subtlety and discretion, never overdoing his bewilderment, always curious as to what Willy means.

But on this day he surprised everyone. He broke off the scene, and raised his hand up to shade his eyes and look out into the dark theatre. "Can I ask a question?" he said. "Gadg? Are you there?"

"I'm right here, Howard," Kazan answered. "What's your question?"

Pointing at the actor playing Ben—Thomas Chalmers, an immense man, formerly an heroic basso with the Metropolitan Opera—he asked with a certain super-intensity that told of a long conflict he had been living through over possibly many days, "Do I see him?"

Kazan kept a straight face. "No, Howard."

"I don't see him at all," Howard Smith confirmed—happily, it seemed.

"Not for a minute, not at all, never. You just don't see him, Howard."

"Good. Okay. That's what I thought."

Apparently Howard had simply been obeying Kazan's instruction never to look at Ben, for what reason he did not really know, and had been puzzling it out for the past days until he could no longer hold back his question. It was a comically embarrassing setback for all the Stanislavski actors in the cast, who, in order to make themselves real, had put all they had into studying the reasons why they did what they did, while the realest one on the stage had not known what he was doing—and it was one of the most difficult feats of acting in the play.

Now, a world away in space and thirty-five years later, here was an actor being Charley again. How odd, yet fitting, that in this time and this place, after revolution and civil war and cruelties beyond the mind's power to contain, this Charley should be asking not why everyone is so bad to Willy but why Charley is so good to him.

I raise the question with the cast whether this play would have been performed, let's say, in 1977 or 1978, and they quickly reply, as though it were obvious, that it could not have been understood by the audience then. I take this to mean that they would not have understood the unusual form. Under the Gang of Four through the Cultural Revolution, they had only Jiang Qing's "Eight Permissible Plays," demonstrations of problems. But in the past five years a few foreign plays have been performed, and the audience, especially the younger majority, are eager for new forms.

"I read *Salesman* to this company in 1978," says Ying, "but they rejected it, sure that it would be incomprehensible. The elements of American society in it had no preparation in the public mind; nowadays everybody knows foreign films and TV and a great deal about how the West lives. We think even the liquid form of *Salesman* has also been prepared for in their minds now. They will be eager for it."

All this reminds me of how much doubt there was about the play when I wrote it. In fact, Joshua Logan, who had invested a thousand dollars in it sight unseen, withdrew five hundred after he read the script. One day during rehearsal Kazan and I ran into him in the street. He was painfully embarrassed, thinking we knew—which was not the case as yet—of his expression of disbelief in the play, and he urged me to remove Uncle Ben and all the elements of Willy's hallucinatory life because the audience would be hopelessly uncertain whether they were in the past or the present. At that time American theatrical experience also was primarily realistic, in the pictorial sense of the word.

I keep pressing the cast to ask questions, not only for the questions themselves but to help me judge where their minds are in relation to the play and American culture. At last the actress playing the Woman in Boston, who occasionally sleeps with Willy when he is there, asks, "Is she a Bad Woman?" This actress has the right voluptuousness, the round Chinese face and a sexy solidity of flesh. Ying quickly interrupts to explain that to Chinese a woman has to be "Bad" to be so promiscuous, and I detect no irony in his voice.

Considering how I am to reply, I think that the actress and perhaps Ying as well and maybe the whole cast are hoping that she is *not* Bad—a prostitute—so it is easy to tell them that she is a lonely woman who has a regular office job and is not at all a prostitute, and that she genuinely likes Willy and his line of gab and his pathos, and so she sees him for dinner perhaps twice a month and they talk and "behave like husband and wife for a night." Great relief on all sides. It would have been difficult to add that she might have a similar relation to a couple of other salesmen from time to time and still not be thought of as a prostitute or even Bad. But this would also be hard to explain in parts of the United States.

I am not sure they accept her behavior as truly non-Bad, but I leave it ambiguous in the hope that she will not try to play a Chinese vamp. I don't trust their notions of Western sexuality, even if I have no experience of the Chinese kind; I remember that on our last visit in 1978, couples did not so much as touch hands in public. Amazingly enough, nowadays they have had to clear a small, dense patch of shrubbery not far from the American Embassy because of its attraction for extrabotanical exercises.

Now that the subject of sexuality is opened up, Happy raises his hand to say that the Chinese would probably not understand his character. This actor's personality baffles me; he is rather small and slight, with straight black hair, longer than usual here, that flows down above his left eye, and a thoroughly pleasant but somehow indefinite, even evasive smile. He seems too young for Happy, about twenty-four, and far too passive for that sexually overheated character, but I keep telling myself that maybe these traits will appear different to Chinese and that I must give him his head. Ying's casting was so right in the other parts, it is hard to believe this fellow is as wrong as he seems at this point.

"What do you think they won't understand?"

Ying intervenes. "He means, I believe, that they will understand the workings of his character, but the play seems not to condemn his womanizing. In Chinese society a man talking about women as Happy does—bowling them over and so on—would be a rotter."

"You mean it will leave them uneasy because he is sympathetic?"

"Exactly. The *i*'s have to be dotted here."

Ying translates our little exchange and the cast laughs, but with a certain uneasiness, as though they are not sure themselves about the matter.

I decide to leave it right there, for the time being. Let their anxieties deepen, it will charge them up all the higher. And anyway I am leaving the country two days after we open.

I ask Linda how she feels about her character and whether such women are to be found in Chinese society today.

"Oh, many, many. There are a lot whose lives are wound around their husbands', and who think only of their men and very little about themselves." The cast nods reassuringly to me. The time has not yet come to tell her that this idea of Linda is mistaken. I am better at working in detail than in throwing out broad generalities.

But in an attempt to fill in my sense of the country—rather than to document the character, which I see somewhat differently than the actress does—I ask whether this attitude, even if so prevalent, is not regarded as old-fashioned now. The cast is emphatic—it certainly is old-fashioned. To pin it down, I ask Biff and Happy, who are seated together, if their generation has women in it like Linda, and they are incredulous that I can have imagined such a thing, and set up a cross talk directed at me through Ying.

"The women," he translates, "earn their own livings now and that's the basis of the whole relationship. In fact"—he grins, pursing his mouth comically again and popping his eyes behind his thick lenses—"it's usually the women who throw the men out, not the other way around."

Everyone guffaws. They are aware of riding a wave of change that has by no means hit the beach and flattened out yet.

I have been catching a certain tone of condescension toward Willy's character coming from Linda and Willy—from him, especially—from time to time. Perhaps it is unconscious; or possibly I misunderstand. It came at me yesterday and again two or three times today, an indefinable but dangerous attitude that could lead to a satiric interpretation, which would leave Ying Ruocheng unable to sustain the role the whole length of the play. (I am not sure he has yet caught on to how physically difficult this part is going to be.) But most important, I cannot let the play become a satire.

"I want to say a few things about the play and Willy now," I announce. They become silent quickly. It is now clear, incidentally, that they normally discuss a play for days and sometimes weeks before trying to do scenes and, like all actors, would—up to a certain point—much prefer interesting general discussions to hard work. But I am coming to realize that in this type of theatre there is no rush to do anything. "You are all aware, I'm sure, that Willy is foolish and even ridiculous sometimes. He tells the most transparent lies, exaggerates mercilessly, and so on. But I want you to see that the impulses behind him are not foolish at all. He cannot bear reality, and since he can't do much to change it, he keeps changing his ideas of it." I am veering close to ideology; I note some agreement here, but it is uneasy. Charley is especially rapt and unable, I believe, to come down on the side of my argument. "But the one thing he is not, is passive. Something in him knows that if he stands still he will be overwhelmed. These lies and evasions of his are his little swords with which he wards off the devils around him. But his activist nature is what leads mankind to progress, doesn't it. It can create disaster, to be sure, but progress also. People who are able to accept their frustrated lives do not change conditions, do they. So my point is that you must look behind his ludicrousness to what he is actually confronting, and that is as serious a business as anyone can imagine. There is a nobility, in fact, in Willy's struggle. Maybe it comes from his refusal ever to relent, to give up."

Silence. It worries me, their never having seen it in this light, the character of this screwball; quite probably they had been moving toward a satiric interpretation, or at least one that would let them off the hook as actors, and the audience as well. I see now why Ying was so insistent that I come and direct; he is especially still, especially open to this apparently novel line on the play, although I have no doubt he has always seen the role as basically a tragic one.

Now Ben has a question. This actor is a short fellow with a certain ferocity in his gaze; the outer corners of his eyes are curled up like those of the Chinese opera villain-masks, especially when he concentrates on what I am saying. Compact and quick-moving, he already has a certain pecky style. Even when he suddenly changes, and bursts out laughing, there is some danger in him—all of this is perfectly subjective, of course; he is doubtless sweet and kind.

"Is Uncle Ben a ghost?" he asks.

"A ghost?"

"Yes."

"I'm not sure what you want to know." I dread misleading him; it will take days to undo some mistaken but—to him—attractive image.

"Chinese plays," he explains, "do not have ghosts."

"Really? I had some idea they did, but it doesn't matter. I realize that you cannot play a 'ghost' but what you should play is Willy's brother."

"Ah!" This seems to please him. "But I am really dead?"

"Oh yes. And you exist in his memory with certain characteristics that are not necessarily realistic. I mean that you must play him as Willy recalls him. He carries tremendous meaning for Willy, and you must learn what that is as time goes by. But for now you can forget the 'ghost' and think of yourself as his elder brother who made a great success in South African diamond mines, okay?"

He has an image and he is happy. A real actor, thank God.

But Ying is not quite satisfied. "What Mr. Miller was trying to say, I believe, is that sometimes Ben has his own character and sometimes he simply voices Willy's thoughts. In other words, he is and is not a real person like the other people in the play."

"That's not a contradiction," I add. "We all remember actual people we once knew but we remember them in a nonobjective way, a way that emphasizes and even parodies some of their qualities. It depends on what they mean to us, doesn't it."

Ying understands, and translates this for Ben, who seems to sop it up, nodding eagerly. So Freud works here, too.

Now Charley is back with another question—I feel good about their being relaxed enough now to leave off raising their hands like students.

"He wants to know," Ying says, "whether he and Willy play cards for money."

I had never thought of this before, but actually they would be putting down small bets, and so I ask, "Do Chinese play cards much?"

"Oh, we love cards but never play for money."

Which brings back a walk I took in Yanan five years ago, when I saw a pretty hot card game going on in the middle of a field on the edge of town, with money on the ground and guys yelling with every card played. I had learned then of the state's prohibition on card gambling, a national vice the government was trying to stamp out. Without raising the political issue, I ask, "Could you play for small stakes in that scene?"

"Certainly, if that's called for." (Whether by design or simply because the very complicated mechanics of the scene made it nearly impossible, no money was ever subsequently used. However, it wasn't in the first New York production either, but it is interesting that the political side of the question was not put to me.)

Still drugged by the worst jet lag I have ever experienced I return to the theatre at seven o'clock in the evening for the first reading of Act Two. I believe they might well turn out to be quite fine, and allow myself a more or less total silence as the reading proceeds. Inge is in tears at the end.

The weirdest part of this day is that in the car on the way back to our lodgings at the end of the reading, I realize again that I had been able to follow the dialogue almost always without using my English script, staying with the actors line for line. Even the lengths of sentences are nearly the same. It is uncanny. Yet, on questioning Inge I learn that the *content* of the lines is very often quite different, involving as it does the imagistic Chinese vocabulary. For example, Willy reports to his boys on his vastly successful selling trip: "Knocked 'em cold in Providence, slaughtered 'em in Boston." This becomes "I tumbled them backwards in Providence-ah, and they fell on their faces in Bos-i-ton!" But it had an uncannily similar sound and almost precisely the same beat.

I fall asleep as soon as I contemplate the bed, but wake every few hours, startled. I am still drugged, numbed, but not unhappy. These will be fifteen-hour days for me, rising at seven to have breakfast and drive to the theatre, with bedtime only after the ten o'clock finish of rehearsals at night. But I am looking forward.

## March 23

We will work only from nine to twelve today because a banquet for the whole cast, Inge, Rebecca, and myself will take up the evening. It will be at *The* Sichuan Restaurant, which according to Ying Ruocheng is the best in the world and the only one with the right to that honorific *The*. I am ready.

I decide to begin our first attempt at an acting rehearsal with the card-playing scene; first, because it involves what I think are our two most accomplished performers, whose success in it, if it begins to show signs of life, will encourage the others, and second, because it is a sitting-down scene that involves a minimal amount of blocking, so they and I can concentrate on their characters. It is also because Ben has much importance in it and I find myself more and more baffled by something impenetrable about this actor. Perhaps it is his absurdly fierce eyes with those half-curled creases of ferocity at the outer corners.

So Ying Ruocheng and Charley sit at the kitchen table and I take a chair a few feet in front of the set, and immediately we have the problem of how to play casino, the game indicated in the script, whose rules I forgot in high school—Lee Cobb and Howard Smith were both fanatic gamblers, so no one had to tell them anything. I confess to the two actors that I have forgotten the game and wonder if they know a Chinese card game they can work into the lines instead, the only requirement being that with a certain line Willy has to break up the game by yelling, "That's my build!" unable to continue talking to Charley once his vision of Ben has moved into the room.

"We could play gin. Would that be all right?" Ying asks. I see no reason why not, and he and Charley sit down and proceed to work out a gin game that can use up a certain number of plays, each connected to a line of dialogue, until an ace is played and Willy can claim it. The whole complicated business takes them a matter of minutes and I am so surprised that I congratulate them both.

"Oh God"—Ying laughs—"he and I did nothing for three and a half years but play gin under a tree all day! During the Cultural Revolution we were both shipped off to a cadre school to raise rice. We can play gin together with our eyes closed."

This gets us onto a question I'd been wondering about: as to exactly how the Cultural Revolution had affected this theatre. It was, it turned

Charley and Willy rehearse the casino game scene, with the cast watching and Miller directing.

out, absurdly simple: all work had stopped for years. The whole company was simply kept off the stage but not stricken from the payroll, so the actors were frustrated and bored out of their heads but less than desperate.

Jiang Qing, Mao's wife, and her entourage stopped all theatrical productions and sent directors, authors, and entire casts to the pig farms and rice fields for the rest of their lives. "We do not need them," she actually said. In her Eight Permissible Plays, the Good were clearly set apart from the Bad, and the very notion of any inner division in human beings was quite simply outlawed. China was to be a country of Good People, and Good People do not read books and think, they know what is good for them simply because they are Good. And so on.

Ying thinks that this practice of continuing to pay salaries to people thrown out of their offices and professions all over the country is what kept such social peace as there was in China. But did the theatre close?

"No, no"—Ying laughs—"Jiang Qing staged her Eight Permissible Plays!" With what actors? "Why the Beijing Opera actors, who never knew what was really happening; they rarely do. They're taken for training at the age of eight and never get an education in anything else. Rather like ballet dancers. They didn't think it particularly odd that a hundred actors were hanging around the back of the theatre year after year."

And so in this very rehearsal room "where we played a lot of gin year after year until they shipped us off," they are playing gin again, and this is why they had worked out the scene in no time at all.

One can't help seeking parallels in Western experience for this extraordinary phenomenon—a government driving people away from their jobs and professions and at the same time continuing faithfully to pay their salaries. The inevitable American analogy would seem to be our short but very passionate McCarthy blacklisting period, but that seems to me to have had more reality, in that people not only were disgraced, in a way not dissimilar to the Cultural Revolution's practice, but were deprived of their paychecks, too. What message was Chinese society attempting to transmit to itself in those weird times? Is it possible that even in the back of the Red Guards' heads was the long subliminal road of China's ever-changing history that promised that this, too, would pass, and so the victims of the moment must therefore be fed and not destroyed? This is tempting, but the truth was that many people were driven to suicide, many were tortured to death, many were nearly killed, many were crippled for life, and in some estimates that I have heard the number of dead passes the million mark for all of China. Ying Ruocheng calls it "our Holocaust."

All I can attest to is that as far as this cast of Chinese actors is concerned, there is a kind of contempt for the era they lived through, but at the same time they laugh about its insane excesses; sometimes, when they compare experiences, they sound like young people talking about the lunacies endured at summer camp. But I expect I will have more on this later.

With these thoughts in the background, I stood there watching Charley and Ying working out the card-game dialogue, matching it with their plays, and it seems obvious why Charley has from my first introduction to him appeared so right for the part, although a bit too ascetic physically, not crude enough; it is that there has been a kind of mutual understanding between him and Ying from the outset, and now as they sit across the table from each other under the gray light from a high row of small windows near the ceiling on one wall, I feel a kind of magical confluence of history's unaccountable accidents: that this play—written and produced in the same year as China's Revolution—should provide the occasion for these two actors to use an expertise that they so unwillingly learned and fruitlessly practiced year after pointless year and in this very same spot.

Since they had been drilling lines before my arrival I am able to work the card-playing scene in a sketchy form, moving Ben into it; I do not expect results so much as a chance to feel out how best to work with them. I find them quick, even too quick, to obey suggestions, often without quite understanding what their motivations are. But they are also trained, it seems, to sort themselves out on a stage, and to move gracefully from position to position, and to keep themselves theatrically alive whenever they are obliged to be silent for periods of time. Ben seems especially graceful. He has an odd curving line to his vocal sound, however, which seems unnatural to me, and at every opportunity turns himself to face the audience. After an hour or so I decide the card-game scene will ultimately work all right with these two veterans, although I am bothered a bit by their mechanical aptitudes in acting first and thinking about it afterward. But better this than actors endlessly philosophizing at me with their rationalizations.

Having explained the underlying psychological process of the scene—Willy's summoning the image of his older brother Ben, whose presence in turn forces him to break up the game—I have nothing more to tell them until they are more familiar with their characters. Suddenly I find myself saying that I would like to start blocking the play from the opening. I had not planned to do this, but I suppose their technical aptitude so impressed me that I thought to approach them through it rather than the other way around, by talking about the story and characters in general. If I block the scenes, it may be possible to occupy common ground, since they are doubtless good at it.

And so for the first time in China, Willy Loman enters with his two valises. Immediately he has trouble with them; they are as enormous as footlockers, and must be changed. He mimes unlocking the door of this mock-up set, enters the kitchen, puts down the valises, and speaks the first sighing lines, "Oh boy, oh boy," rubbing his hands. Whereupon I look for Linda in the bed, but it is empty. Ying looks around the room, searching for her.

She is behind me, just getting into her coat, and telling me with her soft smile that as a member of the city's Revolutionary Council she has to leave now to cast her vote for mayor of Beijing. With a good-bye wave she is toddling off, and that's the end of the rehearsal for her, for not only the morning but the day, since the whole cast will be attending the dinner this evening.

The incident typifies the odd absence of the kind of urgency that is a normal part of a new production in New York. But I believe it is part of the way of life in a state-subsidized theatre almost anywhere. The good in it is that actors get to play all kinds of parts over a period of years, developing their skills to maturity instead of rocketing into the sky in one or two plays and then vanishing forever, as they do with us; most American actors are simply wasted. The bad in it is, however, that people sometimes vegetate in what amounts to a civil-service job from which competition is effectively barred. The older actors, whatever their uselessness to the company, have to be carried on the roster and their salaries paid to the grave, which sometimes means the sacrifice of far more necessary expenditures, and they occupy places that should be going to the young. As in Russia, Sweden, Austria, and some of the German state theatres, the roster is overloaded with gray. (In the Swedish Royal Dramatic Theatre, many years ago, I passed the open door of a dressing room and, glancing in, saw an old actor who could have been in his nineties seated by a lace-curtained window, reading his paper through a magnifier—a touchingly human picture. The dressing room was his for life, as was his salary. But the truth was that the younger people were impatient for him to pass on.)

Our banquet was delicious but uneventful. I was nearly falling asleep. At such occasions as the welcoming of a foreign guest, issues of any sort do not come up, and there is only so much one can say about food. Afterward, however, we—Rebecca, Inge, and I—went to Ying's house to meet his wife, Wu Sheliang. The house nestles in a maze of dark, cleanly swept lanes where lightless figures move silently on rubber-soled shoes. There is no suggestion of apprehension and no police in evidence either. As with a number of other situations, this one mystifies with its contrast to the violence of recent Chinese history. There is a medieval aspect to these narrow lanes, the gray brick houses with their lowering, steeply curving roofs and blank streetside walls that rarely admit a window. As we walk Ying says, "This scene could be a hundred years ago." Then he hurries on ahead to unlock his courtyard door, but really to call an advance warning to his wife inside the house, "I have brought guests!"

Wu Sheliang appears in the doorway of the tiny house, a cheerful, round-faced intellectual whose vivacity is much like Ying's and her English almost as good, too. They met in the university decades ago, and worked together in the theatre where she was an actress. The rectangular living room is loaded with books from floor to ceiling, a great many in English, and also contains a television set that is on, showing a parade welcoming Chinese dignitaries at some airport. We arrange ourselves around the large table in the center of the room, but no one thinks to turn off the annoying screen until I can't help making the move, asking what the program is. Only now is Wu Sheliang reminded it is still on, with the parade-band music a foot behind her ear, and she quickly turns it off—an inurement to sound that is very common in China, possibly because everyone here has lived his life in such crowded quarters and, more, in such a crowded *idea*. In rehearsals, actors will sit observing their fellows working on a scene and continue to talk among themselves in normal unmuted tones and without any noticeable annoyance to the people trying to act. Indeed, during actual performances that I have seen in Chinese theatres, the audience is as busy communicating with itself as it is listening to the play, going silent only during intermissions, probably out of exhaustion. I am assured that with *Salesman* there will be silence out front. We shall see.

I am naturally on the lookout for anything that might throw light on the Chinese relationship with the play, but in this house we are inevitably thrown back to the Cultural Revolution, when both Ying and his wife were in exile, growing rice at a cadre school some fifty miles from Beijing. "It was the world's most expensive rice"—she laughs—"because after all we were still being paid our professional salaries."

"Instead of eighteen cents a catty, it was nearer eighteen dollars," Ying adds.

One has only to look around this room to wonder if this is why a certain surrealism has overwhelmed our way of thinking about Chinese and China. Ying bought the house in 1950, but during the leveling spasm of the Cultural Revolution, ownership of all houses had to be handed over to the state, which, however, took over payments for their upkeep. Only now, as pragmatism once again seeps back into the higher councils, is it becoming a matter of governmental debate as having been a bad bargain. "I hope they don't decide to give me back ownership," Ying says, laughing, for his rent is a pittance now, and the government pays for repairs. Moreover, since it is illegal to dispossess anyone from his home in China, he has all the benefits of ownership and none of the costs. He expects this to change, however.

The original idealism of the Cultural Revolution is something this couple chooses not to forget. Their daughter was not unhappy at first at being sent to Inner Mongolia to be a shepherdess in that vast, barely populated land, for it meant serving the people, she thought. She stayed for six years, listening to the wind and staring at the sky. But gradually doubts set in that she was wasting her mind, and she made her way back to the city to go from one attempt to another in search of a life that could serve both her own development and society.

Except for its surrounding political turmoil their daughter's story would be familiar to any parent in the West, where youth's thirst for moral and occupational authenticity has kept societies seething for decades now. For our twenty-year-old daughter, Rebecca, however, the Cultural Revolution is a mixed image and not at all entirely negative, and one hears resistance in her voice to any total rejection of it, although she is being forced to recognize where it went so wrong. And through her reaction now, so purified by distance, one can imagine how attractive it must have been initially, especially its daring, idealism, and rejection of money values for the sake of human relations, which in China means revolutionary relations. I note Inge also sympathizing with her daughter's frustrations in trying to sort out what happened to China in those terrible years. Ying Ruocheng and Wu Sheliang are likewise not ready to condemn the entire movement out of hand, at least not its initial motives. "One simply cannot erase that idealism," Wu says, "because we need its cleansing power and always will. There *was* corruption to eradicate and there were the dominating habits of officials and so on. But it went crazy. We think that Mao was simply out of it in his last years. You know he couldn't leave his room to greet Nixon, he was practically inert. It was an adventure by a tiny clique around his wife." I think this begs the question of one-party rule, but I keep my silence, knowing that it is not something that can be faced as yet.

## March 24

By ten o'clock this evening, rehearsal's end, I feel exhausted from trying to create the kind of energy in our Happy that the part must have. Alone with Ying at the Lomans' kitchen table in the vast brown room after everyone has left, I try to face the problem with him. Now that I have begun actually to work the first bedroom scene with the two younger actors, the difficulties seem terrible to me, but I soften my worries so as not to throw Ying, who has his own role to think about. But the scene raises a key thematic issue which resonates through the entire action to come—how Biff is to create a life that can gratify him and at the same time pursue what is essentially his father's standard of success. This classically American dilemma suddenly seems far away from the China I am seeing on the streets and in the poverty of our actors' clothes and of what I know of their living quarters and level of life. Is there anything in China now that I can relate Happy to, or is the whole success theme something he will have to imagine as happening way out there across the ocean?

Ying Ruocheng is not only a translator and actor but of necessity a kind of diplomat who, like it or not, represents this theatre before me, and this obligation, I believe, must narrow his field of candor. But there is a production at stake; I am not ready by any means to ask for a replacement for Happy but I sense no way to cut through the suavity. And in addition, to my totally untutored ear there is something odd about his speech. "Am I hearing something different from him, some gliding quality in his way of speaking?"

Ying comes alert, a half-smile playing on his mouth. "It's amazing you caught that. . . ."

"His words seem to have no bite, they flow almost soothingly, and he's got some kind of *zzzjjj* sound . . . he sounds like a diplomat or a radio announcer."

This actor is the youngest in the troupe, about twenty-five or so, with jet-black hair and a slender, handsome face. Offstage he is sensitive and soft-spoken to a fault, with a thoughtless elegance in his physical movements and his fine hands. Physically, he is wrong for Happy—a strapping guy, brash, moody, and sometimes self-condemning, none of the qualities our actor possesses. But he is handsome and suggests a narcissism that might bring out the character's aggressive selfishness. And he does have a certain acuity—on our first day it was he who found the Chinese parallel to Lomanism in the Chinese father's wish that his sons be "dragons." But my initial impression of his ascetic rather than sensuous quality has now sharpened. I have given him a felt hat to try on and a comb to primp his hair during his talk to Biff in their pajamas in the bedroom, but he takes one absentminded swipe with the comb and drops it back in his pocket; rather than admiring himself in the mirror with the hat on, he plops it on his head and takes it off, unable to primp and talk at the same time.

Ying is downcast, far more so than he should be when he has his own part to worry about. "I'm really surprised you caught that odd quality in his speech, but it's true. He has been trained to talk that way, it's an affectation that's not uncommon in our theatre. And it could be especially damaging to this translation because I was trying to break through the formalized diction we normally use on the stage. But I am going to keep at him. I still think he can be good."

He seems even more depressed than I, probably because he so wants not to let me or the production down. Partly to cheer him up I say, "He's not bad in the faster passages, you know, where he just hasn't time for the accent and has to let fly."

"I'll get after him right away. . . ."

So we still have hope for him, I perhaps more than Ying. But it will be a pity if the boy's manner makes the language seem artificial when Ying's whole effort was to create something new, a really contemporary Beijingois paralleling the Lomans' speech. Although, as I have pointed out, and Ying, incredibly for a foreigner, realizes, the Lomans are usually trying *not* to speak "commonly." In fact, their rhetorical flourishes dot the play and are echoes of Willy's vision of himself and Biff transcending into something more classy in life, something like glory.

All of which reminds me that in China art traditionally *means* style rather than any kind of crude verisimilitude; it has always worked to transmute rather than report the visible and audible reality. The problem for the Chinese now is that as they leave behind the ordered "naturalism" of their recent regime-enforced infantilism and begin to deal with life's complexities in the theatre as well as in other arts, a vacuum in their stylistic arsenal appears. I will write more about this later; I see now that their hopes for Salesman are largely based on its exploding the proscenium through its flowing from locale to locale and its bending of conventional time while still moving the onlooker emotionally.

I find myself pressing Ying for his ideas on the issue of success in the Chinese psyche, since Willy is so passionate about it. He believes that it was and is a universal problem for young people—such as his children—who wish to do their own thing and still amount to something in the world. But what about money as a token of success here? "Of course it is," he says. "The more highly trained people make more money, get into higher categories of personnel ratings. Everybody respects and celebrates the working class but nobody is against getting out of it."

I have not had time to press this viewpoint on Happy, not that it itself can help him, but maybe it will get me closer to him, and him to the story of his character. Anything to break down his suavity in that first scene.

In every production the moment arrives when the honeymoon is over and the marriage begins out of which, one hopes, a living rather than stillborn birth will emerge. I still do not understand a word of Chinese, of course, and to be candid with myself, I find toward the end of a rehearsal period a certain grating quality to its general sound, something Inge stoutly denies. I suppose it is as much my frustration at trying to penetrate an incomprehensible gibberish hour after hour as any objective quality of the language itself. In any case, after running and reading Act One two or three times I realize that I have penetrated not the language but many of the actors' intentions, and some of them, I now think, are sentimental, untrue.

Linda, who at first seemed so charmingly devoted to Willy and yet so much herself, so dignified, tends to verge on warbling, especially in her two-page-long aria where she pleads with the boys to help save Willy, who she fears is trying to kill himself. I stop the scene at one point (and only then wonder if I am perhaps breaching etiquette by correcting her before others), and as diplomatically as possible, I remind her that she is talking not about a dead husband toward whom she has these retrospective feelings, but one who is alive in a crisis right now. There is

Zhu Lin, as Linda.

no time to feel pity for oneself in such an emergency situation; she has a task to perform in the scene, which is to get Biff to find a job in New York and begin rescuing his old man from certain suicide.

Looking into her eyes I feel at home, gratified that all actors are the same. She has the spark of recognition, the wit, one might call it, of the aware performer who can turn it on or off almost at will. She is far too experienced not to know what she has been doing—drawing audience sympathy rather than playing the scene—and I begin to fear that she will easily outwit me or wear me down before the end. Nevertheless, she starts again, and this time it is much more simple, direct, almost but not quite free of the warbling. I learn that, like the actor playing Happy, she is of a tradition—in her case, that of the Mother, who in effect is always a warbler. In this play, however, such exploiting of the sentiments will sink them all in a morass of brainless "feeling" that finally is not feeling at all but an unspecific bath of self-love. I suppose it is inevitable that she reminds me of the bits of Yiddish theatre I saw years ago in New York. There, too, the Mother was a lachrymose fount; crying was what Mothers are for. But on thinking about it I see that this is no monopoly of Jews or, for that matter, of Chinese. If one recalls the early movies, most of them performed by actors of Irish background, Mother was always on the verge of tears, too. Lachrymosity must represent some stage in the evolution of society, nationality having little to do with it.

## March 25

Our press conference. I have finally had to resort to this mass interview or spend most of my time saying the same things to the foreign and Chinese reporters who have put in requests. In a large room in the theatre Ying and I face perhaps fifty people packed together, including four or five TV crews from the American and Canadian networks and a dozen still photographers of many nationalities.

For once the bulk of the questioning is not trivial or fatuous. Why was *Salesman* chosen? Was it as propaganda against the American way of life? Is it really possible for Chinese to relate to the very American situation and to Willy Loman's character? Do Chinese actors work differently from Americans in creating their roles? Is the humor likely to register? Are there really any parallels in Chinese society? Will the production be closed to the public, and with "certain strata" let in to see it (as apparently had been the case with some productions in the past)? How much will tickets cost? Are tickets going to be sold to anyone at the box office or distributed to organizations?

I take a positive stance, since we have only rehearsed two full days and I do not yet know all the problems. I tell them that I feel I am quickly learning how to read the actors' signals; that while it is obvious that our cultural semaphores are vastly different, perhaps they are really referring to the same basic information deep within us. I theorize a universality of human emotions; I hope that the production here of this very American play will simply assert the idea of a single humanity once again.

At this point I can only say that the actors seem to have no difficulty in putting themselves into the parts; there must surely be some exotic mysteries for them in this play, but, after all, the Chinese practically invented the family, which is the core of the play, and the social interrelationships with the family struggle have been a part of Chinese life for a very long time.

As for the humor, at least the cast is laughing when laughter is called for, so I presume we have a chance to do the same with an audience. Parallels exist in the play with Chinese society, I have reason to think, assuming that people want to rise in the world everywhere. And if there aren't as yet traveling salesmen in this country, I conjecture that the idea of such a man is easily enough grasped from the text itself. In any case, the salesman motif is in some great part metaphorical; we must all sell ourselves, convince the world of a persona that perhaps we only wish we really possessed.

Ying Ruocheng now takes some questions about the theatre and the production. He is, of course, a star in China, and all the reporters know him and seem to have confidence in his candor. Tickets, he says, will cost one yuan (about fifty cents), and anyone who comes to the box office can buy them, the more the better (a remark in which I sense a little more confidence than he really has). The production will run as long as there is a strong enough demand by the public. He disapproves of the practice of distributing tickets through unions and other organizations in order to dragoon an audience. In fact, "that kind of thing only demonstrates that you've got a flop."

It begins to sound more and more like Broadway, and one of the reporters interrupts to ask me if I had an agreement as to how long they were to run the play. I had nothing of the kind, I said; I expect it to run as long as the public cares to attend, but of course at fifty cents a ticket this has to be a lot longer than my plays have sometimes run at American prices.

Which leads us to ticket prices in New York, a problem I had left behind only a few days before when I attempted to get the eighteen-to-thirty-two-dollar range lowered for the revival of *A View from the Bridge* at the Ambassador Theatre. When I tell them the New York price range—to which Ying Ruocheng adds that he paid forty-five dollars to see *Cats*—there is a gasp of incredulity from the Chinese reporters present. Forty-five dollars is more than a month's wage for most of them and double for some, intellectuals being among the lowest-paid people in China.

I think the best part of the conference is Ying's way of dealing with the propaganda question. "When it was announced that we were thinking about this project for our theatre, there was quite a bit of press comment in Taiwan," he contentedly begins. "They said, 'Cao Yu and Ying Ruocheng must be crazy to think they will be allowed to do *Death of a Salesman* in Beijing, let alone have Miller admitted to direct it.' So you see," Ying continues, "some people apparently think it a different kind of propaganda than others. But actually my own interest in it is basically aesthetic. I think it can open new territory to our own playwrights, since it does break out of the conventions that by and large have held us back. And of course I would love to play Willy, as any actor would."

Inge is then brought up to the front to account for having learned to speak and write Chinese so fluently. She has always tried to learn the language of a country in which she intends to photograph intensively, believing that the linguistic imagery can lead her deeper into the visual. She learned Russian before working in the Soviet Union for the same reason. What she does not say is that she is even more fluent in five other languages.

As a compromise I promise the TV reporters to open the theatre to them all for one afternoon's rehearsal, the alternative being to let in each crew separately, a disastrously time-consuming request. I will pick some afternoon after the middle of April. The trouble with filming a rehearsal, of course, is that I shall have to pretend I am "directing" or it will not seem to be a rehearsal. Actually my physical interference on the set will be quite rare.

## March 26

After yesterday evening's rehearsal Ying Ruocheng, with barely visible irritation, asked me if I would let him run lines with the cast next morning. I would not have to be present, since it would simply involve rote repetition. I was happy to hear this, because scene after scene has been collapsing due to their having to stop to retrieve lines. Ying knows almost all his words and has been the worst victim of the others' lapses. I asked him at the same time to press upon Linda the need to focus her mind on Willy rather than herself and to suppress her bad tendency to weep. I also wanted him to talk to Biff, who I think is now taking on the same sentimentality in spots. Ying Ruocheng, who is fantastically energetic and steady-minded, refusing either to illusion himself or to despair, said he would do his best with both actors. Aware that Zhu Lin's presence in the play will sell more tickets than any other factor, she being the biggest star in the cast, I am grateful that she pulls no rank and is always eager for direction—which of course she does not always use. She dresses in the same brown trousers and quilted brown tapestried short coat each day. In one sense I am glad she and I cannot converse, for she would doubtless have a lot to tell me about her reasons for acting the role as she does. This way, as two mutes, I say what I have to say and she can only nod pleasantly, often with what I take to be pleased surprise. But I am going to struggle with her to the end. She is really too good an actress and attractive a woman to waste her energy on tears.

It now appears that our Happy's speech pattern was not at all an acquired affectation, as Ying had thought, but a way of speaking common in his birthplace, a small town some fifty miles from Beijing. This information encouraged me to stop him in the middle of his first scene with Biff—where he should rather deliciously bemoan his success with women and business. Ying Ruocheng had several times pressed me to give him one simple line of direction rather than any kind of discussion about Happy's nature or his interactions with Biff. It suddenly occurred to me that what he lacked was enjoyment of his dilemma. I called up to the elevated bedroom, "You must be happy, that's all! The character is a very happy man!" His smile was one of relief. He went back to the scene, stood straight, and ticked it off as though he'd been playing it for months, his strain gone and with it a certain overlay of "tragic darkness." But he is still not right temperamentally.

Biff's sentimentality has largely disappeared. At one point he has to pick his old football helmet out of a chest beside his bed and, staring at it, say, "I've always made a point of not wasting my life, and . . . all I've done is to waste my life." The self-pity in it is difficult to watch. I told him that it is an ironical statement, a passing remark rather than something philosophically final. Now he does the speech again but with a grin of light self-mockery, then tosses the helmet back into the chest and walks away. It is really quite good, and gives his character strength. Remarkable how quickly they can shift like this. But it also implies how technical their approach is. I wonder whether our concept of an actor's inner life is at all useful to them, at least at this stage. The whole idea of theatre, it seems, is quite distant from a reflection of actual life, much closer to something formal and ritualistic. That he could change so quickly, and Happy likewise, must mean that they are playing purely by ear.

I must begin working on Act Two on Monday, so the time has come to turn some screws. I get onto the set and take the wild family fight scene, pointing out where the climaxes are and making them drill the cues for me so that we begin to get something approaching the rapid rhythms required. Since I am a head taller than any of them and my voice louder, I yell Willy's climactic line "Big shot!" and Biff's furious response, and Happy's "Wait a minute! I got a feasible idea!" throwing my arms out and belting at the top of my lungs. The shock in their faces tells me that they had never dreamed it went so loud and so far, that the threat in my tone was closer to danger than they had ever anticipated. Nevertheless they seem eager to do the scene again, and this time it goes so wild that the onlooking actors begin making noises as they watch, half-smiling, half-laughing with the excitement, and Ying blows himself out, losing *his* lines in the final tangle. But they seem to catch on to how high it must all reach, and there is some real excitement up there at last.

And so at the end of the first week I think they are capable of creating an American kind of performance, the direct, confrontational style of behavior the play requires. I am beginning to feel particularly good about Linda; on the final afternoon's run she has been far simpler, much more the woman on whom Willy relies, rather than the type to mop up after him. I suppose my hope in her springs from her intelligent, rather nobly commanding nature offstage. It will, I think, lead her to a stringent performance as best not only for the play but for her. At the end of rehearsals I decide it is time to tell her specifically that there is only one moment in Act One when she may actually weep, and that is on the single line "His life is in your hands." She opens her eyes even wider and looks surprised, but she nods deeply. I hope I understand what this means.

Ying Ruocheng's performance is already a joy. A real pro, yet a man full of intelligent feeling who is ready to try anything. He is about the size and shape of Cagney, balanced on short legs, a compact man who is able to come on cold, step onto the forestage and simply call up the feelings and joys of his great moment, decades ago, when through Biff he felt he was within inches of some fabled victory over life's ignominious leveling.

He seems to see Willy more and more accurately, as a little bantam with quick fists and the irreducible demand that life give him its meaning and significance and honor. I found myself standing up the other day and making a speech, to my own and everyone's surprise, and regretting it even as it was happening. But it suddenly seemed to me that with all their progress they were still being actors rather than humans who were privileged to express a poetic vision that lies within the play. They were not moving into the vision. I let myself say that the one red line connecting everyone in the play was a love for Willy; not admiration, necessarily, but a kind of visceral recognition that in his fumbling and often ridiculous way he is trying to lift up a belief in immense redeeming human possibilities. People can't stand him often, they flee from him, but they miss him when he isn't there. Perhaps it's that he hasn't a cynical bone in his body, he is the walking believer, the bearer of a flame whose going-out would leave us flat, with merely what the past has given us. He is forever signaling to a future that he cannot describe and will not live to see, but he is in love with it all the same.

*Death of a Salesman,* really, is a love story between a man and his son, and in a crazy way between both of them and America.

When I finished I feared I'd simply confused them. But two days later, in a car leaving an American Embassy reception for the whole company, Ying Ruocheng, in typical Chinese fashion, simply let drop that he was trying to get my speech written down; it apparently affected the cast, although at the time there was no visible reaction of any kind in their faces. This can drive you crazy, but it is still necessary to simply assert what has to be asserted and hope it has some effect.

There is a certain sensitive diffidence in the Chinese that, I confess, I never really considered before. It is difficult for them to put themselves forward except after some struggle. Ying Ruocheng, for one, does not volunteer to contradict another's mistaken information with what he knows to be accurate until asked his opinion. One comes upon frequent loud arguments in the neighborhood lanes, but I suspect it takes a lot to get their feelings to overleap the bounds, although of course when they do they are wildly passionate. I find that I must persist in drawing out the actors' own views in a way I would not be having to do in America, for example. I sensed yesterday that Charley was still having doubts about the reasons for his kindness to Willy—I can now read their eyes a bit better, I believe—and he admitted in a rather movingly hesitant way that this was so. I told him then what I had forgotten to in our earlier talks: that Charley has a deep feeling for Linda, whom he greatly admires. His face lit up then; he could act that. Paradoxically enough, it is also a kind of envy he feels for Willy's imagination, the condiments with which he sprinkles his life as contrasted with the blandness of Charley's more rational existence. Charley can laugh at Willy as a fool, but he is never bored by him. This seemed to help.

Ying Ruocheng feels that their diffidence, or reluctance to put themselves forward, is a legacy of Confucian self-abnegation, on top of which is laid the second grid of Communist suppression of individual personality, the leveling instinct; in both systems people really exist to serve the higher order, rather than the other way around as the American scheme has it. This may also lie at the root of what outsiders interpret merely as Chinese sexual puritanism. But Ying and others, too, deny that a puritan fear of sexuality is particularly Chinese; it is rather their sense of form that frowns on its public display. And in truth they do attempt to show a cool front in public quite apart from sexual matters. All the more baffling, then, how a monstrosity like the Cultural Revolution could have swept this country, when one of its chief features was to demand public avowals of proletarian loyalty and the most lavish public repentances for past sins against the workers' alleged interests. It actually got to where tens of thousands of people would be assembled in stadiums to witness and enjoy painful humiliations of some of their brightest intellectual and political stars. Ba Gin, one of their most praised novelists (and a major talent, I think), was forced to wear a dunce cap and kneel on broken glass before such a howling mob that packed the stadium.

## March 27

On Sunday, our off-day, a brunch at the apartment of the American Cultural Attaché, Leon Slowecki, for myself and the leading cast members—Happy and Biff left out, I don't know why. The Attaché's apartment is on an upper floor of one of the ultramodern apartment houses clustered together in the "foreign ghetto," as it is called, where foreign reporters must live as well as the employees of all the foreign embassies except, of course, the ambassadors themselves, who live in their own embassy compounds. The apartment reminded me of the Watergate Hotel; everything in place, a lovely view of a superhighway, and the inevitably debilitating sense of the occupants' impermanence.

Some good Bloody Marys, smoked salmon, Polish ham, fried chicken, fresh bread—which the Chinese did not seem to mind as a change, not at all. Deputy Chief of Mission Charles W. Freeman, who heads the Embassy's Political Department, seemed very historically knowledgeable, and both he and the Attaché speak Chinese fluently. Both young—in their forties. I find myself accepting their up-to-date estimation of current Chinese reality, and conceal my own disheartened feelings when Slowecki calmly advises that the Chinese audience will simply not understand *Death of a Salesman* without program notes that simplistically outline the story and how it is to be taken. Ying Ruocheng, who before this had been talking about writing just such an essay for the program, seems—I am not sure I am reading his expression correctly but I think so—a bit resistant to the description of the audience as unsophisticated, if not downright primitive.

Alone with me for a moment at one side of the room, Slowecki says that it is not simply the Communist regimentation of thought but the way things have been done here since the beginning of time. "Everything in China is metaphorical, nothing is what it claims to be. So you have to interpret it for them yourself or all they'll get is what the papers are going to tell them it means."

I suppose he is worried that it will simply become anti-American propaganda, something that concerns me, too. And of course I know about their interpreting everything as metaphor, something not particularly Chinese but Marxist, and not merely Marxist, come to think of it, but Continental; the Anglo-Saxon attitude toward art, especially the theatre, is packed full of unconcern with what it is supposed to signify, it is simply "about" its story and action and characters, inner theme and social implication being left to academia. So by the end of the brunch I am a bit worried, and in the elevator going down ask Ying Ruocheng again to be sure to write some précis of the play for the program, which he agrees to try to do soon.

I had arranged with Alex North, composer of the original incidental music, to have a tape sent that we could use, as well as a score. Alex did so at once but was eager to come himself and conduct the four-piece orchestra in a live performance for the opening, which could then be taped anew. But the expense forbade the trip, finally. On the second or third day of rehearsal I had the sound man run the music on his 1950 model East German tape recorder, which makes me nervous every time I look at it for fear it will break down during performance. *Salesman* cannot be performed without a tape recorder, which carries vitally necessary sounds as well as music. Sounds often cue action and lines at crucial moments. The tape recorder here has vacuum tubes and belongs in a museum.

Ying Ruocheng and the cast stood listening to the small wall speaker, and as the flute solo opened I once again felt its haunting evocation of Willy's longing. It is still the best play score I know of and launched Alex into Hollywood and his eight Academy Award nominations over the next quarter century. As the music played I remembered him sitting down at the upright piano in the basement of Kazan's brownstone house in New York and playing it for the first time, the cigarette hanging from his mouth, the smoke curling up around his large nose and sorrowful basset-hound eyes, and his naive look at both of us as he wondered if it was okay.

I listened only to the first few cues and was satisfied, but in rehearsal later, something nearly absurd seemed to sound from the music; finally I realized that apart from the flute and cello solo passages a big symphony orchestra was entering and realized that it was a tape of the music for the Fredric March film. It sounded silly on stage—poor lonely Willy with his little East German hat being backed up by forty instruments. So Ying is arranging to record a new tape from the score of the original play that Alex North sent. It has to be done in the Beijing radio station, which possesses the only decent hi-fi recording equipment in the city. Hardly a step can be taken, it seems, without some reminder of the poverty of this country.

That symphonic irruption in our tape reminds me of the film, which I so disliked, although Freddy March, who played Willy in it, could have been superb and had actually been our first choice for the role on the stage. I could never meet him in all the years that followed without at some point having to hear how he had to finish this goddam film he was in that prevented his making our rehearsal date. There was always guilt in his eyes when he told me that, but I think the truth was that he never understood the play's moves back and forth through time and had finally feared it would fail.

As for the film, it was the hermetic concept of Willy that defeated it, I think; it made him simply a mental case, and I felt at the time—the early 1950s—that this convenient distortion grew out of a political fear of indicting American society, something that would have been dangerous in those years.

After the film had been completed I was asked by Columbia Pictures to come to a screening of a short that they had made to precede the showing of *Salesman* in all movie theatres. This amounted to lectures by professors at the City College of New York's School of Business to demonstrate that Willy Loman was simply an inefficient salesman, that the profession itself was a sound one, and the whole story of *Death of a Salesman* was merely silly. At the end of the screening the Columbia executives, who must have spent half a million dollars on this stupefying piece of propaganda, asked what I thought, and I said I would sue them if possible, that they had attacked me through the short, and that they were asking for a scandal. The short was never shown, but shortly afterward the Columbia publicity department asked if I would be good enough to sign an anti-Communist pledge for the American Legion before *Salesman* was released, lest it be picketed by the patriots, which of course I refused to do. I suppose that such experiences—there were many others in that period—helped prepare me to understand something of what artists have gone through in China, and it is both strange and somehow logical that I should be directing this same play in a room where more than a hundred actors spent years whiling away their blacklisted time.

My spirits rise but also fall, and as my second week of rehearsal looms I find myself wondering what got into me to attempt this, a difficult, psychologically complex play, with actors to whom I cannot even communicate except with the broadest strokes of overemphatic interpretation. Or so it often seems. I do not know whether I have penetrated these humans, whose faces, with one or two exceptions, tell so little of their feelings. Still, in momentary flashes of optimism I wonder if it is my illusion that as the days pass either they are expressing more in their eyes or I am detecting more there. Nevertheless, it is clearer to me now why China has always been a mirror to reflect whatever the West wishes to project upon it. I think especially of our illusions of socially integrated man, regulated from cradle to grave by basically friendly rules devised by philosopher-emperors or leaders like Mao. These people are all things to us, our sage guides and the same time our helpless, expectantly pure children.

I go into my second week knowing nothing and secure in my understanding that I know nothing. This well-earned modesty refreshes me.

Ying Ruocheng's biggest worry now is that the audience will not understand how life insurance works and, hence, Willy's suicide in order to bequeath money to Biff. There is nothing like life insurance in this country, at least there hasn't been. But I have just read in today's *China Daily* that a company was organized in 1980, the People's Insurance Company of China, that has been doing a fabulous business insuring property and vehicles as well as crops in transit. On a trial basis they are now offering a pigeon-raising policy and have even begun testing life insurance in several provinces. The Western notion of a gratifyingly all-covering social security system turns out to be far from the facts. Older citizens are often in great need even by Chinese standards. Ying is surprised and happy to learn about insurance but still intends to explain how it works in the program notes. These, as in German theatres, are carefully read here and often are elaborate essays on the play. But salesmanship and insurance are at the heart of Willy's situation; how can an audience enter into the play without knowing about them?

## March 28

This morning I blocked Act Two up to Willy's entrance into Charley's office, where he meets Bernard, now a successful young lawyer. I am growing more concerned that the set is to be placed too far upstage from the audience. There is a deep forestage, built on two descending levels, and with a thirteen-hundred-seat house the play may get lost.

Control of this theatre, built in the early 1950s, was initially contested by the Beijing Opera Company, which indeed would find it ample for their biggest productions. But Ying Ruocheng and Cao Yu and the rest of the leadership of the People's Art Theatre, which is sponsoring *Salesman* now, wanted to keep it for plays. Zhou Enlai settled matters by offering to give the theatre to the group that would guarantee to keep it operating three hundred and sixty-five days a year. The opera, of course, could never hope to mount that many productions and lost the battle.

There are blowups of photos in the lobby showing Zhou with groups of actors, some of whom I recognize from this company. He was a close observer of their progress—their patron, in effect. It is not usually made much of, but he and Cao Yu acted women's parts in Tianjin, their hometown, and Zhou was said to be both talented in them and beautiful.

Our first conflict among the actors this morning. In the scene before they all run off to the football game in Ebbets Field, Bernard pesters Biff to let him carry the shoulder guards into the locker room and Biff finally accedes, leaving a very disgruntled Happy to carry the helmet. I was busy studying my script for a moment when shouting broke out behind me, and I turned to find Ying apparently trying to mediate between Happy and Bernard. After a few moments Happy apparently backed off, still looking dark, and Ying explained, trying at the same time to keep a straight face, "Happy is upset because he feels that the shoulder guards are a much more important piece of apparatus than the helmet, and that as Biff's brother he should be the one to carry them." The actor playing Bernard now came over and, pleading the integrity of the script, demanded that he be given the shoulder guards as the stage directions indicate. I could only agree, but called Happy over and explained, through Ying, that as simple as the helmet might look, it was a tremendously vital piece of equipment, maybe even more so than the shoulder guards. He dismissed the whole argument, and, seeing that the older actors looking on were trying not to laugh, he grinned and turned away, regretting the silliness of the whole thing. Incidentally, his sister is a waitress in the best Beijing restaurant, which is also, he says, quite cheap, and has asked Happy to invite us there.

We have been moved to the Bamboo Gardens Hotel, where we shall be more comfortable, they say. We have two rooms at either end of a corridor, both quite small also, but the atmosphere of this place is indeed lovely. It was formerly the palatial home of Wang Dongxing, head of the Politburo under Mao. Jiang Qing had been his "protégée" in her Shanghai theatre days. He is regarded as having engineered her rise to Empress-like supremacy. Fortunately for him, he died just before one of his prime victims, Premier Deng Xiaoping, took office. Like Jiang Qing, the chief leveler, this fellow knew how to live, and Deng's pleasure was to turn this elaborate and beautiful private palace into a hotel for foreign guests. The restaurant is supposed to be first-rate. Surrounded by walls, like all important edifices in China, the complex is two stories high, of gray brick and stucco, and has outdoor covered walks whose columns are high-gloss Chinese red. There are a few large and expensive ground-floor suites, but not, apparently, for us. My only compensation for this whole job is free room and board and transportation while in China, so I guess I must be content with our miniature spaces. Still, we are rarely in these rooms except to sleep, so I suppose complaining is somewhat prideful and illogical. I have heard that Wang Dongxing tortured Mao's enemies in some secret cellar within these walls. The undulating roofs outside our windows are especially intriguing, with their concave, tentlike rising lines. There is a large willow just outside our window, but it is not yet in leaf, and a couple of sophora trimmed in dragonlike shapes. Naturally there is a heavy steel door in the wall facing the street, through which one steps into the *hutong,* and I cannot pass through it without thinking of those who entered in cars, bound and gagged, and never lived to come out. Could one hear screams from our room?

This evening, returning from a walk through the neighborhood, I got into conversation with three Americans whom I noticed at lunch in the restaurant. They had just been in Russia and Japan, where, as here, they sell and supervise the installation of gear-making machines designed in their plant in Rochester, New York. I was agreeably surprised to learn that the Japanese are still buying something from us, but it seems it is cheaper for them not to attempt to master the very complicated technology themselves. The Chinese, these Americans believe, will become a major competitive force in not too long a time. They are thorough, inquisitive, and intelligent. By comparison the Russians are square and do not venture beyond procedures as they are handed them. They wanted to know what business I was doing here and I told them I was directing *Salesman.* They knew the play very well and Willy Loman's name but could not remember who the author was. That pleased me, rather like life after dying.

I have become more and more aware of a tendency to overact, which, I see now, is general in the cast. Stepping back, I see a dreadful lot of pointing and laughing louder than necessary and frowning with anger and touching one another on the shoulder for emphasis. It is open-air acting, I suppose, and reminded me at one point this morning that the Cultural Attaché at the U.S. Embassy reception had said that the theatre audience is only a bit more sophisticated than the population in general. I find, though, that if I simply tell an actor not to point, frown, or touch, he desists at once and without any evident feeling of being constrained; in fact, they seem to agree instantaneously, as though they know that this is a gross habit. But of course I have no real way of corroborating my interpretation.

I have been turning on TV at night in our room out of sociological curiosity and find endemic the same overemphatic performing. This seems more strange, when on the street Chinese seem to behave and converse with a quite British reserve. An exception is their habit of looking over the shoulder of anyone whom they see writing. On a walk I took out my notebook to write the name of my lane in case I got lost, and found two men standing behind me and peering over my shoulder without the slightest qualm, and when I turned to look at them they pleasantly nodded back and waited for me to continue writing. Even in the hotel restaurant, where I have eaten a dozen times now, the waitresses always bend all the way down to watch me sign the check. The sheer act of putting pen to paper fascinates them.

There is a large full-length mirror at one end of the rehearsal space. Yesterday I walked in and found our tall Charley, dressed in an ankle-length robe of blue-and-silver-striped satin, stretching his long arms straight out sideways and lifting one leg in a long gracefully curving stride, then smoothly swiveling about and repeating. He is practicing for a performance in a traditional play. Then he laid his costume in a box and came onto the set with his card deck, ready for his scene with Willy, a lapse of centuries.

At one brief pause while I was trying to locate a speech in my script and the cast was waiting for me to find it, a laugh rippled around the room, and I looked up to find Linda, dressed as usual in her brown trousers and tapestried short coat, stepping down off the set and laughing in some embarrassment. I asked what was happening—she had done an imitation of President Reagan mounting a platform. She demurred when I asked her to repeat it, but finally gave in. She is a rather compact woman, not at all built like Reagan, but she now took on a posture amazingly suggestive of his—the squared shoulders, the rigid back and stiff neck—and strode across the forestage, and then with a little hop jumped up onto the six-inch-high platform and held a pose with one foot gaily raised to the height of her calf while turning to us with his happy, self-congratulatory smile. The lifting of that foot like a cutsie doll had in it all the transparently labored claim to eternal youth that is Reagan's imprint, but it was all done without malice, even with some pity for him, yet another human damned fool among many.

We were working on the restaurant scene: Willy has come here to get what he desperately hopes will be the good news about Biff's interview with Bill Oliver, from whom he wants to borrow money to start a new business. Willy sits at a table with his two sons, and Biff tells him that of course the whole idea of any important businessman lending him money is absurd. Willy goes deaf to this negative news, in effect, and seizing on the mere fact that Biff so much as attempted to see his former boss, begins pumping it up into a veritably successful interview. I kept pressing Ying Ruocheng to be more aggressive in his attempt to inflate the little good there was in Biff's story, and finally he said, "I have trouble with this moment; I mean, my type of person would find it hard to so completely disregard the awful news Biff is giving me."

I quickly thrashed through my sense of his history, at least as I knew it. "Well, let's take the Cultural Revolution time. You could see with your own eyes the catastrophe all around you, the ruin of people, institutions . . . But didn't you at the same time keep trying to—?"

"Oh God, that's it, yes, that's very helpful." And he excitedly explained what I had said to the other actors, the stage manager, and everyone else in the room, and they all started laughing and nodding their heads in a deeply shared agreement. "It's as Chinese as hell"—he laughed now—"we're always doing that—finding some hope where there really isn't any. It's our whole history." And putting his Willy Loman fedora back on, he resumed fighting with his sons. The hat, a green

A rehearsal of the restaurant scene.

narrow-brimmed brushed felt, is from East Germany and somehow landed in the costumer's hoard.

## March 29

The actors expect to distribute themselves on the stage without too much help from the director, apparently. And they do this remarkably well and logically, but now and then they end in a tangle that I have to straighten out. I think they are trained to master a part mechanically — smiling, frowning, laughing, as required — but there is little inner life, or so it seems to me. However, I fear to overload them at this point with psychological directions; I will first let them do what they know how to — learn the moves, words, and requisite "expressions" — and I hope, as days go by, to inject specific motives and feelings to expand their awareness and ultimately relax them into their roles. I want nothing to weaken confidence that they can do this alien and difficult play. Right now the play is their straitjacket, when it should ultimately become an exhilarating liberation of their imaginations. Excepting for some moments by Ying Ruocheng and Biff, imagination is not yet moving across this stage. But I am impatient. We are hardly ten days into rehearsals.

We shall have to bootleg a four-piece orchestra from the Beijing Philharmonic to record the music, but must not list the players as belonging to the orchestra or the theatre will have to pay through the nose. It is a very, very impoverished theatre. I must ask what part of its costs are met by ticket sales. A great deal, I suspect, with very little subsidy.

Sometimes as I watch them indicating and overemphasizing, I wonder if it is simply a reflection of the unsophistication of their audience, but sophistication is a slippery item to grasp. Abel Gance's *Napoléon,* Griffith's *Birth of a Nation* and his other films, Chaplin's whole canon are full of overacting by contemporary cosmopolitan standards, yet no one can call these artists unsophisticated. Bernhardt in her film about Queen Elizabeth is about to die, and stands up, hits her forehead with the back of her hand, then clasps both hands over her heart, then clasps her cheeks—while attendants quickly bring on dozens of cushions to spread around her, and when everything is arranged she simply falls over and dies with a downy bounce.

Inge and Rebecca have just returned from a three-day trip to Luoyang, where they climbed the sacred mountain and spent the night trying to keep from freezing in an allegedly deluxe hotel, finally finding a bottle of wine to sip and a pack of cigarettes to keep their noses warm. Neither of them is a smoker. They climbed seven thousand stone steps to get to the top. People make offerings to little god statues on the way up, and the great moment is to see the sun rising from the peak, but it rarely can be seen through the clouds. I think Chinese are still close to their poetry; when I referred to *Salesman*'s being a poem essentially, the actors fell silent, and as I elaborated this concept by pointing out the integration of the parts into a single symphonic line, they moved easily and deeply into this mode of thinking and offered examples of their own, each seeing his own role as part of the other's. Realism—the naturalistic kind—came very late to them and is already on its way out.

Ying Ruocheng said that Chinese drama contains all the forms of the English, including tragedy, comedy, lyric, and song, and I conjectured that this must indicate a common human mechanism creating these forms everywhere. He saw it, rather, as a parallel social development but with one vital difference: feudalism in England and Europe was spotty and in most places was never a national, long-lived system,

Biff.

whereas in China it succeeded in creating a strong national government with a single language and philosophy. The bourgeois revolution had no chance against it when it did attempt to rise, and thus the modern era of scientific thinking and popular democracy never developed. The country sees itself as still grappling with its feudal heritage; one hears this everywhere. I see it in the actor who is playing Hap. A rather light but well enough built young man, he cannot manage the free-swinging, up-front manner of not only an American but even many young Chinese nowadays. He walks with his hands at his sides, turns his head with what seems suavity, as though under the pressure of deep water, when I suspect he is merely a shy fellow trying to play a very extroverted part. Biff, on the other hand, is eager to throw himself all over the place. He has a vibrant, outgoing face that becomes devilish-looking when he gets angry, his eyebrows slanting up and his lids narrowing. His problem is the opposite of Happy's—he follows his emotions headlong and forgets what the scene is about, thus blowing himself out of breath very often. But it will be easier to shape his performance than Happy's, which has hardly more than an adept mechanical quality.

The stage manager suddenly arrived with a wavy brown wig for Ying Ruocheng, designed to make him look Western. I told him it seemed distracting to me, in fact absurd. The problem, which the stage manager demonstrated on his own hair, is that Chinese hair does not absorb gray dye and ends up looking like white straw. We must come to a solution of the principle we are to follow in this. I shall continue trying to persuade them to leave their hair alone, but here the cultural question arises: What will the audience make of them if they are Chinese in this so American play? I am only sure they mustn't try to disguise themselves as Westerners. I must find out how they play Shakespeare. Probably in whiteface. Here is where I wish I could get inside them and look out. I realize that I have taken on some of their Chinese reticence by pretending not to notice that despite my great speech against wigs they are continuing to experiment with them, but I will find a way to stop the business soon.

One of the best rewards for me in this project is to be able to get to know Ying Ruocheng better. Instead of less, it grows even more stunningly incredible that he and his wife should have been kept in a cadre camp—in exile, quite simply—for more than three and a half years, wasting their lives. There is something medieval in the whole conception of this kind of incarceration away from society, which at the same time is not a concentration-camp situation. That kind of punishment seems more modern, even more rational in a sinister sense. The idea here was to remold the intellectual, but in actuality, as it turned out, it was to punish him for being an intellectual, not a manual worker. The whole thing was a war upon the mind, upon thought itself. And this is still a strong motif here: many engineers and other trained people are reportedly leaving China because of humiliations in factories at the hands of self-styled proletarian types who have been able to hang on to important posts. It becomes clearer that part of the urge to bring *Salesman* here, and to have me direct it, was to show an ambiguous situation on the stage, one in which the audience would find itself understanding and even sympathizing with a man who is not particularly "Good," or moral. In short, to let the real world into Chinese art. And apart from my being able to lead them through the play better than a Chinese could, I think my being a foreigner is important as a signal that their isolation is, and should be, over with.

Walking through the neighborhood this afternoon with Inge, I was reminded of postwar Europe again. Almost everything is in short supply and vital foods are rationed. It is a country coming out of a war, but a civil war, in reality.

Without some historical sense it is easy to misinterpret everything here. The streets are much better swept than in most American cities but there are public latrines on every block and a man could find his way to them in pitch-darkness by following his nose. It is an acrid, ammoniac stench that, oddly enough, one almost gets used to. But it is necessary to imagine what it must have been like here before such latrines were even built, when the streets—as they were in southern Italy after the war—were running with shit in which children played. At the same time, it is also necessary not to excuse everything for historical reasons; in fact, the most energetic of the officials here are impatient with that kind of condescension. The Beijing leadership intends to build sewers and bring in gas for cooking as soon as possible, history or no history.

The way the people in the neighborhoods use the streets reminds me of nothing so much as Coney Island in the 1930s—not the amusement park but the adjacent streets where I used to have friends and where my school, Abraham Lincoln High, is located. With its proximity to the ocean, the area attracted thousands of roomers who were satisfied with any kind of shelter as long as they could get out and run down to the beach. The overcrowding was unbelievable, with large rooms divided and subdivided by partitions until they were hardly big enough for a single bed. Beijing neighborhoods are jam packed in much the same way. And nowadays, just as in Coney Island, people are extending the fronts of their houses out onto the sidewalks to create yet another tiny room.

As we walked, lines formed in my head about Mao—"After such struggle to break the grip of the past upon them, did he know as he lay dying that the past was he?" I had just glimpsed a man filling his little basin from the common cold-water faucet in his courtyard. But it is all passing away; one can look up almost anywhere and see an anonymous apartment house being constructed.

I have broached the idea to Ying Ruocheng of his wearing a wig that will simply look like his own hair turned gray. I keep watching in the streets for gray-headed, sixtyish men and discover many with full heads of hair like his, whose graying looks just fine. I have reported this but he is still hesitating; the convention must be stupendously powerful that requires wavy Western hair and the white makeup I find so ghastly. But at least he is now talking about perhaps wearing a wig with a receding hairline. But what color does he have in mind, and will it be wavy? I await surprises.

## March 30

After much hesitation I begin the evening rehearsal with a speech. The only director I have known whose speeches seemed to energize and excite rather than confuse actors was Harold Clurman. He could stand there rubbing his hands together greedily, talk about anything that flew into his head, and end by making the play at hand seem the most important enterprise ever undertaken in the history of the world. However, I did think this cast needed a general overview of where they were at this point, the tenth rehearsal day's end, and how far they still had to go.

Having now blocked the whole play, I say, we have the outer shape of a body but this is not to be mistaken for its soul. To approach its spirit each actor must begin to really listen to what the other has been saying and begin to be dissatisfied with merely behaving in a generally suitable way. Having detected no sign of Stanislavski training in their working methods, excepting for Ying and Charley, I have decided against suggesting any of its techniques for achieving relaxation, but will simply hew to the play's psychological life, taking each actor as close as I can to a fresh confrontation with his part. My eye happens to fall upon poor Happy, who, I am afraid now, is hopelessly miscast and can sink us all. I ask him whether he is perhaps too shy by nature to easily play as extroverted a fellow as Happy, for if this is the case we had better face it now and see what can be done.

Looking a bit tense and embarrassed, he struggles for a long moment and says, "No, I am not normally shy. Only in rehearsals."

"Well, then, in that case your job may be easier, don't you think?" At this he affects a pale grin while his big eyes softly open and close as he waits me out. As the youngest in the cast he probably feels he is thrown in with some heavy hitters and doesn't want to say the wrong thing in their presence. All that even slightly encourages me is that I did think he relaxed the other day after I told him that the character has to be happy and joyful. But his air of constraint and caution has returned—it would fit him perfectly for the part of a man from the Foreign Office. I press on, trying to crack his formidable composure, which I also find pathetic. "Do you think Happy's character could conceivably occur in a young Chinese?"

He gives this a stubbornly long thought. The company watches with imperturbable composure. Happy nods, finally. "Yes, a Chinese could have his character, but not his behavior."

"Ah! Then maybe you have to see him as a Chinese, but the first of his kind in the history of China!" Everyone laughs, and the actor with them. "I say that because I still think you feel you must be American. But you don't really know any Americans, so all you can hope to have is a manner. It's like Americans who try playing Orientals by putting their hands into their sleeves and hunching up their shoulders and taking tiny steps." I stop there. For the time being.

To Biff, who is quite good in the part, or might be by the opening, I tell another tale. "You mustn't feel that every time we rehearse you have to reach a performance level. You lead with your emotions, throw yourself into it, and sometimes forget what the scene is about and what you are doing in it. First feel out the structure of what is happening in you and the others; then you will find it easier to gather together your emotional life."

For Linda I can only diplomatically repeat the old admonition but in a mercifully—I hope—different form. "She is not a woman to follow meekly behind her husband, wiping up after him. She has strength; she has held this family together and she knows this very well. She has the intelligence to run a large office, if that had been her fate. She knows the contribution she has made . . . etc." In short, she must not warble but confront problems standing up. "After all, it is she who keeps the accounts, it is she who is marshaling the forces, such as they are, that might save Willy." I tell how Linda has gone with Willy on some of his winter trips, sitting beside him in the little car to keep him company. How she has walked miles to pay the gas and electric bills and save the postage. "She is determined, not simpering." Linda nods, wide-eyed. I am not sure where I am getting. She is taking notes.

I ask for questions. No one, Ying and our Charley excepted, of course, has asked me anything so far—a bad sign. Bernard, of all people, raises his hand. Of the whole cast he seems to have had the least trouble making something of his role. He and Biff move much like Americans, in an easy, loose-limbed way, but he is smaller and ten years younger than Biff, with a cheerful countenance and quick, intelligent eyes.

"In my scene in my father's office with Willy, when I am older and successful, do I notice that he is distraught? And if so, why do I rake up that story about Biff coming back after his Boston trip a completely changed boy? Wouldn't I spare Willy that?"

Bernard.

"This is what I was referring to earlier—you must study what the script is telling you and listen to what your partner, in this case Willy, is saying to you. He has several lines pressing you to tell him what you know about Biff's becoming pessimistic and losing heart. And read your own speeches, like the one where you yourself reveal how curious you've always been about Biff's sudden change—'I've often thought of how strange it was,' and so on. But the pressure is coming mainly from Willy: it would be very hard to refuse him. Besides, it might help him to know what you know."

He seems surprised that the answer to his question is in the script and immediately opens it and begins reading to himself.

Biff has a question now. "If I say I like it so much working out West with horses, why do I end up saying I don't know what I want?"

"You are not reading the script. You have been saying the correct line yourself for days now, but you are not even listening to yourself. You don't say 'I don't know what I want,' but 'I don't know what I'm supposed to want,' and this is a key idea. Biff knows very well what he wants, but Willy and his idea of success disapprove of what he wants, and this is the basic reason you have returned here—to somehow resolve this conflict with your father, to get his blessing, to be able to cast off his heavy hand and free yourself. From Biff's viewpoint the whole play is about how he came home to try to resolve his conflict with his father and his father's screwed-up values."

As always the whole cast is seated more or less in a row behind the tables facing the set in this sad, high, ballroom-sized space. Ying interprets all my directions for everyone to hear, even those that apply only to his own role. If I tell him that he is being too vehement at some point, he stops and addresses anyone around and says, "He is telling me to stop being too vehement." Now, with these critiques of Biff's and Happy's performances, Charley, his long legs crossed under the striped silver-and-blue gown he is still wearing after doing some exercises for his traditional-play role, offers Biff some advice. He feels Biff is verging on self-pity in his attack on Willy in the last big scene of Act Two, when he should be totally preoccupied with Willy's salvation rather than his own hurt. It is a fine line, and Biff quickly appreciates the older actor's straightforward criticism. In fact, as Charley speaks, the lighting man, the stage manager, and one of the costume people nod vociferously. Along with the actor's own ego there is the company's common identity to take into consideration; they are all involved. The last time I experienced this caring unity among actors and technicians, lighting and scene people, and even the stagehands was in London in the mid-1950s, when a special dress rehearsal of Peter Brook's production of *A View from the Bridge* was performed for the stagehands and theatre personnel and their families. Afterward the wives and the kids inspected the scenery, their carpenter and painter fathers showing off the fine points. This is inconceivable in New York, where any such show of feeling on the part of the staff would seem to threaten its concentration on the pay scale.

## March 31

On arriving this morning I discover a dozen or so bewigged dummy heads standing in rows on some tables pulled together, the cast trying them on with the fervent advice and aid of four or five women and one man from the theatre's own wiggery. These specialists are all, of course, dressed in the standard blue trousers and plain jackets, the man wearing his blue cap as befits wigmakers in a workers' theatre. Ying is trying on a scraggly mouse-colored wig with a receding hairline; a hairdo like that would get anybody fired from his job for sheer neglect. To my amazement he is studying himself in a mirror with serious deliberation. Worse yet, I spot two platinum-blond wigs that are undoubtedly intended for the two women in the restaurant scene whom Happy picks up. In other words, they are intending to "whiten" themselves for the play even though I had stated in my first day's lobotomized speech, without any demurral, the principle of their not trying to imitate Americans but to play as Chinese doing an American work. Admittedly, this places them in a never-never land, ethnically speaking, but at a minimum it is a more beautiful sight to see than Chinese with blond hair, something that can only convince an audience that the actor is capable of wearing a wig. Of course I am leaving out their conventions, but I am doing so purposely since I cannot honestly judge by a taste I do not share or even understand. In any case I have a gut conviction that Westernizing the cast will vitiate the production.

Ying asks my opinion of the wig and I tell him it is all wrong, and he is easily convinced. In his case a wig is necessary to help age him and that is all. But it must have a pre-Beatles look, unlike the long

Ying Ruocheng, in wig and costume as Willy, with the wigger whose hairdo was copied for him.

hair he had been trying on. It has to be reminiscent of the fairly close-cropped businessmen of the 1950s, 1940s, and earlier. If a salesman can be ruined, as Charley says in the Requiem, by a couple of spots on his hat, a scraggly haircut would have sunk him without a trace.

From nowhere—we are now a milling mob of actors, wiggers, technical people with opinions, the sweet and aged doorman with his point of view, and me in the middle with bewigged Ying walking around and looking as if he could frighten bats—a small wigger woman appears with a fat illustrated book of Great Movies, which I open to a picture of Jimmy Stewart in *Mr. Smith Goes to Washington*. Stewart has the standard American haircut of the period. "That's it!" I yell. Whereupon I find myself facing a large, jolly, rather overweight, cherry-cheeked man—a wigger—in his late fifties who is just taking off his blue cap to scratch his head.

"*There's* your hair, Ying!" I call, and at a glance Ying is taken with it: dense, silvery white hair clipped short all over but in a distinctive, efficient-looking way that is not quite conventional and yet could be. Immediately, of course, all the wiggers object that it is too short for Weelee. It is the old story—if you can make a wig, make a big one, something that *looks* like a wig, or why else bother? And so I must fight off wigs for Biff and Happy, whose own haircuts are perfect, with Biff's rather short cut quite right for an athlete, and Happy's about the style of Adolphe Menjou, very black, carefully shaped, and natty. My suggestion that Biff shorten the length of his sideburns, which are halfway down to his jaw, arouses his instant defensive indignation—"My jaws are so wide I must have these sideburns to make my face narrower!"—and I give up quickly without argument. And he does, I admit, tend to bulge toward the jaw hinges in rather a pear or punching-bag shape.

Speaking of which, as we finally settle down to begin running a scene, and everyone is getting back to his tea or taking position on stage, the tall doors to the outer corridor open and a monstrous shape begins moving into the room, its gait shuffling, its progress a few inches with each shove from the rear. The entire cast turn, as I do, transfixed by this apparition. It appears to be brown leather, about six feet in height, and as big around as a large culvert, with great brass grommets set around its open top through which a veritable hawser could have been threaded before it was separated from whatever might have been its normal abode. It is with sinking heart that I slowly realize that this is supposed to be the punching bag that Willy bought for his boys in Boston and brought home as a surprise in the trunk of his little Chevrolet.

The thing now ceases to shuffle into the room, and around from its rear appears a small man in the usual blue, his cap and shoulder whitened with the dust of the bag that he has, incredibly, been pushing single-handed, God knows from what distance and over what boulevards and even mountains. "I think that's the punching bag," Ying says with typical Manchu understatement, staring up at me with his thick lenses, doubtless aware—at the least—of a slight awkwardness in my coming attempts to stage the moment when Happy will rush onstage carrying this object in one hand. The man now comes forward, I suppose to claim his credit from the great star and the Foreign Expert for having accomplished the impossible. I refuse even to imagine what they must have gone through even to locate this thing in Beijing. An ordinary punching bag, of course, is about the size of a lengthened basketball, and a sandbag is about four feet in height and perhaps a foot in diameter. This thing could only have been fabricated in prerevolutionary times, probably from a description of one seen in a New York or London gymnasium by a Chinese businessman who was extremely small.

But I know that Chinese are tough in the face of discouragement—how else could they have endured their history of suffering? "That is not the right punching bag," I tell the man, as quietly and forthrightly as possible, and draw him a picture of a light bag suspended from a round board. The stage manager suddenly recognizes this and explains it to the moving man, who, looking stunned, nods vaguely as he is led out of the hall into the corridor. Another day another dollar, as my father would say.

During one of our ten-minute breaks for pee and tea, Ying Ruocheng approaches with a surprising request. The theatre wants me to write out a "rehearsal schedule" specifying the hours when I will require the use of the theatre in the days prior to the opening. When we do not intend to use one of the "three periods, morning, afternoon, or evening," they intend to rent out the premises for other uses, such as organization meetings or the showing of films. The stage being very deep and the set placed well behind the curtain line, they can easily drop the curtain to conceal it.

I have not the slightest idea of the time periods when I will or won't be needing the theatre so close to our opening. I tell Ying Ruocheng that I had never heard of a company not having the use of the theatre for at least a week before opening, full-time. He himself is not happy with this arrangement but cannot bring himself to say so, for such is the poverty of the country that, to literally the next-to-last day before opening, the theatre will continue to be used for other purposes in order to take in a few more yuan. I suppose that their persisting in having a theatre at all under such circumstances is a credit to them. I have no idea how to resolve this problem and simply leave it lying there.

Now on top of this news, Old Feng, the lighting designer, a spunky little guy with a short 1950s haircut, has sat me down and gone through every scene of the show to outline his lighting plot, and politely informs me that their equipment cannot handle more than eighteen light cues in succession without replugging. To replug they will have to go to a blackout, when absolutely nothing is lit, whereupon they can resume after some fifteen or twenty seconds. This is like driving along in a car at sixty miles an hour and crawling out on a fender to change spark plugs without stopping. Another problem that I simply refuse to think about and I leave it right where it lies.

To escape from all this good news I go over to Charley, who is doing his lonely tai chi exercises, and mime what he is doing, much to his pleasure and everyone's amusement. Standing erect, feet apart about the same width as my shoulders, I raise both arms slowly forward as though my sleeves were doing the lifting, arms relaxed and wrists hanging. "You will begin to feel your fingertips swelling because all the air inside your body is flowing into them." I do. They swell. It is astonishing. He then leads me through a couple of presses; the open palms are pushed against nothing as though to compress the air. A surprising flexing of the whole body takes place, quite as though an obstacle were actually being pushed.

Moments of real feeling and poignancy are beginning to happen in the scenes, but they are forever being broken off because someone has lost his lines. This is especially aggravating in the passages with lots of short cues, where no build is possible without fluency. So I sit everybody down for half an hour and run lines. They are improving but the quietest passages are still shot through with breakdowns. Ben is busy being a ghost again, I think, and he forgets what to say. I am about to land on him but there are other things to do first. Maybe the problem is my pressing them to speak more rapidly than is customary, but I am convinced it is necessary.

Suddenly at the end of yesterday's rehearsal, when the Chinese language began to sound like five cats in a barrel going over a gravel road, something wonderful happened. I had been after Linda every day to cut what still remains of her warbling and to straighten up and play some strength. She is interested in women politically, she must have some feminist convictions, it seems to me. Suddenly, talking to Willy in the first scene of the play—where she is saying that he must talk to his young boss, Howard, and demand that he be taken off the road and given a job in the New York operation of the firm—she sounded like a woman comforting rather than pleading with her man; a woman, moreover, who sounded deeply in love with him precisely because she was being so strong with him. The change was startling. And reminded me that I had completely forgotten to tell both Willy and Linda how in love they really are and always have been. And later, as I finished staging the last kitchen fight, the suicide, and the Requiem, when she made the long walk downstage to the grave, helped by Happy and Biff, and sat on the step that in this theatre separates the forestage, she again brought me to tears, along with my wife and daughter beside me. What this production can become! There was no weeping by her until the very last words, "We're free . . . We're free . . ." and even there she seemed to thread an irony through her anguish. If only she holds it now. I gave her a kiss, I was so moved. She seemed unsure what to make of it. But I guess she knows.

Now I have time to work a little on the opening scene in the bedroom and I tell Linda and Willy how theirs was a love match. Ying translates all this with warm eagerness—that her family disapproved of him because he had no money or prospects and that she, in effect, had run off with him. Both Ying and she take it as great news that they are still physically in love and that she means it when later she is to say, "Willy, darling, you're the handsomest man in the world." Hearing this she lifts her very mobile eyebrows with a large surprise—she can act that. Today she is wearing some definitely better-made clothes, a wine-brown little double-breasted worsted jacket over a matching dress and brown velvet pumps on her tiny feet. A sign of her optimism?

But by the end of this period the big fight scene in Act Two has fallen to pieces again. Everybody is blowing lines. I leave for lunch with one last look at the giant leather bag still standing near the doorway like a lost bear.

Two tremendously encouraging developments this evening, and one bewildering one.

I had run the last fight scene in the kitchen. Usually, up to this point, I have stopped and gone back over other work, avoiding the Requiem, which I dislike seeing them do in a mechanical fashion. My hope has been that one day they will truthfully perform the final climactic battle and when that happens I will let them into the Requiem, filled with their truths, but not before. I have put them through the Requiem two or three times merely to block it, but this, so to speak, is the quietly sanctified end of the song, where a false voice is most painfully obvious. This time, having approached a certain validity in the climactic kitchen scene, I let them proceed into the Requiem.

Linda is miraculous. I sit in an armchair hardly ten feet in front of them—Bernard, Happy, Linda, Biff, and Charley at the grave; all at once I realize that Willy is "dead," is never going to be present in their lives anymore. I miss him! It has to mean something real has happened. Linda sits and does "Help me, Willy, I can't cry. . . ." The restraint, the purity of her concept of the woman, the valor of Linda and her anguish—everything comes together so simply, in such restrained elegaic lyricism that I cannot help weeping. I give her another big hug and kiss afterward. She is no longer warbling. Clearly she has the character straight now. I think we may have a show, after all. And better than anything, I believe the others have caught the power of her feeling; this more than anything I can tell them must help them to gauge their distance from reality in their own roles.

The second piece of good news is that Biff, after what for Chinese actors is a very short rehearsal period, says he has particularized, narrowed the area of mystery in his relation to Willy; it comes down to the question why he feels he has to return home at all when he knows how hard it will be to get along with the old man. What is Biff's need, what is the burden that only his father can help him unload? (As noted, I had been after all of them to begin breaking into their "generalized" behavior.)

I explain once again that this is a love story; that away from home he sometimes feels a painfully unrequited love for his father, a sense of something unfinished between them bringing feelings of guilt.

The actor says he understands this, that it is very Chinese.

"But why are you guilty, can you say?"

"Because I condemned Willy. I turned my father away," Ying translates.

"That's it. That's wonderful. What else?"

The actor shakes his head, says something to Ying Ruocheng, who tells me, "He doesn't know."

"It's like needing somebody's blessing before you can enjoy doing a certain thing. You want Willy to say, 'Yes, you should live in the West, you should not have to chase after the dollar, you should live your own life.' In other words, your love for him binds you; but you want it to free you to be your own man. But Willy would have to turn away from his own values, wouldn't he, to give you his blessing?"

He nods to me, says he understands this, and he seems excited by it, but I know there is something more to be said, something that will fill him with the anger he needs at the climaxes. I need something personal, intimate, something Chinese for him to grasp and use. The cast, as usual, is looking on and listening; it occurs to me that once again the Cultural Revolution might be an apt analogy. "It's like the dilemma of the Cultural Revolution; Jiang Qing's leadership was also full of self-deluded demands on you, wasn't it?" They all come alert as Ying translates.

"She also claimed to be acting out of devotion to China, and that may have been what she felt, for all we know. Just like Willy, who believes he is trying to help you, not himself. But no matter how you tried to obey her and come up to the regime's expectations, you had to see that objectively China's economy was falling apart, her arts, commerce, the whole civilization going down the drain. And your father, Mao, seemed to be backing her, isn't that right? The point is, you felt a powerful frustration, didn't you, an anger that nobody was able to tear away that complex of half-truths and deceptions to raise up the truth before the people—before Mao himself!—the facts of the destruction going on. And maybe this is why Deng Xiaoping is using the slogan 'Truth from Facts,' rather than from ideology." A laughter of recognition up and down the row of chairs. "Biff is trying to do something very similar—tear Willy away from his ideology to face himself and you in detail, as a real individual who is at a certain time in his life. You can use the same Cultural Revolution frustration, that feeling of anger and the violence in you, in this role. The same thwarted love."

He seems moved. "I understand that frustration." There is a hum of talk around us. They are profoundly politicized and see themselves as parts of a society; in isolation they cannot, I think, even study themselves, let alone imagine resolving conflicts. By politicizing the Willy-Biff conflict, I think, I have brought the play into their terms and made it more familiar, perhaps more Chinese.

At ten o'clock, quitting time, I emerge from the theatre into a broad driveway beside it and find Charley, Willy, Biff and Happy, the Woman in Boston, Bernard, and some of the crew mounting their bicycles and riding silently away into the Beijing night. As a biker I envy them, but they must sometimes ride through rain and snow, too, and the roaring Gobi sand-driving wind, and this brings to mind their salaries. The two Loman sons, the youngest members of the company, are earning about twenty dollars a month, the seniors about eighty. Ying Ruocheng sometimes makes a lot more by working abroad in movies and television, but he is exceptional. Even so, such income is taxed at ninety percent, which would not be quite so objectionable if some of the tax went to support the theatre in its dire need. They are milking the artists who are just about the theatre's sole support. Nor can one easily accept this pay scale as being entirely due to the poverty of the country. Is it also, or even primarily, a way of keeping these "intellectuals" in their places? After all, some have spent a lifetime learning their art and end up making less money than novice factory workers.

But I am not sure that money does not have a somewhat different meaning for them than it does for us. Life is Spartan but costs are very low, too. A pair of good jeans is about three dollars, food is cheap, bus tickets about three cents a ride. All this is bound to change, I think, as the new economic policy raises incomes and starts customers bidding up prices. When there was nothing much to buy, money had little importance.

Large items like refrigerators are sold on time payments. They will understand that element in the play, at least.

China's war on her intellectuals—meaning anyone with book-learned skill—is apparently not yet over among the people even if the armistice has been officially declared. In yesterday's *China Daily* it was reported that in 1980 the Huashan Hospital in Shanghai finally managed to open a canteen to serve hot meals for doctors after they performed surgery. At the time this was big news because in the Cultural Revolution—and since—they had been provided only with cold meals. As late as this February a middle-aged doctor in Ruijin Hospital performed an operation on a cancer patient from eight-thirty in the morning until three o'clock in the afternoon, after which she either had to cook for herself or eat cold food in the dining room because the kitchen had been closed for hours, or try to satisfy herself with some steamed bread and water.

"Year after year," the report concluded, "there are news stories about hot meals for doctors. This to some extent reflects the difficulty of reforming leaders' workstyles and the implementing of the Party's policies on intellectuals in some units. Leaders of hospitals should be ashamed if stories like this continue to be news."

Sometimes as my cast runs scenes I find myself musing on what they have seen in their lives that outsiders can never even imagine. One morning in the wild 1960s, both Charley and Willy, along with the whole company of more than a hundred actors, were confronted by a Red Army Educational Detachment that simply settled into this theatre to oversee their reeducation. The problem was that the Detachment could barely read and write. Charley and Willy, among others, were promptly assigned to the theatre's boiler room, where the "honest workers" found them getting in the way and finally asked them, since they were literate, to write up some kind of report on themselves that the Party had demanded the workers send in. This kind of jolly waste of every kind of brainpower was devastating and continued for a decade.

At lunch in our hotel restaurant the retired President of Cornell University, Dale R. Corson, stopped at the table. We had met in the early 1960s. Now he is Chairman of the International Advisory Panel, Chinese University Development Project. With a two-hundred-million-dollar grant from the World Bank, his group is attempting, as he put it, "to begin the reconstruction of a higher educational system for this country." The same story—"They have a long, long road to go, the destruction even of what they had had was complete." One cannot help seeing the grim comedy in this. I happened to be in Paris in 1968 when the French students exploded onto the streets en masse, cut down the old chestnut trees, ripped up cobblestones, flung themselves against lines of club-wielding police—all to condemn the bourgeois system that had devalued human beings. And Mao's name was on many of their lips. China's alleged simplicity, her communality, is indeed still appealing to visitors who have been sucked dry by their alienation from their own so complicated societies in the West.

At just about the same time as those Parisians were throwing rocks, however, the actors in this theatre in Beijing were coming out with hammers and fine picks to chip away at Mao's sayings, which had been painted in enormous letters across brownstone fascia that flank the entrance doors of the theatre. For the Great Helmsman had happened to opine one day that he actually was opposed to people trying to make him into some sort of god. Seizing on this as their license, the actors instantly began chipping away. The pitted surface can still be seen. I find in discussing this odd event with actors here that without exception they think a play written on this subject would have to be a comedy. Of course at some times in some places you can get killed by a comedy, too.

## *April 1*

This morning I arrive to find Ying Ruocheng sitting at the kitchen table on the mock-up set with the actors somberly facing him from the line of chairs and tables stretched across the long wall. He is wearing his East

German felt hat and a cardigan under his jacket. As I approach him I notice a slump to his shoulders and he seems to sigh as he says, "I have some bad news. Our Happy is in the hospital with a fever of a hundred and three that they can't diagnose." I note and feel remorse for the want of alarm in my heart at this news. Other actors assure me he will be back to work on Monday the fourth—something I do not believe, not after that kind of temperature. Since there is absolutely nothing I can do about the problem, I settle in to rehearse around him, which gives me plenty to do for the day.

## *April 2*

Ying the magician has produced another Happy, whom he has sprung from a play in rehearsal. This man, I now learn, was his original choice but had been tied up in a film when our rehearsals began. Best of all, he is obviously an old laughing-buddy of our Biff, who now horses around with him, guffaws frequently, and in general behaves like Biff with his brother Happy.

It is fairly wonderful to be reminded again what differing instruments actors are. This new Happy has read the play only once, in another translation some time ago, and at seven this morning glanced through his part with Biff, but when I put them both up in the twin beds to stage their first scene, he already can do whole series of speeches with hardly a glance at the script. More strange, his voice and manner are a lot like Cameron Mitchell's, the original 1949 Happy Loman. He is clearly a lovable rogue, sincere as all hell and in headlong flight from any commitment to anyone except, possibly, his mother. He is stocky, with a full, round, cherubic face and devilish black eyes that always are on the verge of laughter—even when he is most seriously avowing his direst confessions of moral conflict. I can just see this one on Brighton Beach in July with a babe under each arm, making both of them as happy as clams. I feel we are now in business. The one really false music, which I could never hope fully to conceal, has gone. However, Ying has arranged for the first Happy to understudy the role when he is feeling better.

With our new Happy I go through the whole play from the beginning to block him into his positions, but I hardly need open my mouth; the

The new Happy.

other actors move him with a gesture as required, or he himself senses where he should be positioned. This is one part of the Chinese actors' training that I much appreciate: every one of them assumes he is responsible, provided the director agrees, for positioning himself logically on the stage. I have never seen this done with such ease and certainty, although I do change their moves about half the time. But mine are mostly small adjustments for the sake of a finer clarity of meaning or for emphasis in a script that is still, after all, about another civilization. In a play of their own I doubt they would have to be told very much at all about the blocking. By the end of the first three-hour session Happy has become part of the whole, although of course with the script still in his hand. He will study all day tomorrow, Sunday, and I expect he will come in with the whole part learned on Monday. I cannot help marveling, when in addition it is all in Chinese! This is not a mere quip—for it must be a painfully uncertain process for these actors to slip into not only alien characters but an exotic way of life of which they know next to nothing. For example, Willy is desperate, yet he owns a refrigerator, a car, his own house, and is willing to "settle" for sixty dollars a *week!* And those were the fat dollars of decades ago. This, in China, is nothing short of fantasy. It is, incidentally, for this sort of reason that Ying, responding to a question at our press conference, said that the play cuts two ways as propaganda, for if a man can have reached Willy's standard of living and still feel in bad straits, it can't be as awful a system as is sometimes advertised.

But of course such numbers have little weight in putting together a picture of any reality here. Foreigners are still charmed by Chinese cities in which most of the inhabitants bathe from a single cold-water tap in the courtyard and have to use a public latrine the smells from which could float the Graf Zeppelin. If one is charmed by the housewife carefully emptying a tin bowl of dirty water into the street, it is well to remember she is doing this because there is no drain at all in her house. And those who walk the lanes of Beijing after the dinner hour may find it heartwarming to see young parents patiently tending small romping children in front of their houses, but their serious purpose is to get the tykes to defecate or pee on the open ground before bed. But they are indeed patient and loving even if there is little question they would prefer their own toilets.

What is turning out to be universal—unless I am going to be brutally disappointed on opening night—is emotion rather than "facts." Linda, for example, is thoroughly on target now, no longer Willy's whimpering doormat. She has told me that she had the wrong idea of the woman to start with. Instead, she has become, as he calls her, "my foundation and support," who is fighting off his death from the outset, the only one who knows that he has attempted suicide and has connected a device to the gas heater that, should the mood overtake him completely, he might use. Linda's part has often been weakly played, as though she were a mere follower, but that is unlikely to happen when the actress keeps herself aware of what the script has told her she knows. The "fact" in this case is a completely exotic gas heater for water, something that these Chinese have never seen (and, indeed, has probably ceased to exist anymore in the States) but which they easily understand once I describe its design and operation. In any case, its strangeness does not for an instant interfere with our Chinese Linda's eventual understanding of the kind of woman she has to play—the kind who is strong by concealing her strength. Perhaps we conventionally overestimate the profundity of technology's impact on our lives.

It rained all day, and in the evening we took Linda in our car instead of letting her find one of the last buses home. As we rode, she in the back seat with Inge, who interpreted for me, she told of the time in the 1940s when the Japanese were ravaging Beijing and she had to hide her little daughter under a blanket to keep her from being taken and murdered by soldiers. "The blanket was suddenly handed to me by an American. He stayed by me till the troops had gone away. He refused to accept it back. I will never forget him." That was forty years ago. What burnings, rapes, horrors has she witnessed—this lady who often plays queenly parts in the grand Chinese manner with glittering robes and golden crowns and fingers covered with rings, and now Linda Loman in her little Brooklyn house—how many women are in her? No wonder she hardly reacted when I kissed her on the cheek after her so affecting rehearsal performance of the Requiem—what was this achievement compared with some *real* scrapes she'd gotten through alive? But—I have now grown accustomed to this—Chinese simply do not react to praise in any open way, although they adore it like anyone else. Inge, in fact, thinks Americans are the only ones who respond to a compliment with a thank-you, all other peoples affecting to downgrade their achievement rather than to openly acknowledge it—in bad taste.

I have taught Biff, who had never laid eyes on an American football before, to throw a tolerable spiral pass to Happy—something I want them to do in the scene of Willy's homecoming in Act One. Unfortunately his aim is not always that great, and this afternoon, while I was busy looking at a lighting diagram, he threw one across the stage and hit Linda square in the jaw. She refused not only aid but any of our attempts to comfort her, although the shot must have hurt. Biff, who has a manly, stoical nature, did not so much rush over as walk in a purposefully rapid stride to her and apologize. I thought to ease the moment by saying that she was the one who ought to be wearing the helmet I had brought from America and that she was now the first football injury in Chinese history. She is a great lady who was able to laugh, and there was never a flash of resentment against Biff at the accident. The ball, on my unfortunate instruction, is pumped up hard.

There has now been set up in Beijing a Department of Civic Virtue, with offices and a large staff, to promote the end of spitting, improvements in conduct on bicycles (of which there are three and one-half million in this city alone), public politeness, the giving of true weights by vendors of meat and other products who evidently have had their thumbs on the scales, and so on. Nowadays a great many items are sold by private enterprisers, who in time-honored fashion may have been bilking their public. However, the papers often run stories of employees in state stores who ignore customers, serve their friends the best cuts of meat, conceal items in scarce supply, and steal from the till.

Interesting, too, is the play being given reports of individuals who have set themselves up in small businesses and have succeeded in making it big. One fellow, inspired to leave the city for a chick-raising country life, was discouraged from doing so by the Party and friends who said he was crazy—nobody in his right mind in China has ever chosen to live on the land rather than in the city, where he can "eat out of the iron pot"—the state-industrial payroll. But this man, according to *China Daily,* persevered, started selling chicks, then chicken feed, to other farmers, and last year netted himself ten thousand yuan (about six thousand dollars). He has now brought his brother into the business and intends to expand into pharmaceuticals for chickens, and other supplies. "I intend to make it big," he is quoted as saying, "and there is nothing wrong in this because I am working for my money and providing value and service." The newspaper—and presumably the Party—approves.

I have begun to hear a hollowness in Ying's way of delivering certain speeches. He is a marvelously adept actor, quick to incorporate almost any suggestion that he can visualize himself doing—which means almost all I have offered him. But he has been unable to swing two particular stretches that are important for the character to make credible. Both involve Willy's romanticization of the past. The first, when he tells his boss, Howard—who will shortly tell him he is fired—that he had once nearly decided to go to Alaska to follow his brother Ben, when he met a salesman in the Parker House, an eighty-four-year-old named Dave Singleman who could still simply pick up the phone and call the buyers, and "without ever leaving his room, at the age of eighty-four, he made his living. And when I saw that, I realized that selling was the greatest career a man could want. . . ." This long speech is a kind of elegy for a way of life that did once have its reality. "In those days there was personality in it, Howard. There was respect, and comradeship, and gratitude in it. . . ."

Even not very able actors—Americans, that is—can create an image with this material, but Ying, who has been far better with lesser moments, seemed unable to generate an inner life that can only come from conviction, from truthfulness. Once again, in Act Two, he seems similarly hollow when he tells Charley that "if a man was impressive and well liked" he could never really fail in life.

Ying Ruocheng, once I noted his straining to create these moments, was quick to admit that he was not able to find a line into them and we got to talking about the social reality to which Willy is referring. Of course, I said, he is romanticizing as he always does, but there is something real underlying his feeling. "In the era he is talking about, the buyers for the stores he sold to were either the owners themselves or had held their jobs for many years and knew him. You know, there was actually a man named Filene, a man named Gimbel, R. H. Macy—and, for that matter, Louis Chevrolet, Buick, Olds, Ford, Firestone . . . these were actual human beings at one time, and if Willy did not really deal with them in person, their reality was part of his reality, and their beginnings in poverty and their rise in the world were the pantheon that circled his mind. The era of the salesman as mere order-taker whose canned pitch has been made for him on television and who has no options as what to say or charge, this was not yet the case in his time."

"I would never have imagined that," Ying Ruocheng said, rather blaming himself for being not wholly prepared, "it would just never have occurred to me. In other words, there was really a basis for rugged individualism."

"Oh absolutely. In fact, I had a friend and neighbor, T. K. Quinn, at one time Vice-President of General Electric, who used to say—this was way back in the early 1950s—that the spread of giantism among corporations was going to strangle American business one day by creating an inertia in place of the competitive spirit. Those were boom times but he foresaw a crisis in the quality and technological datedness of American products because small business was being squeezed out. He had been in charge of the Small Business Administration in World War Two and came out of the experience convinced of the depth of the problem. So Willy is not blowing bubbles, not altogether; he is recalling a different era."

I couldn't but realize once again that it was by embracing sociopolitical realities that one could make the emotional life of Willy Loman and his crew clearer and, so to speak, more Chinese. "I will work on it from that angle," Ying said, and with some eagerness now. "But, you see, there was nothing remotely like that in Chinese history. A businessman here always put up a screen before his name, called his shop 'The Heavenly and Peaceful Drygoods Store,' or something like that. They were embarrassed by any public identification with trade."

What we are skirting again, of course, is the differing development of feudalism in China and Europe. To the feudal mind the trader and businessman is hardly more than a louse preying on the body of society. The exemplar is the soldier whose code is honorable and beyond the reach of money and selfish advantage. In China the honor went to the scholar. China's feudal state was far more successful and all-embracing than Europe's, where there was an endless struggle between local magnates and national governments, such as they were, and this crippled the development of a middle class. The current hope is that if a controlled amount of private enterprise is unleashed, the national wealth will multiply. In Chinese terms, it is an unacknowledged recognition of what has long been denied: that it may be necessary for a bourgeois interval to precede socialism, that primitive accumulation and development is necessary, after all, before there is something worth socializing. But as contradictory as it sounds, the values of Communism and feudalism are kin—the stress on selfless service rather than individual aggrandizement, the concept of fealty to a hallowed leader or social unit rather than a one-to-one relationship between the individual and his inalienable rights, and higher authority extending up to God. I am beginning to feel now that while the Chinese audience may well experience a familiarity with Willy's feelings, there will have to remain a gap in their understanding of his very Western experience and the mythology he carries in his head concerning this kind of individualism. On the other hand, what resonances escape us as we watch Shakespeare, in whose plays innumerable political and social inferences lie that no longer have any life? It seems not to matter too much, but we shall see.

We have gone to a play much talked about that is on in the small auditorium on the top floor of our theatre. *Warning Signals* has an almost totally youthful audience, and the two-hundred-seat house is always packed. The set is a platform raised four feet off the floor, with black iron pipe indicating the outlines of a railroad signal car in which the trainmaster has his desk and oversees the train's operations. He is played by a middle-aged, rather roly-poly actor with great warmth and fatherly gentleness. His usually uneventful night's ride is interrupted this evening by a young rogue, the Gangster, whom we see tempting a decent young fellow, the anti-hero, to join in his plot to halt the train at a certain point between towns so that his fellow gangsters can board it and somehow . . . One never quite understands more than the plot's general drift and neither of my two interpreters, who were fans of the play, could explain it either, but it hardly matters for the point of the play lies elsewhere.

Blackie, the anti-hero, is an unhappy youth who cannot find a job. This is already rather a shocking fact to bring before an audience. He is also much in love and would like to marry, but his girl's parents refuse him because his prospects are nil. Surly and bitter against a world that has no place for him or his generation, he cannot be reassured by his girl that her love does not depend on his worldly goods, and becomes so dissatisfied that he makes the decision secretly to join the Gangster in his plot and boards the train to help carry it out. The girl does so, too, but is still unaware of his criminal plans. There is a fourth character, the Trainmaster's Young Apprentice, who also loves the girl and who forms the third leg of the triangle. But he, while sometimes youthfully inattentive to his duties, is still a good sort underneath, just as Blackie, the other suitor, is.

It isn't necessary to follow the plot any further to understand why the young flock to this simple melodrama. It is remarkable because it openly voices the protests of Chinese youth against unemployment, for one thing, and on top of that warns the Trainmaster, the older generation, that it has its own right to its experience and cannot find spiritual nourishment in the preachments of the old about responsibility and patriotism. Nevertheless, by the curtain the plot sees to it that Blackie, never more than a half-willing ally of the Gangster, reforms his attitudes at least enough to reconcile him to the Trainmaster and accept his advice to have patience and not expect things to change in a day and to keep faith with old values.

Theatrically, it is hard to conceive of another country where such a play could find an audience anymore; it is so naive in its psychology and so extreme in its melodramatics that it would bring laughter in its most serious moments. The Gangster, for example, literally leers through very large horn-rimmed glasses; the hero—or heroes, for the girl ends up not having to choose between them but remains a faithful friend to both—looks into the future with teary eyes and vaulted eyebrows reminiscent of nothing in Western performance later than dauntless William S. Hart in the earliest cowboy silents.

The flashback, still another hitherto unknown dramatic device here, causes much excited comment. The general lighting dims and actors cease moving to stare into spotlights, thus transferring themselves backward in time while the action on the train is suspended. In the more lavishly emotional moments recordings of the scores of movies like *Three Coins in the Fountain* or American pop orchestrations of the 1950s are turned up in the background. Jack and Harry Warner would be delighted not only by the production but by the play's highly moral philosophy, not to speak of just the right degree of suggestion that the heroine has in fact slept with both her suitors at one time or another (yet another astonishment in a Chinese play).

The blatancy of the overacting is so unabashed as to raise the possibility that it represents a consciously overwrought style in itself, which, like most other Chinese failures, one tends to ascribe to a kind of curdling of ancient tradition. If their acting has always acknowledged its divorce from realism, it has not necessarily fled from reality; it is merely a presentational account of moral and social meanings rather than a representation of the inner life of characters—something that Brecht, for one, appreciated and indeed stole for himself. And of course in this case the Gangster is Bad and there is no point in underplaying his Badness—even though one may wonder how any Good person could be inveigled by one so obviously worthless. But if the old agitprop method of "acting-the-meaning," and of giving the audience no right to choose what it is to believe about a character, is implicitly obeyed here, the play is still an electric experience to the audience. Its shock and novelty is that it appears to skirt skin-close to denying support to the advertised presumptions of the regime. If Good and Evil still wear white and black hats, there is no guarantee that decent but frustrated young people will not fall into the claws of the Black Hats. The warning signal is that they are no longer satisfied to repeat the sentiments of revolution when real life does not allow them the chance for self-realization and work.

One has to wonder whether this began, as is customarily believed, in the years of the Cultural Revolution, or much earlier, with the Liberation itself in 1949. The wooden inflexibility of such melodramatics can never succeed in portraying the complexities of human life, whatever the society, and one has finally to judge it as an insufficiency of imagination and a failure to confront experience. The melodramatic urge is basically an authoritarian one in art, as it tries to command what the viewer is to make of what he sees rather than give him choices as to what things really mean. This play, on top of everything else, makes me wonder if the Cultural Attaché was right, and that Chinese audiences are indeed extremely unsophisticated.

It is jarring to remember that down the street the Beijing Opera is playing with a kind of sophistication most Western acting never touches. The compartmentalization of the human mind is a fearful thing to behold. Yet, I suppose that in its indifference to psychology this production of *Warning Signals* has a cultural continuity with the opera, which in a different manner also presents its stories in ways unabashedly broad. The thing that is so hard to absorb, however, is that the actors, director, and author of the play think they are being real, although I am told the author would say that he is forced to write down to his audience in order to make things clearer.

I wonder if this is the harvest of so many years of indoctrination, when any play, indeed any artwork, has been regarded as hardly more than a thinly disguised political statement. I know that those who have invited me to put *Salesman* on here are desperate to at last break out of this kind of bone-dry liturgy masking as drama, but I must wonder whether they themselves are cured of their lifelong habits of obedience to political demands made on their art. I have the sense of a struggle going on within them to free themselves as well as the audience.

## *April 4*

This morning, after yesterday's day off, our new Happy came in with most of his Act One words learned. He is a magnet for direction. Ying and I climb up to the second-level bedroom with him and Biff and I find it a pleasure to see how quickly he has got the point of the character, his brag and his sentimentality and his narcissism. We all find ourselves laughing together, as Chinese and American bragging recognize each other and merge.

As for this evening's rehearsal, it's the first to fire off some continuous lightning, and it has a wonderful effect on the cast. Our new Happy is almost fluent in the part now, stumbles only occasionally, so it seems time to try to create the rhythms of the scenes rather than merely lead the actors through the psychological realities. I cannot tell if the audience will follow us at our bracing velocity of speech, but now that it has been reached in some passages, it seems undeniably right. Especially in Willy's scenes of recollection, I have pressed them into a style of falling and rising cadences, which, to be sure, are not natural but somehow signal that they are memories rising out of his anxiety. And so I drill cues with no pauses allowed, everything compressed into a stream. In life, after all, we don't experience memory in ordered trains of words and images but in compacted, overlapping flashes. What takes five actual minutes of playing time should seem to streak before us in a few seconds. In any case, once they had reached this nearly breathless pace it was possible to pause suddenly—as when Willy, trying to stall Ben's departure, takes his arm and tours the stage apron to point out the woods around the house, saying, "It's Brooklyn, I know, but we hunt too. . . . There's snakes and rabbits . . ." and with this sudden slackening of speed, frame and elevate his lyrical longing for the lost promise of the past. The actors felt the spell of this happening and were excited by the discovery of the psychological truth behind the pace.

And I have now got Biff to tuck the football under his arm as it should be, rather than pressing it against his side like a package of bread. He is a quick, well-made actor, his eyes full of fun and feverish truth-seeking. Our new Happy is another version of him. I have now gotten to the point where I can yell, *"Pow, pow!"* and Biff runs in a halfback crouch across the stage instead of breaking up in laughter at my suddenly using this Chinese word for "Run!" This evening I tell them that both Lomans were Boy Scouts as kids and took their oaths with great seriousness, and that there is a nearly military aura to the loyalty in the house, as though the Lomans were a little armed camp in hostile territory. The actor playing Biff was a Young Pioneer, the Chinese version of the Scouts, and understands at once—with some laughter at the memory of his own childishly sentimental vows of eternal faithfulness to the highest ideals.

Happy is getting so good that I take him aside to inquire what image he is using for his characterization, for in actuality he is as a person a good deal more sophisticated than Happy and can see around the character, so to speak. "Is there a Chinese type that you are drawing from?" I asked.

"Oh yes, they exist. I am thinking of the unemployed youths now who get into shady deals, smuggling and the like, and get themselves apartments and the Honda bike and the girl, and once they have it made, go around asking what they're living for. We have plenty of them now, especially down in Guangzhou and a lot in Shanghai, where the smuggling is more common. But they're here in Beijing, too." Then he adds, "They're not bad fellows. Happy Loman isn't bad either. He's just empty. If there's a major difference here it's in the Lomans' fanatic interest in sport. We don't have that as intensely as this family."

In the restaurant scene I had instructed him to inspect his clothes admiringly as he is talking to the waiter while waiting for Biff to arrive. I mimed running his forefinger and thumb down his trouser crease, adjusting his shirt collar and tie, unfolding a handkerchief and putting it into his breast pocket, and told him to feel free to invent whatever he could in that line. What he added at the next rehearsal was shining his shoes on the backs of his trouser legs, not quite the thing for a Happy wearing a hundred-and-fifty-dollar suit. But how to convey this to him, when he would probably have to work nearly half a year for that kind of money? Still, he can probably make the calculus for himself, so I will try.

The set-building shop intends to build the set in two days. According to Ying Ruocheng, the whole technical side of the theater is behaving extraordinarily well because they sense the special importance of this production for the theatre. The evidence is that the lighting designer and set designer have both attended several rehearsals and have already, three weeks in advance, worked out their schedules and diagrams. Normally they don't show up at all even for discussions until a week before a show is to open. I could be wrong but I sense there has been in the past a lot of slack indifference, and I can hardly wonder why, considering the unacknowledged irrelevance of so much of the work. Once again I think I understand why they so wanted to do this play and to have me here supervising it. It is undoubtedly an attempt to blow some excitement into their work. Ying apart, there seems literally no awareness of the theatre world beyond China, a sleeping beauty. What can an audience fed on the unexceptionable, if not soporific, be expected to make of my play? Yet the actors feel, or like to feel, that the audience is secretly prepared—way ahead of them, in fact.

The director of *Warning Signals* is working in the small theatre upstairs on another play by the same author and has been stopping in for a look at my rehearsals every day or so. One night after we had finished work and the cast had gone, I asked him to sit and talk for a bit, with Ying doing the interpreting. He is about twenty-eight, I would think, quite thin, tired and hollow-cheeked, but wearing corduroys and a brown zipper jacket of wool rather than the common blue cotton outfit. I have found myself thinking a lot about some of the stylistic extremes in *Warning Signals* and was eager to ask about them. But first I asked what he and his audience felt was so novel about the piece. Was it the style or something in the story—perhaps the strong suggestion, for instance, that the heroine and hero had slept together?

He answered with care, and at first I thought it caution and I felt I was speaking across half the world with him. Gradually I began to wonder if he really understood my emphasis on stylistic questions, for apart from the manifestly speeded-up physical movement and the novel use of spotlights, the play, he felt, was acted realistically, the acting represented how people behave more or less in life. "But the Gangster," I persisted, "seems to be so utterly sneaky, evil, and flicks his eyes left and right and zips around on his sneakers . . . is he realistically portrayed?"

He thought for a moment. I had the feeling that he was not so much embarrassed as at a loss how to explain. Finally he threw caution away: "The character is very superficially written."

"I see. Because he doesn't seem believable—a real gangster has to be able to deceive people, he has to seem good or at least not too menacing to a young fellow like the hero. This gangster wouldn't fool anyone, I don't think."

"But you should have seen the part before we cut it. It was much worse." Which meant that they were not, as I had pressed myself to theorize, trying to create a new version of the traditionally outspoken moral-pointing style, but simply had not been able to break away from the old kind.

Yet the play was clearly persuasive on some level to its young audiences. "It is the first time on the stage that a story has shown the feelings of the young. The older generation has nothing to say to them—

the future is not with them; all they can advise is patience. Meantime, life is going by. The love story is not the new thing; it has been done before. But this generational conflict has not been."

And yet the Party passed the play for production, and the Party is surely the older generation. The play, in fact, leaves the generational issue unresolved, for the reassurance of the Trainmaster that time will heal everything must seem more of a palliative than a resolution—and that is also news.

As for what this young man knew of the European or Western theatre, he had read plays by Ionesco and Beckett, also Albee. He seemed most taken by Beckett. It occurred to me that they should be interested in *Rhinoceros*—Ying suddenly reminded me in his stubby physique of a modest version of Zero Mostel, who did a phenomenal Rhino. But it was impossible to tell from the director's mere nod whether he agreed or not. How telling is one's social environment when estimating any style of art or even thought; here in China, I believe, Ionesco's attack on the human capacity to rush into mindless conformity would appear as a militantly progressive political statement, whereas in his own time he seemed like a forlorn warning of individuality forsaken by bourgeois culture. *Rhinoceros,* I suspect, would not pass Party vetting, at least for a while.

There is not, at least not in Beijing, although I suspect there may be signs of it in Shanghai, anything like an avant-garde, as this director confirmed to me. He was one of the new, younger group of directors—the older ones did not show any interest in *Warning Signals,* which gave him his big chance. What he wished to tell me, I thought, was that he knew the play's limitations perfectly well, that one had to proceed a step at a time in opening the Chinese stage to the unprecedented moral and political risk-taking going on in the country. Something of what they are up against came through when he told of a discussion in dialogue between himself and the play's author that was to preface the published version. In it they discussed the characters, the style, and other elements usually dealt with in introducing a play to the reader, but there was some strong criticism from conservative Party people that they never so much as mentioned the message, something that is always of the first importance, overshadowing everything else.

"But the message," said Ying sharply, "can be put in a single sentence. Unemployed youth are bitter and alienated and the older generation has nothing to say to them. You can hardly fill up a whole preface with *that* subject!"

As we parted, I found myself feeling more warmly toward *Warning Signals* and its naive, even primitive, level of art. It took great determination, even imagination, to manage its confrontation with very delicate issues; and to have guided the project through the sieve of controls and finally to move its young audience, as it unquestionably does, is an honorable achievement. In talking to theatre people here, one hears very little more than nineteenth-century names as representing good theatre—Chekhov, Gorki, Ibsen, Tolstoy. It seems to have all been caught in amber. Yet this is not altogether the work of Communist censorship shielding the artist and public from the West's bad influence. It is phenomenally difficult to translate literary works into Chinese, although somewhat easier the other way. It is not merely the totally different syntax, if that word even applies to Chinese, but perhaps more fundamentally the Chinese tendency to speak in images, and better yet, images of startling density and complexity. "I don't like to rush through an art exhibition" becomes "I don't like to ride past pictures on a fast horse." Nor is this lovely tendency confined to the intellectual classes; the endless changes in government policy are known among the peasants as a "change of sky." In comparison, everyday English seems unpoetic in this metaphoric sense, more fact-bound.

The young director of *Warning Signals* and its author have a right to find it a daring challenge to portray a young man who enlists in a criminal plot yet is Good underneath. Their Trainmaster, epitome of social and moral authority, is also a shocker, for he is shown to be at a loss as to what to tell the young, and if he doesn't know, who does? It may be nearly pointless for an outsider to note that the acting is still not truthful, the emotions not grounded but reached for, and the staging innovations old-fashioned by the standards of other countries. One has to start from somewhere. And so, much is at stake with *Salesman*'s reception, for Willy is not Good, and yet one is supposed to feel pity for him and perhaps even fear that he will die.

The notion of an avant-garde is a contradiction where art must be supportive of the regime almost by definition. But apart from that, an avant-garde is unlikely where there is simply no money with which impromptu groups might set up small theatres or even ad hoc productions of new and unorthodox work. Poverty thus strengthens the official grip on theatre life; I could be wrong but I sense a dead weight at the top even now, despite the encouragement for innovation in all other fields.

With some surprise I learn that up to three quarters of this theatre's expenses are subsidized, the other quarter coming from the box office. I would have thought it the other way around, given its seeming lack of any money at all. But the conservatism of the repertoire is understandable. Change can come only by the inch. But more than political control enforces this conservatism; it is also the Chinese moral vision, which demands that art be "clear" in its moral choices. It is doubtless the people themselves who want to understand quickly and easily who in the plays they see they are supposed to support. It may simply be an old-fashioned country, something like the United States before World War I. Indeed, the charm of Chinese opera rests partly on its naive and underscored signaling of every character's position on the moral seesaw—the gloriously imaginative makeup is just such a system. This does not necessarily require that Good people win out in the end, but they must not be mistaken for Bad people. The moral reassurance this provides is reminiscent of *Everyman* and the medieval mystery plays, in which the issue is less a question of what happens than of the sublimity of style in which the story evolves.

Willy is a lot of things but he is not particularly Good; it may even be that his faults and failings dominate him altogether. But at the same time the play obviously presents him sympathetically. I really had no clear idea of how remote the art here is from acknowledging any sort of ambiguity, the very coin of the world's contemporary literature. In our handfuls of audience looking on at rehearsals I sense at times a confusion no play can surmount. Already one young onlooker has told Ying Ruocheng that if Charley's role were eliminated it would be a much better play—that is, if his capitalist virtues were not allowed to cloud the picture of a thoroughly malign American society. Trouble ahead.

## *April 6*

Today it is even clearer that the level at which *Salesman* is to be interpreted is a rope that two sides in the artistic hierarchy are tugging at. *Xinhua* has published a narrow description of the play as a condemnation of monopoly capitalism, period. But the actors and others around the theatre seem totally undisturbed, dismissing this as inevitable and as something nobody reads but foreigners and newspapermen. In any case, I sense I am being shielded from this ideological conflict; everyone around the production wants the play to be received and felt as a human document applicable to China. And that is how Ying Ruocheng is trying to sell it to the reporters and politicos, I think, in order to keep it from becoming a political bone of contention.

## April 10

I took yesterday and the day before off, and tomorrow I will return with a three-day holiday behind me. I had begun to lose concentration. For two or three days I had not had to refer to my English script at all—I knew where they were, even within speeches, almost all the time. But this took additional concentrated effort, for on top of having to keep up with what line they were speaking I also had to try to register what emotions they were connecting with it. Yet again I found them creeping back to their old habits of indicative acting; noble ideas make them turn out to the audience with noble expressions, in moments of pathos they bat their eyes. Cropping up again was the tendency to point at themselves or at others at every opportunity in what Ying has called the "outdoor acting style." But they were thankfully quick to cure themselves when I pointed out what they were doing, and Ying would have none of that either. But he never got ahead of me in this, unsure, possibly, that he was not being oversensitive to it. But in the climactic scene of the play, when Biff flies across the stage in what seems like an attack on Willy and then embraces him in tears, our actor sank to his knees gripping Willy's body and crying, "There's no spite in it anymore, I'm just what I am, that's all," and twisted himself around to face front, and threw his arm out in a wide operatic gesture. I had withheld correcting him, wondering whether what seemed so excessive to me might not seem appropriate here.

During a ten-minute break, which is required every two hours and is rigidly adhered to, I asked Ying, who answered succinctly, "It is too much anywhere." It was a simple matter to get the actor to embrace his father and weep on his shoulder for a moment.

I had been having a problem with Happy when he reminds Biff, "The trouble with you in business was you never tried to please people," and goes on to recall how on Biff's last job "Bob Harrison said you were tops, and then you go and do some damn fool thing like whistling whole songs in the elevator," the passage ending with, "I'll tell you something that I hate to say, Biff, but in the business world some of them think you're crazy."

First of all, Happy could not understand what was involved in Biff's whistling in the elevator. "Why does he whistle?"

"It expresses his longing to escape."

"But is it musical whistling?"

"Yes, he whistles some popular tune."

"And is it undignified?"

"Exactly. It is as though, let's say"—and I reached for some absurdly extreme example that at the same time would not include elevators, figuring most of their offices don't have any—"it might be like a young and ambitious undersecretary in an important Party organization who is waiting with other officials for transportation, and while everybody is trying to stand there looking businesslike and responsible, he is off by himself whistling a tune."

"Really! Biff would have done that?"

"Something like that, yes."

This seemed to strike a note; he nodded deeply, an excited look on his face—such behavior would indeed seem a little crazy—and he at once delivered the speeches with a better mix of admonitory indignation and self-satisfaction with his own sanity and social discipline.

Still, it is difficult for him to stand face-to-face with another man and call him crazy. It is infinitely impolite and un-Chinese. So he performs the line purely by imitating me and accepting it, I believe, as something real in America.

Reverting to metaphorical or analogous situations is of course common in directing anywhere, but the Chinese actor seems to fire up far quicker and with more excitement when given an image than I have ever seen American or British actors do. Image, after all, is what their language is filled with.

For two weeks I had been watching in slow agony Biff boxing with Uncle Ben upon the latter's challenging invitation, but at a loss as to how to give the fight some kind of conviction. For one thing Chinese don't use their fists in fighting. The scene is part of Willy's reverie of the long past when the boys were young and his brother Ben did indeed stop by on one of his voyages to far places. Willy, trying to rise to Ben's brave confrontational life in the African diamond fields and Alaskan forests, with a miraculous gesture produces Biff from behind the proscenium and boasts, "That's just the way I'm bringing them up, Ben—rugged, well liked, all-around. . . ."

"Yeah? Hit that, boy—hard as you can"—with which Ben pounds his own stomach and awaits Biff's attack.

The two actors playing Biff and Ben had tried developing something like a trading of punches ending in a fall, with Ben standing over the boy, his umbrella pointing into Biff's eyes, and growling, "Never fight fair with a stranger, boy. You'll never get out of the jungle that way." But Chinese, it occurred to me yesterday, seem most stylized in portraying violence on the stage, and perhaps this was why the fight had no conviction in it on any level. They thought they had to make it American and realistic.

Rehearsing the fight scene.

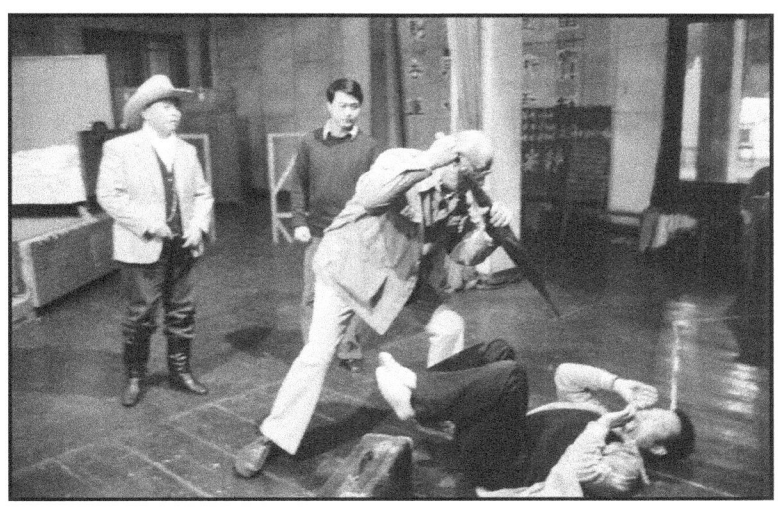

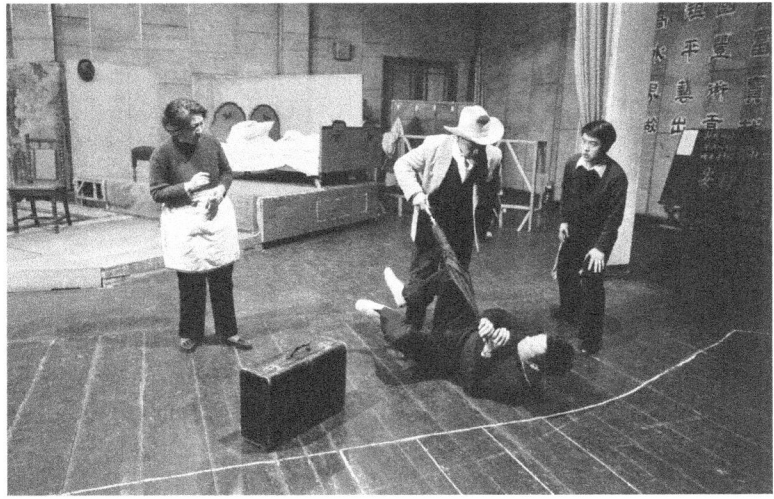

Rehearsing the fight scene (continued).

Suddenly I recall the marvelous choreography of the Beijing Opera battles, where nobody loses his aplomb, nobody is actually hit, and yet the effect of battle is amply produced. "This is a dream," I say. "It is Willy's adoration of Ben's superhuman power. It is all magic! It is the Beijing Opera!"

Delighted laughter. Ben, under these new dreamlike instructions, really pounds his belly instead of politely indicating how hard it is; and Biff comes on like lightning, his fists flailing at the air; and Ben, chuckling imperturbably, faces his charge, and with two quick gestural blows to Biff's forehead, which he never of course touches, sends the boy flying to land on his back and spin slowly around with his knees and hands raised defensively in front of his face; and Ben is on him instantly with his umbrella pointing into his eyes.

Ying has great technical facility, so that it takes time to realize when he is "delivering" a speech and when he is doing it truthfully. One of his final speeches has been troubling me with its lack of conviction and I resolve to tackle it with him. He is planting his garden at night, flashlight, hoe, and seed packets in hand, when Ben appears. Debating his suicide with himself, he is using "Ben," in effect, as the devil's advocate to remind himself that Biff might call him a coward, a damned fool. "He'll hate you, William," says Ben, forcing him into a speech of intensified longing for the loving past. "Oh, Ben, how do we get back to all the great times? Used to be so full of light, and comradeship, the sleigh-riding in winter, and the ruddiness on his cheeks. And always some kind of good news coming up, always something nice coming up ahead. . . ."

Ying, I think, is achieving only an intellectual recognition of a hopeful time gone by, but not the taste of it, the smell of it, the vision of something concrete and real. He agrees, "It is hard for me to imagine such a time."

"For Willy it meant the American 1920s, the time when it all seemed to be working, expanding, opportunity everywhere, the dream in full bloom. . . ."

"Well, of course, we never had that. China was still carved up by foreigners in the 1920s. But I hadn't been thinking about it in those terms exactly."

"You were thinking only in personal terms?"

"Well, I hadn't concentrated on the social meaning, but obviously that is what he is talking about." He thinks for a moment in silence.

"Actually, we did have a few years of prosperity and peace although not in my lifetime, but I think I can use those." The speech now begins to fill with the fervent texture of recall rather than an objective and cool quality alien to it.

I have also been troubled by a certain reversion to vehemence in Ying's delivery, which seems to me to threaten his performance with repetitiousness. I have hesitated to mention this until I was more sure that it was not some linguistic peculiarity, and indeed I realize on thinking about it that for my ear Chinese does have a vehement kind of emphasis. It is akin to the abrupt imperativeness we associate with German, although quite different in its actual sounds. Finally, I checked the lines on which he sounded unintentionally angered, found ten or twelve as examples, and presented them to him for a solution. In each case it turned out that, at this relatively early stage in rehearsals, he had not really worked out what he was feeling and thus had been fleeing into a verbal violence to produce something that sounded strong and definite to cover inner uncertainty. In short, there was no particular Chinese element in the problem.

Actually, it was not merely the repetitiousness of the sound that bothered me but that it tended to make Willy seem petulant and irritated rather than a man in pursuit of his "strange thoughts," someone who senses the nearness of death and is desperately searching for meaning in his life. If Willy can be a nuisance at times to his family and friends, he ought not be a petty one. He is extraordinary in one sense at least—he is driven to commit what to him is a consummate act of love through which he can hand down his selfhood, his identity. Perversely, perhaps, this has a certain noble claim if only in his having totally believed, and dreamed himself to death. Petulance is nowhere near enough for this.

The vision of Lee Cobb, the original and I think the best Willy, keeps returning. I hear his baritone voice occasionally, I see his mass and his so moving, depressive slump—a man who was born old, whose very laughter was sad and somehow filled with a bottomless kind of wanting for love, admiration, friendship. The other day I watched Ying as he stood at the edge of the forestage looking front, with Linda in the kitchen mending a stocking, and saying, "I don't know why—I can't stop myself—I talk too much. A man oughta come in with a few words. One thing about Charley. He's a man of few words, and they respect him."

LINDA   You don't talk too much. You're just lively.

WILLY   Well, I figure, what the hell, life is short, a couple of jokes. I joke too much! I'm fat. I'm very—foolish to look at, Linda. . . .

For Lee it was one of the moments when he reached a rarely achieved relaxation, a private calm that at the same time was filled with anxiety. It was quite miraculous to me at the time. I tell this to Ying now—that he is really talking to himself here, that he is as isolated as a star in space. He had thought he was talking to Linda, who does indeed have interrupting lines, but he sees at once that this is not so. Like Ben she is at this moment merely a contrapuntal voice that Willy summons up in order to both "correct" his anxieties and confirm their reality. Ying tried it again—how quickly he can change an attack!—and did take a step in the right direction, but we must work on this more.

Yesterday afternoon Inge and I drove to the Yong He Gong temple, which houses The Five Hundred Buddhas. Statues of five hundred larger-than-scale, robed men, covered with gilt and dust, sit in long somber rows, each with a distinctively different face. Inge found one with a remarkable resemblance to Ying Ruocheng, a square, flattened face and much the same kind of intelligence in the faint grin. To think of Willy played by a Buddha's descendant!

I have my second meeting with Old Feng, the lighting designer, a trim and witty little man in his forties who seems a bit happier with me than during our first meeting, when I sensed his apprehension about my making demands he could not meet. Now in discussing Act Two we dispense with having to move through it cue by cue as we had the first act, and concentrate instead on three or four problem areas. First is the business of flooding the stage with the shadows of leaves to indicate that Willy has made the mental leap into the past, when there were trees rather than apartment houses surrounding his backyard. I can recall an afternoon back thirty-five years ago, with Jo Mielziner and Kazan, when one of us—I no longer recall who—dreamed up this idea of the leaves. It was a response to the frequent skepticism in the play's earliest readers as to whether the audience was going to follow when Willy moves in and out of the present. For me, it was hard to believe there would be a problem, but others did. When I first saw the leaf effect and forever after, it seemed very doubtful, more like a failure of the electrical system than an evocation of a leafy neighborhood. The problem, as I now tell the Chinese designer, was that the distance from the lights to the stage so diffused the leaflike pattern that it lacked real definition. He agrees, but says he has one trick he would like to try but that I should not expect too much. I tell him I always had doubts about the effect but invite him to try his luck.

We then proceed to the worst problem, their equipment's inability to handle more than a series of eighteen cues without replugging, which would require a total blackout of some twenty seconds. In Act Two he has counted up to eighteen and found that the blackout has to come between the scene with Willy and Charley and the restaurant scene with Biff and Happy. "That is exactly where the one full blackout has to occur," I say. He is very happy to hear this, but asks if it could last twenty seconds, a long time for the stage to be dark. "Oh yes," I say, "we could even go longer because there is a long music cue and I want a kind of breathing space just before the disastrous restaurant scene." This makes him even happier, which prompts me to add, "In fact, I originally wrote it with a long Chinese blackout in mind." Ying translates, and the designer's eyes widen in a shock of surprise; then, looking at my poker face, he catches on and gives me a medium laugh.

Actually, his problem is not unknown to me; in 1949 the Morosco Theatre on Broadway had not had a computerized console to control lights either. And I remember our electrician (whose last name, to my shame, I no longer recall — but his first was Dick) stretching to move his light-level handles while touching up another light with his shoe toe. He, like this Chinese electrician, had never had a play with so many cues. Nowadays, of course, everything is run through a civilized console and one operator easily moves the various level controls or can preset them to adjust themselves automatically.

I am also being conditioned not to expect hard-edged spotlights, which the Chinese do not possess. The equipment in general is about thirty years old and its design older than that. But they are quite abreast of equipment available in the West — aware of what they cannot yet have.

The paper is running stories about the infanticide of female children. But statistics are now provided that show a burgeoning imbalance between the sexes in some provinces, so that twenty years hence the young men will actually find it impossible to locate a spouse. *Economic Daily* reports that in Hubei Province, "Among babies under one year the sex ratio is 182 males against 100 females; among infants under three years old, 384 against 100; among children under five years old the ratio is 503 males against 100 females." The newspaper *Renmin Ribao* attributes these murders to feudal thinking that downgrades the female but also to the introduction of "the one-child-per-couple policy." In other words, if more than one child is heavily frowned on as unpatriotic, there is a strong impulse to make that one a boy. But there is doubtless an additional irony in that the new encouragement given private initiative and market-pricing instead of fixed prices has placed a premium on more production, which in the countryside means favoring men, who are regarded as stronger in the fields and generally more productive. One is entitled to suspect, too, that with more money — and the peasants these days are making a lot, in Chinese terms — there is the impulse to keep the family assets in the family. Girls marry into other families and are thus not to be given inheritances that will only end up in strangers' pockets. Money is in the air in China, far more so than it has been in a long time, anyway.

Remote as the connection may appear, I cannot read such evidences of feudal mentality without wondering whether it will help or hurt my play. On the day the world is blown up, the playwright whose show opened the night before will be leafing past the news section of the *Times* to find his review — as he ascends through the stratosphere, oblivious.

Last Thursday evening we ran the play through from beginning to end for the two musicians who will be conducting and helping to perform the play score. The film music I have definitely discarded as too lushly orchestrated. Also present were a thirtyish American lawyer, Jamie Horsely, who practices in Beijing, and her young Chinese driver and his friend. The play apparently devastated them, and Jamie, too — although, despite her fluent Chinese, she found it hard at times to keep up with the speed of the speech. There was also Liu Housheng, one of the triumvirate running this theatre, the former actor now in his sixties, who was overwhelmed. None of the Chinese seem to have any trouble understanding anything. Can this be possible? I reassured myself that both salesmen and life insurance are surprisingly well explained, in effect, in the play: Willy tells exactly what he does and how he does it, and the insurance procedure, oddly enough, is also laid out quite understandably.

It occurred to me only now that this may partly explain why the play can be done so successfully in so many different cultures, but I am still prepared to experience an audience here that does not connect.

An interesting short discussion with Ying the other morning on China's isolation led directly to a talk about the two thought-systems China has laid upon herself: first the Confucian, and on top of that, the Marxist. (I hadn't been aware that the trader or salesman occupies the very lowest Confucian category of worth.) Correct behavior is decreed from cradle to grave — obligations to family and state, relations between the sexes — a veritable web is woven in the Confucian system to catch the individual wherever he tries to move. On top of this grid another, the Marxist, set of obligations is overlaid. But the heavy emphasis on chastity in Chinese Marxist practice is unique — chastity, that is, as a social good. After all, Marx had an illegitimate son and Engels several children out of wedlock.

I can't help thinking of chasteness as I watch Ying acting the scenes with the Woman in his Boston hotel room. The actress who plays the part, Liu Jun, has invented all her business, I having left her to herself out of a fear of overstepping bounds of Chinese propriety in this sexual encounter; I have no idea what they might find distasteful and what erotic. Left to herself, she enters with the music, a long white scarf draped along her outstretched arms, as she slowly turns and turns, approaching the self-absorbed Willy, and at the same time softly laughing. At one point, where the script calls for them to kiss, they have arranged for her to revolve into his arms with her face and mouth turned from the audience. When not on stage, she practices dance steps, watching herself in one of the long mirrors that stand against the walls. She invited us to come to her house, an hour's bike ride out of Beijing, but when we accepted the invitation she flew into a frightened frazzle because they have only one room. But I am interested in her actor husband's sideline — he raises some species of large fish. Perhaps she will still let us come. She appears in one of the large blown-up photos of actors with Zhou Enlai that hang in the theatre lobby.

I have been working with Ying now and then to age him. He hasn't an athletic body but he is obviously not in his sixties. Aging is part of Willy's story. He is practicing a heavier step, a habit of sighing after any effort, but it goes too far at times, as it inevitably would. With his white wig he may have an easier time of it. But I caught him doing a knee-bend when he was setting the seed packets on the ground in the scene with Ben near the end. When I pointed this out to him he looked at me quizzically. I then realized that Chinese do a lot of squatting throughout their lives. People rest that way even at street-corner bus stops, and in fact it is a wonderful posture for relaxing if you can manage it. I won't mention it again.

I was just leaving the theatre at noon when I saw Ying, looking unusually tense, hurriedly trying to back his bike out of the mass of bikes parked near the door. He had just received word that his house door was wide open and that probably a robbery had taken place. "It sounds like New York!" I said. He gave no answer and pedaled rapidly off. That evening he told me that his mother had gone out and left the door open but that nothing had been taken. He had been worried about his TV set and record player, and a TV tape machine that he had borrowed from the Cultural Attaché at the American Embassy to play the tapes of some films he wanted to watch. "So the virtue of socialism is intact!" he said, laughing.

There has been a severe shortage of fruit, especially oranges and bananas, which have been scandalously left to rot on the trees, and one hears talk of sabotage by unrepentant adherents of the Gang of Four, and/or opponents of the current economic line who intend to help it to fail. It is not hard to picture a certain revulsion at the cupidity that the new incentive production system has unleashed—as one European woman, resident here for half a century, said to us, "It has released their instincts for gain, the worst part of them." I have also heard distaste expressed at the sight of able-bodied men peddling trinkets on the streets. In fact, selling or even serving the public in any Marxist state has a tinge of the ignoble about it; in the Soviet Union, waiters can stand a yard from one's table for half an hour before strolling over to contemptuously show the menu. The Cultural Revolution, among its other meanings, expressed the yearning for the purities of equality when none would serve another. It ended with everybody serving a psychopathic dictator-lady. Service in China, however, is usually cheerful, if erratic.

But the papers never cease to berate stores for purposely ignoring the customer or ill-serving him or cheating. It all keeps reminding me of Huey Long's main slogan—"Every Man a King"; in many ways he strikes me as our first Cultural Revolutionary, preaching a leveling egalitarianism and getting rich at the same time. He was our Jiang Qing, rising as she did out of an economy that had stopped working and a people without hope or direction.

Yesterday the Chinese Government announced that it was canceling all cultural and athletic cooperation with the United States because of the Hu Na affair. This nineteen-year-old tennis player has decided not to return here. Guests at lunch in the American Embassy the other day quite obviously considered that the Reagan Administration's way of handling the case had unnecessarily fired up Chinese national pride. There was no call to declare the girl a "political refugee," as the Administration did, there being no indication that she had the slightest political interest and could not be described as a target for punishment if she should ever return in the normal course. In fact, hundreds of Chinese sent to study in the United States have defected over the years and while this may upset the regime it has never raised so great a fuss; their loss to China is seen as a cost of production. But Chinese apparently are offended now because the U.S. Government itself has in effect challenged them to be, since Deng himself asked that her defection not be politicized. Worse, President Reagan has apparently declared he would adopt her himself if he had the opportunity.

This picture of a forlorn little girl tennis player is something nobody in the Embassy takes seriously. No one would say so, but she has probably been gotten to by people who make a business of trying to disrupt the relationship between both countries. One did not have to be supersensitive to gather that official Americans here are appalled at having been pitched into a battle in which we are wrong and will ultimately have to lose. And of course among the lesser consequences will be our necessary reluctance ever to allow the return of the girl to her home, which, for all anyone can tell, she will one day want to do. She has an older sister, a brother, and, to judge from photos in the press, a mother and father who are still quite young. From this distance and particularly from this ancient culture, Reagan looks callow to the point of arrogant ignorance, a veritable Know-nothing.

Nevertheless, it is also true that certain well-known artists have found it is impossible to get permission to go to Hong Kong with their spouses lest they defect, as some significant numbers have done. As one Chinese old-timer here put it, "There is a widespread idea of Hong Kong as a perpetual banquet. Of course there are many who make good there, but a lot end up trying to get back if only for a meal they can enjoy, preferably cooked by Mother. Chinese food is not the same outside." For Ying Ruocheng, who calls himself a minority in this, Hong Kong is the depths of vulgarity, where poor Guangzhou peasants, lured by dreams of wealth, end up exploited and spiritually broken.

This being the third and last day of my holiday, I am trying to think of how to proceed over the next weeks of rehearsal. I believe we could open as sharp as a tack in no more than ten days, even less. There is a danger in being over-rehearsed; a boredom seeps into the performances. Perhaps we can sit down and talk about the play for a while, and about America and China and the subtler adjustments the actors are making to play these characters. I am still finding it difficult to see the play and the America that stands behind it as they do. Unless, of course, there is something one can call the basic man—what the French have named *le moyen homme*—who operates on the same principles everywhere.

Inge and I spent three hours bicycling through the lanes and main avenues of Beijing again this bright sunny morning and every few blocks came upon clots of people, and sometimes quite large and dense crowds, shopping at pushcarts stationed at random on the sidewalks. A variety of goods was being sold, all of it cheap and in the West doubtless unsalable except to the poorest people. But trade was brisk, especially in white cotton cloth that the tradesmen were selling by the meter, first snipping the selvage edge and then ripping it across the width of the goods. Quite young men in their late teens and early twenties were hawking balloons and children's dresses, grandsons of the Revolution turned salesmen. After so many years of indoctrination that cursed the arts of trade and the trader, years when goods were sold only across the official counters in cold and cheerless stores, here they sprout again, the ones who buy low and sell higher and incidentally distribute the goods where they are needed, greeting the passerby with the glad hand and the inviting spiel, fluffing up the goods to keep them looking fresh—how did they learn these tricks, from what germ secreted in the blood in this place where they were for more than thirty years forbidden? It is the bazaar again, the primordial excitement of purchasing, taking it home, trying it on, and hoping it will change your life. The immemorial lust for shopping. To be sure, these young businessmen have been forced by unemployment into what for stricter Marxists is an ignoble type of work, but there is nothing dispirited about them, and their eyes are quick with the classical avarice that the salesman sublimates in his pitch and the customer learns to cease suspecting for the moment it takes him to shell out his cash.

We cycled past a long gray wall, over which could be seen large buildings in a compound. Now there is an imposing gate with large brass plates beside it, and under the Chinese lettering is written in English: "Security Force of Beijing." It reminded me that I have yet to see a cop, a police car, or the least sign of police, excepting for the traffic cops on station at the busiest intersections. But the press, with its newly won candor, speaks of rising crime. Each neighborhood has its committees to deal with juvenile delinquency and routine disturbances, like family squabbles and petty pilfering, which thus never get into a courtroom or onto a police record. For more serious matters they summon armed police, who do in fact cruise the city in motor tricycles, but only at night. The army is also stationed in the city for major problems, and foreigners have no doubt that numerous secret police are scattered everywhere.

At the Foreign Languages Institute, where I spent an hour in the afternoon with a dozen faculty and thirty or so graduate students, I learned that there is really no set system behind their decisions as to what foreign works to translate. Heller's *Catch-22* is now very popular, and Bellow's *Humboldt's Gift.* Agatha Christie, however, beats everyone else, with at least five different translations of the same book. These were put out under different titles by different publishing houses, and more than one reader, they told us, complains to the bookstores that he has already read what purports to be a new book.

From all I can learn they do not have the Russian Glavlit system of censorship, which requires every manuscript to be vetted in a crushingly orderly manner. Rather, there is a self-censorship that everyone insists is more and more relaxed, although there is no denying that anything advocating the overthrow of socialism, for example, would never see the light of day. I have no doubt either that at any one moment a work dealing with a sensitive subject could be stopped without too much difficulty since they accept the superior authority of the Party as a principle. So if there does seem to be a kind of vacuum at the moment, a new hard line could at any time be laid down once again. China is not finished changing.

The Foreign Languages Institute is not, as such a school would be in almost any other country, a cultural adornment but rather a dire necessity. If more people on earth speak Chinese than any other language, more people do not speak it than any other, too, and are not likely to try. (Inge, who is fluent in all the European languages and very good in Russian, had to study Chinese daily for eight years in order to reach a good level of fluency, in addition to taking classes every week at Yale University.) Thus the Chinese studying English, for example, are vital to the state and its business quite apart from literature or the arts, and language students should thus be expected to have a rather good level of intelligence.

Inge, Ying, and I faced some seven or eight teachers, most of them in their fifties and sixties, and forty or so students in a room where chairs were set along the walls in an informal way. The building is of the 1950s "Dungeon" Style common to Chinese institutions, dark domed hallways with peeling paint and the ammoniac smell of the sewer spreading for yards on either side of the toilets.

This meeting took place in the afternoon between our morning and evening rehearsal periods, and both Ying and I were tired, so we asked for questions rather than trying to lecture. There was a long, timid silence until a painfully intense nineteen- or twenty-year-old fellow, speaking reasonably good English, said, "I cannot understand how a girl as young as Abigail [in *The Crucible*] could have such complicated and terrible thoughts"—laughter begins but he presses on—"to be so sexual at that age, and then to cause people's deaths. . . ." His anguish as much as his naiveté breaks everyone up now, and the department chairman advises him, "You must live a little more, you are still too young to understand that sort of thing." Chastity is still with many of them, and the little boxes containing moral categories. And these are not only sexual. (Ying told me later that he played a run-through on Saturday night, when I was on my weekend holiday, to some fifty people who work in the theatre, and the young especially were weeping, something not usual for the Chinese. But the older ones, he thought, although they also were affected, "were a bit less willing to get involved." He theorized that the play's refusal to fit into the usual moral categories might have been the reason, but more likely Willy's scenes with the Woman in Boston.)

Unfortunately, between the Foreign Expert and Ying Ruocheng, the students seemed rather overawed, but after some jollying up, a discussion of sorts began. The general view was that poetry is in very bad shape; as one professor put it, "Poetry is ambiguity; if not, why bother? And ambiguity is something we have not been accustomed to for some time." There was no dissent at this and no comment either. Stories and short novels were being written that they estimated fairly highly, but there was a holding back of real enthusiasm about new Chinese literature. They seemed to think the new, more truthful literature is a young and not yet vigorous plant, but a promising one.

They were particularly interested in my experience before the House Un-American Activities Committee in 1957, which I tried to put into perspective, saying that I had been subpoenaed after the crest of the wave had begun to fall, and that I was psychologically strengthened because I worked in theatre rather than in movies and thus had a certain independence that movie people did not have. But they took this as mere modesty, preferring a purer, unadulterated heroism. For unalloyed villainy they melt together Salem, the Un-American Activities Committee, and the Cultural Revolution—parallels driven home by the production last year in Shanghai of *The Crucible.*

All this time I kept glancing around and wondering which of the professors was the one who had so fiercely persecuted an aged lady of our acquaintance, a resident here for half a century, who was shut in a room in this very building for nearly two years and threatened with the execution of her children, denied the use of the toilet, and starved nearly into coma. The man, we have learned, has been promoted two or three times since. It was impossible, of course, to guess which of the sixtyish faculty he might be, especially since the eight or ten of them present were all looking on with such intelligent gentility.

Perhaps my awareness of this contributed to my feeling that students and faculty here had no great forward motion, no driving philosophical concept, out of which to form new ideas. It was not an atmosphere of fear of expressing unorthodox thought but of not having any, it seemed to me. Nor do I think this is confined to China these days; the world is not being inspired at present by any vaulting conceptions that I know about. But nevertheless, the atmosphere here was, at a minimum, docile. Perhaps they or their friends and parents had been burned too many times, and dead caution seemed most wise.

Nevertheless, there was some animation on my asking about the surprisingly large number of new magazines being published. To judge by their laughter it would seem that some are far-out.

One starts a magazine by getting a "unit" to nominally sponsor it—a trade union, school, cooperative, any legally recognized agglomeration will do, for most magazines do not reflect their sponsors' special interests. The same procedure holds for sponsoring theatre groups, although any little-theatre movement is definitely still in its infancy. But a nascent off-Broadway type of play space is beginning to appear, and from two of them plays have made it to the big-time Capital Theatre, where *Salesman* will open. *Warning Signals* being one of them.

I left the occasion trying not to be depressed; I warn myself that it is only a few shades less luminous than other academic environments, which, in my admittedly narrow experience, seem to reproduce what has been reproduced from what was reproduced before. Besides, it takes time to draw people out.

At a luncheon interview with two American reporters I try to check out Ying's statement that there are hundreds, perhaps thousands of new magazines, many of doubtful standards but many with far-out viewpoints. The reporters have read some of these and agree that the lid may not have come off but that it is not being clamped down. But this is a high sea the Chinese ship has ventured out on, and everyone seems to be waiting for a new crew to wrest away the wheel and turn back into the old harbor again. The *Salesman* production, they believe, will be a lodestar in China for many years to come.

Yesterday, Inge and I rode through the city on bicycles for three hours. Regardless of the signs of its backwardness and poverty, the city seems so intimate with itself; there is much verbal contact on the streets, streetside shopping, window gazing, babies and old people being cared for, bikes being repaired, purchases being compared, and every kind of thing being carried on the bike from a bunch of greens to large plywood sheets. In comparison the new blocks of housing projects seem cold and isolative, far less human than the ancient little courtyard and its dirt floor and everybody inspecting everybody else's plants and doubtless minding everybody else's business. I recall Ying again, when we arrived and passed this type of apartment housing on the road in from the airport, saying, "Those are the apartment houses Willy Loman hates, right?" Are they heading, in some wild ironical trajectory, to Brooklyn? But perhaps no such connection will be made by the audience at all.

The reporters tell us that a number of housing construction projects have been brought to a halt (as we have noticed) by what are in effect strikes by cadres—the leading workers, usually the most skilled and, more than likely, Party members—who have refused to proceed without being guaranteed that they will be the first to get apartments for themselves regardless of others' needs. Rather inevitably Happy's speech in the Requiem comes to mind—"All right, boy. I'm gonna show you and everybody else that Willy Loman did not die in vain. He had a good dream. It's the only dream you can have—to come out number-one man. . . ." This is one speech I have the feeling they're going to understand with no problem at all.

To dinner with Jamie Horsely and an economist with the U.S. Embassy here. The four of us were concerned by the recent breach in U.S.–Chinese cultural relations. Senator Goldwater is reported demanding we "derecognize" China—something like derecognizing the moon. The depth of ignorance in the States about this country is depressing. It makes it all the more important that *Salesman* succeed and perhaps illuminate our common humanity.

Jamie's apartment and offices high up in the modern, plush Beijing Hotel look out over Tien An Men Square and the rather dimmed rows of streetlights that were just then turning on. The sky was yellowed by the everlasting cloud of Gobi desert dust. Somehow the lusterless streetlamps, doubtless using lower wattages of electricity for economy, seemed to symbolize the generally slower pace of Chinese living. It is this rhythm, reminiscent of ours in parts of the American South, whose loss is regretted by many an emigrant to helter-skelter New York or Chicago. People do stop and talk in a leisurely way on the streets, and the whole town seems a congeries of villagelike neighborhoods. Only for a block or two around the big hotels is there the anonymous feeling associated with life in a capital city.

To my questions about the health of the economy, the economist says it has declined on the consumer levels for the past year and a half because "the heavy-industry guys have been grabbing materials for themselves." I wonder whether the plan—there is always a plan—calls for this. But he replies, "How can there be a plan when they still haven't any deep statistics? The Cultural Revolution simply abolished statistics (no doubt as the work of 'intellectuals') and they are only partway back to having anything useful. The idea of a planned economy is ludicrous here; it's simply impossible without pretty complete statistics and they aren't close."

Our dinner at a Mongolian restaurant is hot and delicious—in the middle of a large empty room there are two tremendous mushroom-shaped grills fed by open fires on which the customer grills his own thin-sliced buffalo meat after dunking it in a sauce and sprinkling herbs on it. This is preceded by crabmeat, duck, and a spicy dish of fresh-water scallops. (Inge slept for about five minutes after this repast and I about an hour.) Mongolian workers are the customers in the large front section where tables are covered with white oilcloth while the more secluded rear room has a couple of tables of Japanese and us; I doubt the prices are not vastly different as one crosses the threshold between the rooms, our dinners costing about nine dollars apiece including several liters of beer.

Whether speaking to foreigner or Chinese, one is constantly told that most of the people support the Deng program. At the same time there is always a line of applicants at the American Embassy seeking emigration visas. This may be not so much a contradiction as proof that there is less difficulty and stigma connected with emigrating than there was before Deng Xiaoping took over. Nevertheless it is hard to believe that the current encouragement of profit-making and a market economy is not enraging some part of the bureaucracy, which doubtless sees it all as a liquidation of socialism. The papers sometimes reflect the uncertainty; peasants refuse to attend a "commendation meeting" called to congratulate them on their production and high profits, their rationale being that "the Communist Party always fights the rich to help the poor," which means that sooner or later as wealthy peasants they will be criticized again. The paper points out that this is a mistaken idea propagated by the Cultural Revolution's levelers, who "linked the word 'poor' with revolution and 'rich' with revisionism. People then did not dare make money or wear new clothes, and ate good food only in private. As a result there was the prevailing concept that the Party liked the poor and disliked the rich, which is certainly not true. . . . The Party supports and protects those who become rich through hard labor and scientific knowledge. At the same time it will help those who are not rich yet—not just by promoting egalitarianism—to get on the road to wealth." There is an obvious relevance in this to Willy and the play; indeed, the whole psychological atmosphere is changing as we rehearse, and no one is sure of anything, something which may help keep minds open about Willy as a social animal.

## April 11

Curiosity about American society is intense in the cast of *Salesman,* as was indicated this morning when, for the first time since we began, I decided to fill them in more thoroughly on the social and historical background of the play, its characters and themes. In this kind of partially subsidized theatre, where a production may take six months to prepare, they are accustomed to such sessions, but I had not wanted to indulge in background talk until I had a clear notion of what their questions are and before they had a grasp of the play itself and some confidence in their ability to do it. During my three days off, Ying not only drilled them on lines but had begun to go into questions they had not dared to ask the Foreign Expert that might reveal their naiveté or ignorance. For instance, what was really involved in Happy's trying to pick up the woman in the restaurant scene by telling her that he got his nickname at West Point?

As Ying had explained, West Point was the U.S. Military Academy, but in Happy's mind, I added, it would represent a very classy background; he seizes on it, however, as guaranteeing his reliability as a companion for the evening, because for a Loman this image of reliability is of course the opposite of his chaotic nature and his tendency to run out on obligations.

"Is there any parallel in China?" I asked. "What would a guy say to a girl he wanted to impress under some similar circumstances here? What lie would he tell her?"

Biff and Happy, the two youngest in the cast, guffaw in recognition and Biff volunteers, "He'd say he's an actor." And adds, "Especially if he wasn't one."

But Happy is unsatisfied. "I'd say I have a father in Hong Kong." This brings the house down; a few bang their hands on the small tables that stand before each chair.

"That has the glamour?"

"Oh yes"—Ying translates Happy—"it means he's got money."

We all settle down again. The actor playing Ben—he speaks his lines with what to my ear is a sharply etched, stylized sound of steel on

Uncle Ben.

glass—has a question, and it strikes me oddly now that I no longer see the formation of his eyelids as I initially did: as reminiscent of an operatic mask, with their upturned, half-curled corners; maybe I am no longer looking at his face but into his eyes and finding him a quick-minded, rather serious man who normally carries himself with a certain trim elegance. He has found a pair of calf-length black leather boots, and Ying has loaned him a ten-gallon Stetson that he was given last year in Texas, and he wears these at all times.

"What does it really mean," he asks, "that Biff wants to go to the West and work on the land? How is my character involved in the West? What does it mean to me and to Willy? Were those who came back from the West looked up to or condescended to?"

God only knows what he has in mind; I believe he may still be thinking of Biff as emblematic of a whole movement of young people who "went West." Maybe it is impossible in this country of a billion people to think of one man making this kind of decision all by himself. My guess is that the actor is confusing this with the westward movement of the nineteenth century—which would put his sense of American history about on a par with ours of Chinese history, or perhaps better, since there is comparatively little of ours to misunderstand. But I am beginning to feel we are wandering away from anything they can *act,* so I begin to maneuver the discussion toward Biff's feeling of guilt for having failed his father's expectations—when it comes to acting, a certain amount of history can go a long way—but there is such an uncustomary silence among those actors who are not being used at the moment, and the pens of our half-dozen observers are so expectantly poised over notebooks awaiting my reply, that I finally decide to answer the question. The American West, I think, may still remain the most fascinating American myth for Chinese.

"Biff sees the West in a way Americans have traditionally seen it, as both an escape from the mean city and the commercial civilization and as a place of great opportunity. It is our romantic arena where you have to prove yourself as a man rather than where you dominate by controlling pieces of paper. This was never wholly true, of course, but I am speaking of the mythology now, which can be even more important than the reality." There is much nodding at that, their having so recently come out from under a mythically unreal regime.

Surprisingly, Linda lifts her hand. There is a look of imaginative fervor in her face, as though she had been captured by a new and moving thought.

"There are many changes since the Cultural Revolution," she begins. Shen is interpreting; Ying needs to rest his strained voice, but he polices her rendering carefully, I notice. "Years ago—before the Cultural Revolution," Linda continues, "I would not have hesitated to help my husband pack up his things if he had wanted to go out to the country to help in agriculture or to some hard frontier area to do his bit to build it up."

Silence as she touches her dry lips with her tongue, her eyes filled with emotion. "But now I would not even agree for him to leave this city for any reason. And I don't understand it; I don't understand my own psychology."

In her look of perplexity I see how deeply she is buried in her own—all their—past. For me it seems rather simple; she no longer believes in what she once did. But in their poverty and life of sacrifice they have necessarily lived for the future, far more so than more satisfied people, and it is terribly painful to raise to consciousness one's loss of faith, which was all that sustained her. But I believe her—she really cannot fathom her psychological change.

"In 1958," she continues, "many workers left to work without even a salary in places where they were badly needed, just for food and water and a place to sleep. One reason, of course," she adds without much emphatic conviction, "is the big difference between the city and the hardships of country life, but—". She breaks off inconclusively.

Biff interjects, "I think in 1958 things were even worse." Again laughter and a babble of cross talk as they each try to interject their own confusing experiences of the past twenty-five years. Biff, now thirty-eight, was an actor in an army theatre but had the bad luck to "back the wrong side" in the bitter Party-line feuds of the time and couldn't get anywhere until he drifted off into this theatre about ten years ago. He is, despite his intensity of feeling and a certain inner seething quality, a happy-go-lucky type who can always land on his feet without spilling his drink. He shares this temperament with the much more roguish-looking Happy, who was a soldier, too. In fact, he was assigned to guard the cadre school where Ying and Charley had been kept as exiles during the fateful period. Ying remembers Happy as a joker who spent his evenings catching frogs for frogs'-leg banquets in the dormitory. They still talk about the night he caught two hundred.

We are led somehow into the subject of opportunity that is so central to Willy's thought, and I attempt to lay out a picture of the American salesman of the 1920s and earlier. He was a vital force in building the trade and commercial network of the country. The salesman needed little or no education, but an engaging personality and a faith in the inevitability of next week's upswing. Every salesman knew some other man who had hit it big, opened his own business, and died respected and rich. The myth of the salesman exemplified the open ranks of a society where practically overnight a man could leap to the head of the line. I think then of the stage, the American expectation that an actor might have to train no longer than a year or two before he lunges for the big chance. "Here," Ying puts in, "he passes through grades from bottom to top, gradually, over years."

"Like an army," I say, and they all nod ironically and laugh. I talk about explosive beginnings on the stage like Marlon Brando's—how he had not really worked very long before people gravitated toward him and his seemingly mystical concentration, his "selfness." Willy believes in just that kind of quick, smashing beginning. And so his sons are never trained, have no patience with the whole process of forgoing and delaying the slaking of whatever thirst is on them at the moment. They are narcissists and would, in the sociology of the 1960s, exemplify the narcissism of the consumer society.

To this the reaction is ambiguous and uncertain, as though I have touched a nerve. I know that Chinese banks, for example, are bursting with the savings of people holding back on making large purchases like washing machines and refrigerators, waiting for higher-quality merchandise to come into the store. Not long ago they would gladly have accepted anything, but sophistication about goods is swiftly spreading. These actors are living through something new in China, a buyer's market, which means that the consumer may feel a power he never had dreamed of before. More, there are installment plans now for purchasing large items, so that that feature of Willy's life has crossed the Pacific. In short, their reaction tells me that it is not so easy here, not as yet, to identify a common enthusiasm for life-improving goods and inventions with narcissism, which better applies to surfeit and waste. At the same time I am aware that here, too, Things are climbing into the saddle to ride Mankind, and it worries people, as it always must in every New Jerusalem emerging from its state of siege.

Questions about the nature of Biff's "ideals" keep cropping up, and I sense an uncertainty in these Chinese actors when we talk about idealism at all. Among many other things the Cultural Revolution began as a veritable paroxysm of idealist militancy, a brutally manic drive for egalitarian uniformity, and these people seem to shy from having to comment directly on idealism as a concept. Bluntly, they want to get on with building up the country and not get waylaid in any more theoretical talk.

Thus the story of *Salesman* may be moving and interesting to them, not for any adverse reflections on American society but for its family relations, in which they see their own. Referring to their small audience at the back of the room on Saturday night, when I was off, Linda remarks, "Most of these people shed tears because their lives are like Willy's, especially his hope that his sons become dragons."

To this Ying Ruocheng adds, "They have no hopes of becoming rich or famous themselves, they are ordinary men and women. But this gap in the play—this generation gap—they can identify with, it is absolutely Chinese."

As for whether Biff's disgust with the city rat race represents an American "movement"—Ben's question—I answer that in 1948, when the play was being written, most Hippies were in diapers or not yet born, and that this is Biff's own reaction, not something he picked up somewhere in a magazine. I am aware, of course, that the actors see the Cultural Revolution as also a revulsion against a society of order that required forgoing, that insisted on slow progress up the prescribed ladder to maturity and achievement. I wonder now whether they are searching me out to locate Biff's position vis-à-vis *that* catastrophic revolt, so I emphasize, quite truthfully, his apolitical mind. These actors are politically more sophisticated than most American or European casts, however, and are soon satisfied that Biff is not in the play to infiltrate some political message.

Trying to press home their political concept of the play, Ying Ruocheng tells how "the principles and emotions behind Biff's rejection of business broke into political form only fifteen or so years later in the United States." Now he grins. "The ultraleftists began what they called the Hippie movement. Most of them were the children of affluent people." The actors raise eyebrows in amused surprise and some break into uncomprehending laughter. "These people dressed like the proletariat, let their hair grow long as a way of defying the businessman, who was shaved and barbered."

I can't help adding, "After a while, though, the bosses also took to wearing their hair long and in their time off some pretty powerful people took to beads and sandals—everybody was getting into the act. . . ."

Suddenly, through the laughter, I hear Ying. "Bob Hope's producer wore a T-shirt and really did look like a Hippie, and he was a millionaire!" Heads shake; giggles and laughter. Ying had acted as interpreter for the *Bob Hope Special* from China and had warmed up the Chinese audience for him. He had also fixed up some of Hope's less inspired witticisms for Chinese consumption.

Our Biff has stopped laughing. "But did Biff go in for that kind of business?" he asks me, no doubt still alarmed that he is to impersonate an incipient Hippie, which in Chinese terms is very close to a Red Guard.

"No, no," I quickly reassure him, "Biff's reaction is strictly his own. But since we're talking about Hippies I should say that like the Cultural Revolution this movement also began as an authentic critique of the dehumanization of the society." This brings silence; many of them remember well how they welcomed the early bursts of what seemed a new freedom to criticize bureaucracy, deadhead professors, stultifying regulations of every kind. "But it degenerated into simply a new style of life, and for some a new form of selfishness and power-grabbing based on baiting the middle-aged. With you, of course, it went a lot further—"

I break off, sensing that they do not wish to confront history directly; we must keep this a play, and that is fine with me.

Howard, Willy's boss, wants to know how big his company is, and I tell him it is a medium-sized place for that period, with perhaps twenty or so salesmen who travel to various cities. He also wants to know if when he took over the company from his father it was prosperous or failing. It was prosperous. He seems to prefer to have built it up by himself.

Ben is still curious about his character's social position: Why, for instance, does he seem to condescend to Willy's being a salesman? Ben, I explain, is the aggressive, adventurous explorer who risks his own skin and transforms the earth, cutting down forests, digging up gold, and so on. This type can feel only contempt for stay-at-homes who basically do no more than exchange goods and skim a profit that way. "It is perhaps related to your feudal contempt for the merchant as opposed to the soldier, who is always at the top of the heap in feudal societies. . . ."

"Except in China," Ying corrects me, not without a note of pride. "The top here was the scholar-philosopher, although the merchant certainly was at the bottom."

"In any case, Willy has to compensate for his calling, which is certainly a less than noble one even in his own eyes, and so he romanticizes Brooklyn for Ben, and if there aren't bears and tigers, there are rabbits and snakes, and Biff has courage, too, enough to go and lift lumber from a nearby construction site and bring it home, a true pioneer." Laughter at this. I now broaden this view for Ying's sake. "He also romanticizes the salesman's past."

"Let me tell them about that," Ying asks, and for a few minutes I sit silently as they listen spellbound to his summary of my story of the salesmen of old, when the rugged individualist had some reality.

In this hiatus I recall a luncheon banquet given us a few days ago by the top man of the cultural establishment, Yuan Yingnan, the old revolutionary who had served in Yanan with Mao. Having studied in Germany in the 1930s and having been married to a German woman, he knew something of the West. He had remarked, "The audience will understand your play, although we have no traveling salesmen. What we do have plenty of is traveling buyers. Every major industrial plant has people out scouring the country for materials. Even the city of Beijing has men on the road buying up vegetables. This is a big business, and these people are getting rich at it, too." I never got to ask him how, but I can imagine.

It now occurs to me that more and more of the questions are revolving around a single theme: the alienation of Biff and Willy from capitalist society—the son by turning away from business, and the father by assuming the guilt for failing in it. So I talk a bit about David Thoreau and Walden Pond, his rejection of the progress which set Things in the saddle to ride Mankind. "The very sound of the railroad depressed and angered Thoreau because it threatened nature, the source of all good." I can see their conflicted bewilderment at this; here, in a country that needs everything so desperately and is reaching out to all foreign countries for technology to modernize, it is impossible to imagine seriously rejecting all that. In many ways China is living a century ago, American time. "I am not, and the play is not, advocating Thoreau's philosophy; but there is a strain of agrarian romanticism in our American thought, a looking-back to a simpler time when relations were more personal. Thoreau was reflecting an end to the era when the independent farmer was king; he saw heavy industry moving into its dominant position, carrying with it a new culture and new values of commercialism and what Marx called the cash nexus. Willy's brother Ben lives in his mind as the free man, the wealth-creator, all that has strength and range and the joy of the adventurer. And unwittingly he has primed his own son Biff for his revolt against what he himself has done with his life and against what he has come to worship: material success. Yet built into him is a distrust, even contempt, for relationships based only on money."

I turn to the actor playing Howard, a former romantic lead, now in his early fifties and partially bald, who I think has been fouling his performance with an imitation of what he conceives is sophisticated American aplomb; but his native excitability keeps breaking in, and he is suddenly waving his arms and laughing at the wrong places and creating "activity" that amounts to little more than embroidered emptiness. "That's what Willy is trying to tell you—that the impersonality of business is destroying him; and what is your answer?"

This actor, while I am speaking my English, turns to chat with his neighbor—he adores chats, and even when Shen, my translator now, is repeating my speech in Chinese he fails to listen. I call him to attention, order him to listen, and explain again. "Your answer is that you are helpless to do anything for him. You are both caught in the same machine." He nods blankly. I am going to have to take him gently by the hand and walk him through the part step by step.

"The play," I conclude, "does not have the solution to this problem—the alienation brought by technological advance—because I don't have the solution. What I present is the price we pay for our progress. Perhaps—you will know this far better than I—there is some relevance for China in this issue." I have of course been trying to teach the play, but it is clearer to me now that the main obstacle, apart from the usual ones in any production, is my difficulty in seeing the play and America as they do. Perhaps I am too suspicious, but their very ease in slipping into these characters is to me a sign that they have done so only superficially; so that later, when the time comes for deep feeling, they will have only technique. I must probe farther to the deeper places where they really live their Chinese lives, and to do that I must tempt them to emerge and reveal even more of their own references that parallel events and ideas in the play. Action that is not personal tends to mock itself and reveal its shallowness when performance time arrives.

I see, thankfully, that the question of its relevance for China has started a long discussion between Ying and almost every member of the cast, and I wait for the translation. Ying's report is succinct and given with his Manchu smile, his pursed mouth and grinning eyes. "They're saying that we're commercialized enough now—you have to pay for every damned thing!"

"Are you referring," I ask, after we have all burst out laughing, "to what I've noticed the last few days on the streets—small crowds of young people digging up plots in front of apartment houses and smaller homes to plant trees? They look to me like neighborhood folks who are just pitching in without pay—are they?"

"Oh yes," says Ying, "that sort of thing still goes on. But the truth is we have both systems now, the commercial set of values and the socialist, cooperative set, all going on together."

"But do you foresee that as the society becomes more commercialized, specialists will be called in—for example, to be paid for planting trees?"

"Yes, certainly. They already are in some places. Why," he recalls only half-humorously, "you can hardly get anyone to do anything anymore except for money. Journalists go out to the country now to interview peasants and they agree but want to be paid for their time! And that's because they're making profits now, and time has become money, so why should they give it away free of charge?"

Everyone is grinning and chuckling in recognition of this troubling new commercialization of life in China; the question seems unsettling for them. Perhaps it's that it means progress but at the same time is hardening them in their relations with one another. In any case, I think Ying Ruocheng has an aristocrat's suspicion of money; he has referred several times in a favorable way to how little one needs of it to live here, and one afternoon we looked into the etymology of money-as-excrescence, applying it to Willy's psychology. Willy teeters between idolatry and contempt for money. In Freudian psychology, I pointed out, money is like feces, and in Chinese folklore, he tells me, it is the root of evil. As actor, he seems to absorb such ideas as strengthening reassurance; I also think they lend the part dignity for him.

Often, when the actors seem to lose concentration and a scene breaks down, I ask Ying Ruocheng for an exact translation of the Chinese. In the scene at the end of Act One, Willy instructs Biff, who has decided to try to borrow money from his ex-boss, Bill Oliver, to wear a business suit, not a "sports jacket and slacks when you see Oliver." But in Chinese, "suit" can only be "Western suit," which would be ridiculous, since they are supposed to be in Brooklyn. So he has had to translate as "your blue set," which means a matching jacket and trousers, or Western suit—although not necessarily in every usage.

A touchier problem is brought up by the actress playing Miss Forsythe, the woman who enters the restaurant where Happy is waiting for Biff and Willy. She wants to know if she is a prostitute trying to pick up men, and, if not, what can she be doing in this restaurant, ordering an alcoholic drink and smoking a cigarette all alone?

I must make a quick choice—if I say she is a call girl, as Happy suspects, I will have the job of explaining that such women look and act exactly like any other woman in this situation, something that I suspect will disorient this actress, leaving her with no image to imitate or play. On the other hand, if I say Miss Forsythe is a prostitute, I am afraid she will inevitably feel she has to mime some glamorous American *houri* never seen on earth or in heaven. So I tell her she is a photographer's model, as her dialogue indicates, and that she has had a hard day at work and is now stopping by for a rest and a drink. Chinese love to rest; the *shu-shi* is one of life's profoundest compensations; I am constantly being told to take a *shu-shi,* and in fact am shortly to discover that I have been working these actors much too hard.

My explanation seems to relieve her of having to characterize an immoral type, and one she cannot ever have encountered. She is a tall, good-looking woman around thirty-five with a chubby, naive-looking face, who has taken to wearing a pathetically shabby green cotton tam-o'-shanter cocked over hard to one side to indicate her slam-bang, risqué personality. Of course she is still in her baggy brown trousers and a sweater, and rides to work on her bike like everyone else.

"In other words, the things she says to Happy about her being on a magazine cover—all this is true?" On this being confirmed she is emphatically satisfied—now she knows where she is.

But to reinforce this tenuous, if—to her—gratifying, explanation, I feel I have to add, "It's only Happy who says, speaking of her, 'There's not a good woman in a thousand,' but that's *his* idea. For Happy a woman is either good, like his mother, or close to a prostitute. . . ." The onlooking actors laugh in such a burst of recognition that I know I have struck home. "It's the sime the 'ole world over," as the Cockney song had it.

In approaching Miss Forsythe to pick her up in the restaurant, Happy takes on a certain noble posture and his gestures become rather elegantly formed; I can just see him in robes with long wide sleeves. But I cannot bring myself to naturalize his behavior, so to speak, because it looks so damned beautiful. There is only one problem: the moment he sets his body into that form, his eyes begin glancing out front. If I can get him to do one without the other . . .

There are Chinese hand-signals they tend to use whenever numbers appear in the lines, but the onlooking actors always burst out laughing when they see this happening in the supposedly American environment, and so it is gradually falling away from their performances. Happy uses a wonderful gesture when he says, "I told you she was on call!"—with hand turned up, he flaps all four fingers quickly against his palm. I'm leaving that in; it will probably tell everything.

We have been captivated by the routine of living in Beijing, so much more relaxing than the rigors of sightseeing. The tourist mind presses attention outward, but living in a place lets things in. Merely to traverse the same streets four times a day to and from the theatre is to notice changes—different vegetables for sale from one day to the next; blankets suddenly appearing on a line strung between trees across the sidewalk; a made-to-order-furniture maker planing his framing in front of his house, there being no room within; a tent raised over the sidewalk inside which two young fellows are compressing wool into flattened sheets for bedrolls, which they sell at a profit. (To reduce youth unemployment the government has encouraged them to start their own businesses.) All the cabinetmaking is done without power tools and the ripping is managed with a hatchet, which they handle quite delicately. The planes probably go back to Kublai Khan, with hornlike handles sticking out on each side. The furniture made on the sidewalks is done from customers' sketches on slight, one-by-two framing to which is glued a very thin, perhaps one-eighth-inch, plywood that looks like the so-called Philippine mahogany, or luan, a cheap softwood that can, however, take a stain quite nicely. Like cabinetmakers everywhere, these don't mind being watched as they work. Most of them are certainly under thirty, many much younger than that.

There is a tidal flow of faces day after day, a surging toward one and away like pebbles rolled forward and back by waves of the sea. Impossible to forget, ever, that their number stretches from these streets into the vastness—one billion of them out there, each keeping his secrets, each seeking something better now. Yet they are not unruly in their multitudes—if one didn't know better, it would seem a city of philosophers, such is the repose in so many faces and the quiet gleam of an inexhaustible intelligence. A young cyclist halted beside us as we were walking one late afternoon and in surprisingly adept English asked where we were from, and after a little talk I asked what work he did. He was a truck driver on his way home for dinner. The proletariat by all accounts is far from an illiterate mob, having had much more education in the last few years especially. Indeed, their problem is to find work appropriate to their academic level, a dilemma from Cairo to Rio now.

The street life is wonderfully open to the cyclist now that the Westerner is no longer the surprise that he was even five years ago. In fact, we are often completely ignored. The best time to move about is around six-thirty in the morning. Beside a street roaring with early traffic a man is brushing his teeth over a sewer drain, his elbow inches from the flank of a passing bus. Over another drain a baby is being held in a midair squat by her mother, and the bedding-beater grandmas are starting a busy day. Later, the older men—never the women—will start their sidewalk checker games, usually three men to a board, one kibitzing. And on one corner a bookseller crouches, his two or three dozen books standing on boxes, and a couple of men squatting alongside, reading from books they have rented from him for an hour. Somehow it brings to mind my father's stories about the old Lower East Side at the turn of the century and his tenement with its outhouse in the backyard, the philosophers congregating on the stoops, the future gangsters and judges and songwriters yelling across the areaways. . . . The one great change since five years ago, apart from the far higher level of sheer energy in the Beijing streets, is the reduction in the amount of spitting. Still, Jamie Horsely told me she continues to give a wide berth to people who are coughing as she jogs past them every morning, and has "Don't Spit" in Chinese across the front and back of her jogging suit.

Inevitably, there is the story of the peasant caught spitting by a cop, who fines him two mo and demands payment then and there, as the law provides. But the peasant has only a five-mo note and the cop has no change. So the man spits again and gives the cop the five. Speaking of cops, I learned that our stage manager had been the enforcer, so to speak, for the Red Guards, and kept discipline among the acting company during the Cultural Revolution. Yet there seems no animus against him now, even though he had played rough with them from time to time. Nor do they wish to talk about his "mistakes" in the past. This is one more example of a determination to put the past behind and get on with building China, a task that has been sidetracked by internecine fights. The man, I must say, is always sweet to me, but when it is time for our break he does enjoy springing up and charging toward me with his forefinger violently jabbing at his watch, as though I had already broken the rule. He is a roly-poly fellow, always refilling my teacup, and is probably not a bad guy.

## *April 12*

Leaving the theatre this noon, Ying and I emerged into bright sunshine, to be confronted by NBC News, asking what we thought of the U.S. giving political asylum to the tennis player and the consequent severing of our cultural relations by the Chinese. I said it seemed "completely unnecessary," referring to the U.S. action, but a moment later wondered if that could be misinterpreted to refer to the Chinese reaction to it. But I continued on into our car rather than risk involving the production further with this stupid contretemps. Ying and I both told Sandy Gilmore, the reporter—as he was walking backward, leading his NBC cameraman, both of them nearly falling over the bumper of the car—that *Salesman* had not been involved so far and that it probably wouldn't be, since it was privately sponsored. I am not at all that sure now.

In a spasm of optimism I have written a letter inviting Premier Deng to the opening, but people don't think he will come, due to the strained relations between China and America now and also his lack of interest in theatre and his passion for bridge.

It is wonderful how Zhu Lin, our Linda, has logically extended her new fix on the role, so that she is really alarmed in the opening scene when Willy comes home, his selling trip aborted. Nor does she show the slightest tendency anymore to play out to the audience, something that fell away in a matter of days.

I worked Howard for half an hour in the evening session. He actually owns a complicated hi-fi set, which he bought in Hong Kong, and demonstrates it to all his friends with tremendous pride.

On hearing about this several days ago, I thought to relate him more to the wire recorder that obsesses the character as Willy enters his office to ask to be transferred to a New York job. But I apparently managed to relate him so profoundly to the wire recorder that he no longer pays much attention to Willy at all. So now I must run him backward. I jump up in frustration and act for a moment myself, and this has a good effect on him—he mimes me quite well. Maybe that's the way to make it happen with him. He has the right shallowness for the role, but it is still scattered, unfocused. Yet he is eager.

I have been trying to move Ying Ruocheng toward the mystical kind of wonder I have always felt at meeting someone whom I have not seen in years, who has since grown up. He needs this feeling when he comes out of the scene-in-the-past where he is rushing off after Charley, who has mocked his excitement at Biff starring in the Ebbets Field game. Now he suddenly finds himself in Charley's office facing Bernard—whom we last saw as a kid, and who is standing there now, a grown man, a lawyer. It is perhaps the most magical transformation in the play, partly because it is so quick yet so logical, but much of the effect depends on how Willy realizes this agonizing stretching of time, how he looks at the young lawyer and literally twists his mind to focus upon him. Somehow in our discussions Ying was moved to say, "In China we congratulate a person because he looks much older than the last time we saw him, but in the States you're always telling people how wonderfully young they look. We have a saying, 'Never entrust important matters to a bare-chinned man.'" Nevertheless, he really seems to fill up with happiness when at last he realizes he is face-to-face with the grown-up Bernard.

Reading novellas by Chinese women writers before bed. There is a surprise here, a new tragic tone rather than the boring "socialist realism" boosterism. Still, it is sad to think that it has taken so many years to arrive back at the beginning—where one admits that life has not been "solved." And so characters emerge now who resemble people one may not know but can imagine. It reminds me of something a congressman from Cincinnati said to me at my hearing before the Un-American Activities Committee, of which he was a member. "Why," he asked, looking down at me from his raised seat at the table, "do you write so sadly?" On the whole, the private lives of politicians are so wretched, but as wielders of power they all demand tones of progress and joy. Thinking of optimism I think of opium—one can't help trying to imagine what this city can have been like before the Revolution ended the opium traffic—and that brings me to the Timothy Leary types and their optimism. Or was that only an American reaction to drugs? Every new thing we do makes us happier, it seems.

Probably as a result of word-of-mouth from our tiny run-through audiences—six to fifteen people at most—a scramble for tickets has begun. Much attention is always given to rumors about new shows because tickets for the better ones are quickly sopped up by organizations, but also because people do not rely on what papers say about plays—except to rush to those that are condemned as in one way or another antisocial.

## *April 14*

A poor run-though last night; Willy strained, his performance haphazard, his soul not there. Is he overdirected? Did I give him too much to remember? Is it time to leave them alone?

Charley reminds me of Henry Fonda, with much the same sort of imperturbable goodwill and the same tendency to lapse into sentimentality. I can see that, like Fonda, he always plays good guys, but he is really a better actor than that. In the play the character conveys common sense, and it seems to me now the danger is that he will play it with a bit of a subliminal wink to the audience. I have to toughen him up, emphasize his ignorance, crudeness, even stupidity—which is not easy for so intelligent an actor to play. Funny, though, how they all try in one way or another to ingratiate themselves with the audience. But he is still very, very good. . . .

Happy has been having trouble exploding with "Wait a minute! I got an idea. I got a feasible idea," when he moves in to halt the fight between

Charley.

Biff and Willy toward the end of Act One. It is very un-Chinese to have to begin from a standing start and in one line reach a roaring crescendo that will outyell his father and brother. And on top of that sustain the energy behind his crazy plan to go down to Florida with Biff, organize two basketball and water-polo teams, and play against each other and publicize a line of sporting goods. After a couple of attempts on a purely technical level, I sat him down and with Biff, Ying, and Linda, discussed what he is really saying—I had the feeling we had a cultural disconnection here.

"First of all, do you believe this is possible?—to start this kind of a business?" I asked him. He half nodded, shrugged, laughed uncomfortably.

"The idea *is* absurd," I explained, "but that is what is so persuasive about it. Most such ideas actually fail in America, but that doesn't stop people. I guess it's because they do succeed often enough to make it seem that absurd ideas can be brought off successfully." The whole cast seemed taken with the poetry of this notion. "It still is that way, you know—small businesses go bankrupt at a great rate but they also start up at a great rate. The idea of creating something out of your own head and making it happen still goes on in America. For a lot of people there is still that kind of promise in the air, even if statistics disprove the likelihood you will really make it." I thought that they did not want to hear about the failing, only the succeeding. And in fact this tack turned out to be useful for Happy, who got up and did the scene the best he'd ever done, with the Loman passion for the unlikely full on his lips, selling himself on the idea at the same time he was spitballing it for the family.

I asked Ying whether there had ever been a Chinese parallel for this kind of near-delusionary youthful ambitiousness or whether society had always presented a more or less fixed bureaucratic ladder of promotion.

"Oh, very definitely—that's what the Cultural Revolution was all about, kids coming into a place and demanding to take it over instantly—and succeeding!"

Again the nodding and laughing at this, to me, incredibly materialistic interpretation of something I had always thought of as political idealism gone amok.

"But what was their motivation? In Happy's case it's money and power and women. . . ."

Ying laughed. "Exactly! They wanted to go up in the world and fast! And they decided to do it with muscle. Why, one day right in this room a twenty-four-year-old guy walks in with his little gang—" A bubbling-up of recognition all around me at this well-known catastrophe, which, however, they appear to look back at now as if it were an escapade at a summer camp. The absurdity that this power grab actually succeeded for a full decade must numb their minds. "—And he says to me, 'We're going to revolutionize this place!'"

"And what happened then?"

"Well, the first thing was that all our productions were brought to a halt. The theatre simply died. And that's when we started playing gin rummy year after year while the Beijing Opera was dancing around out front in the theatre," he said, indicating the back entrance of the theatre down the hall, "and some of us ended out in the country raising rice, and him"—he indicated laughing Happy—"catching frogs for our banquets!"

I caught what I took to be a somewhat embarrassed look in their faces now. I knew, for example, that Cao Yu, then in his sixties and head of this theatre, was pulled out of his office by the "revolutionaries" and made to work for four years as the gatekeeper, admitting cars into the alley next to the building. I could not help recalling, incidentally, Cao Yu's saying to us in our house in Roxbury, Connecticut, after just seeing *After the Fall* at the Arena Stage in Washington, how moved he had been by its "truthfulness." "I wanted to kick myself for having wasted so much of my life attending meetings when I could have written the truth," he had told me. In fact, he had written two or three landmark plays in the 1930s in Shanghai. I have read them and found them works of depth, with fully developed characters and grand, sweeping stories of the underbelly of a decaying Shanghai before the Revolution. The women in them are especially well written, with no tendentious loading of virtues for or against one or another social type. Cao Yu had spent a year in the United States in the early 1930s and had fallen in love with O'Neill's work, on which he molded his own. He now spends most of his time in Shanghai with his forty-five-year-old actress wife, writing his memoirs or, as is said, "editing the past." At the time, I was curious about his remark and asked what in *After the Fall* he found so truthful, assuming it would be the relationship of Quentin and Maggie. But it was a certain particular speech that Quentin makes on learning that his old friend Lou, a former Communist being hounded by the Un-American Activities Committee, has committed suicide; he has taken on Lou's legal defense, even though it frightens him and might well cost him his position in the firm and in society. He is shocked on hearing of Lou's death, but also relieved that a burden has died and that once again he has managed to be among the survivors. Ying Ruocheng, who had attended the Washington performance with Cao Yu, says that the old man kept repeating that this was precisely what had happened to people during the terror of the Cultural Revolution: the same pressure to turn one's back on the publicly condemned, the same secret relief that one had escaped, and the consequent guilt.

Not all by any means escaped, however. Now I learn that in the courtyard next to the Capital Theatre, on the very spot where the car drops us and picks us up each day, Red Guards rounded up some forty people who worked in the various departments, as well as actors and writers—most notably, the novelist, short-story writer, and China's best and most prolific playwright Lao She, whose *Rickshaw Boy* had been a great success in America. As Ying would put it, "Every actor in this theatre—in China actually—was bred on Lao She's plays." Lao She's *Teahouse* is to this company what Chekhov's *Seagull* was to the Moscow Art Theatre under Stanislavski—their nurturing ground. Then in his sixties, he had had some running disagreements with these ardent Maoists, who finally, on this night, marked him out of the group in the courtyard, berated him, sneered at his contemptible bourgeois ways, his plays, his pretensions, his character, enraging themselves to the point of starting to physically abuse him. A Beijing policeman intervened before they could beat him up and, assuring the young militants that he was as outraged as they by Lao She, managed to talk the writer out of their clutches and into custody. He kept him until later that night, when he felt it was safe to let him go back to his home. Instead, Lao She went to a certain pond near Beihai Park, where people saw him walking along its shores in the darkness seeming very despondent. But apparently no one intervened, at least not decisively enough, and next morning his body was found floating in the water. Thus was this theatre "revolutionized." In addition to betraying a genius, this movement produced nothing in the next ten years that anyone will ever want to put on the stage again.

It is quite strange, but after better than two weeks of listening to the play in Chinese I realize from time to time that I am seeing them as Americans. I no longer even notice the slant of their eyes and it actually takes some effort to remind myself that some of their gestures and mannerisms are not at all American.

I don't think it is merely that I have grown used to them. They have changed, too, and being required to behave far more informally with each other, they have, I think, taken on something akin to American body movements. "Almost everything the sons do in the play, everything they say, is conceivable in Chinese sons, except to call their father 'sport' and their mother 'pal,'" Ying once said. But if I detect a kind of willowy slouch in them to accompany this kind of informality, they have probably done it without thinking, and so by now it seems perfectly native to them.

What still startles me, though, is the entrance into the rehearsal hall of two or three of the young actresses in classical costumes—they come to us in the intermissions of an historical play going on inside the theatre. Coiffed with ten-inch-high wheels of hair standing up from one side of their heads, suave in their gold-embroidered long gowns, and their cheeks blazing with bright red makeup, they tiptoe in to quietly sit and watch the Lomans fighting it out in Brooklyn. I learn that my own cast is following a highly unusual practice by sitting behind me and watching when they are not needed on stage, forsaking their time off.

I find it ironic now that Brecht should have been so inspired by what he took to be the Chinese desentimentalized style of acting when he first saw it in Moscow in the 1930s. Of course what he saw was Chinese opera, which indeed is sanitized of all naturalism and involves a system of mutually recognized signals, not to be found in life, by which the story is "distanced." Emotion is also far more discreet in the opera than in the Chinese "talking theatre," where sentimentality is both its sin and its attraction for the public. I am quite sure, in fact, that part of the reason for their insisting that I direct my play here was the hope that I might break through the conventional tearfulness and make emotion happen out of real, not idealized, behavior, tricks of overemphasis, and rafter shaking.

Nevertheless, yet once more I think the old devil is slipping back in Linda's by now lovely performance, and Biff's, too. But I will warn them as many times as it crops up that this is one Chinese tradition we will do without—indeed, they laughingly agree when I point it out to them and instantly leave off making "noble" and/or "pitiful" effects while at the same time taking those touching little glances out to the audience. But I nevertheless wonder what the show will look like when I am long gone.

This said, I still find that I must keep correcting my prejudices toward melodramatic acting; Chinese people do have a habit of nodding

Willy and the Woman from Boston.

overemphatically when agreeing with something, especially with something funny. There is a danger I will tame their native reality to make it conform to mine.

The Woman in Boston, for example, enters Willy's memory of the fateful night when Biff discovered him with her, in a baroque fashion that would be on the very verge of the intolerable by conventional New York standards. On her line "Whyn't you have another drink, honey, and stop being so damn self-centered?" she slowly circles him as in a dream, offering a drink with a long white silk shawl flowing over her back and outstretched arms. It is so un-American that I begin to reject it, but so beautifully naive and so chaste compared with the customary crude sexuality with which the moment is usually played that I am about to decide to keep it in. Perhaps her obliqueness will be even more erotic than our normally more blatant rendering.

This actress has all but completely invented her blocking in this scene and it keeps changing, but I don't want to set it too soon. The poetic fantasy of her moves has sent me back to rereading her dialogue and Willy's in their two scenes together, and after a quick glance, it is obvious that I indeed had originally intended an hallucinatory surrealism which had somehow gotten lost in the various productions, including the original. We had always tried to force some realistic sense upon dialogue like:

> THE WOMAN: Whyn't you have another drink, honey, and stop being so damn self-centered?
>
> WILLY: I'm so lonely.
>
> THE WOMAN: You know you ruined me, Willy?

They were clearly intended to be not so much talking to each other as stating their dreamlike, disjointed, and intensively compressed positions—a frightening phenomenon but a common one in fear-ridden visions. It is the process itself that should be fearful, and so I have begun to change my earlier approach, which required them to behave as though their speeches were logical responses, in favor of one emphasizing their uncommunicating disjointedness, while at the same time they must appear physically connected by sexual desire. I think this shift has clarified and relieved both their minds; for the first time now, they repeat the same staging quite exactly. Until now it never seemed to settle into a pattern, and I suspect it was because I was unthinkingly pressing them toward a more naked and realistic show of sexuality than the world within them would allow.

## *April 15*

Another particularly dispirited run-through tonight. I think they all realized this. I have a sense of not having made a connection with them on any but a formal level—as the Foreign Expert who should never be contradicted in any serious way. I don't understand how they could so completely have lost their concentration. It was all a mere rote rendering, with the loud and soft pedals pressed as commanded but little or nothing inside. Ying's Willy seems unconvincing to me, the worst kind of "little man" typology; it reminds me of Paul Muni in the 1950 London production, which even Kazan could not bring to life. Muni, too, played the "type," going so far as to record the entire role on a gigantic reel of tape under his wife's tutelage and then imitate himself in a rendition of the "American Salesman," with the wooden smile and the "glad hand." Ying is by no means doing that, but all his emotion is going into his throat and his vehemence has returned. Which means he is not "seeing" and not "hearing" any longer. I have done something terribly wrong.

At the conclusion I have a hard time keeping my eyes open, but decide to not dismiss them without saying something to confirm what they must have sensed in the performance but at the same time to avoid leaving them in despair. I tell them that they have lost some of their concentration and that we must begin once again listening to one another, and I lay the blame on the enormous amount of technical and sociological information they have had to absorb. But I am not sure I believe this.

Looking at the calendar, I am slightly shocked at how few days I have been working with them—only about twenty-five. And here I have been running the play from top to bottom every night! Why have I pressed them on so quickly? I suppose I feared they would come to the opening unprepared, especially Willy. In past years I have had some involvement as an adviser to two fine American actors in the role who simply ran out of steam somewhere in the first quarter of Act Two, and I didn't want this to happen with Ying. It is a monster role, as exhausting as Hamlet, with so much of it demanding to be done at a high pitch. The play is without transitional scenes, when an actor can coast along for a while. Each scene begins at its latest possible moment, which means that Willy almost always enters in high gear.

Still, this does not account for so much of Ying's energy straining his throat. But rather than attempting to analyze him into a more relaxed approach, I take specific speeches where he is pressing and ease him back. He responds at once, and we rehearse these particular sections with one purpose now, to back him away from any suggestion of vehemence. Thus, "The boys in?" in the first scene, which he had colored with resentful disappointment, becomes a simple question without vocal emphasis. As a result a real and searching exchange begins to form between him and Linda, rather than two separate performances, and he senses his own truthfulness in this change and pursues it more and more through the scene. The pressure is now measurably less on his throat there. I must not forget, however, that Lee Cobb also lost his voice in the part and to everybody's horror asked for a vacation after "only" three months in the part. He was right but no one in those days would dream of letting a star of such a hit take a couple of weeks off, and so he had to be let go. And became a sheriff in Westerns.

## April 16

I think things are coming together again as I drill them more on bits instead of launching into larger sections of scenes and whole acts at a time. They want to be stopped, it seems, precisely when they are wrong rather than be allowed to continue and be given my notes later. I recall something Ying said to me at the outset—they normally are given a schedule of which scenes are to be rehearsed on which days and at which hours—a veritable railroad timetable that allows them to prepare before rehearsals. I never got around to this. Without too much thought I simply launched them into the full sweep of the story and the development of the characters from moment to moment. They are staggering now, but I am not sure my attack was wrong. We shall see. It is not their customary method of working by spending weeks simply drilling lines and learning the play rather than being dumped into it to flounder around as I have made them do. I believe the floundering is creative and will build the muscle to support Willy's monster role. It is also a kind of recapitulation of what the author—and later the director—has gone through to grasp the whole. It must not be made too easy. Nevertheless, I suspect they are getting saddle sores.

The closer they come to transcending technique and the memorization of lines—the closer to really beginning to act, in short—the more Chinese they begin to seem. Happy now approaches Miss Forsythe to pick her up in the restaurant with a wonderful formality, his back straight, head high, his hand-gestures even more precise and formal, but with a comic undertone that ironically comes closer to conveying the original American idea of the scene than when he was trying to be physically sloppy and "relaxed"—that is, imitating an American. I think that by some unplanned magic we may end up creating something not quite American *or* Chinese but a pure style springing from the heart of the play itself—the play as a nonnational event, that is, a human circumstance. But how will an audience see it?

Linda, I'm afraid, may be a problem with lines right down to the deadline, if not into performances. Naturally, she does her long arias, several pages of long speeches, without a mistake, but during those speeches she needn't worry about cues and, besides, she is comfortably facing the audience. But I am beginning to stop her now and drill her weak sections if only to make Ying feel better, for her stumbling distracts him more now that he has come closer to a performance level.

Sometimes during rehearsal I get so tired I can't hear anything anymore and wonder what the hell got into me to attempt this. Although I must say that while I don't understand the language and never will, I can still surprise them time and again by picking up a line if they are misinterpreting it or even altering its proper color. I suppose I am hearing Chinese like music, for which I have a good ear; one does not have to be a composer or musician to know when a familiar passage is being played too fast, too slow, or too dispiritedly. And having placed them on the stage in relation to their lines I can easily tell where they are in the script by where they are on the stage and what business they are performing.

In moments of exhaustion, I think for some reason of writing an autobiography—proper work for tired artists—but every autobiographer must secretly believe he has triumphed in life. Maybe, incidentally, that accounts for the paucity of women's autobiographies—they know better. "My Autobiography—How I Failed" is not likely as a title, at least not in our dear America. A good friend, Louis Untermeyer, poet and biographer, wrote three autobiographies—one at sixty-five, another at seventy-seven, and a third at eighty-eight—each more cheerful than the last, and died in the agony of his nineties uncertain of anything, let alone his life's meaning and still less its success. Among his last words—"I wrote too much."

A most affecting scene: we were biking around "Back Lake," a serene artificial lake of some ten or so acres behind an active market, when we came on a small, new-looking park built on a rise above the water's edge. It was midafternoon, and the real kings of China, boy babies of ten months to a year, were being paraded around the lake by their grandparents, and in a latticed pavilion sat a man who looked to be in his eighties, facing four or five others of his generation and singing to them in a frayed thread of a voice. Inge listened and after a few moments translated—he was extolling the beauties of his home landscape somewhere in Shanxi. The sun warmed the little group and one could feel their pleasure at his sung description of mountains and falling water and the unique color of the sky over his homeland. His hand, gnarled with time and work, formed the shapes of the hills. He was seeing it all in his mind's eye and drawing the landscape for them to see it, too. It was the real culture—a form of trust, and charged with necessity.

With all the brutality of their history one sees on the streets many fine gestures of gentleness and caring. Perhaps it's that their crowdedness has bred into them an etiquette necessary to survival. And doubtless for some, socialism is still ethics.

Suddenly, while looking at television from bed, I realized I was watching commercials that I did not recognize as such because the techniques are still so primitive. But Chinese television does advertise crackers, candy, absorbent cotton, theatres. It is noticeable, also, how sentimental their own modern symphonic music is. Yet the same audience appreciates Mozart. In all things they are living in a spread of different centuries, it seems.

## April 17

We drilled all day to set lines, feeling that this is the main obstacle to our progress at the moment. Very boring but necessary. They seem to love this kind of work, I suppose because it gives them reassurance. The objective of the director, like that of a parent, is to make them less and less dependent.

Our little "audiences," whom Ying Ruocheng has invited to watch, say nothing at the end of a run-through or a scene, simply close their notebooks and, with a word to Ying, leave. Nor does he tell me what they felt or said. Nor do I remember to ask. I guess something inside me has contracted to do all it can and let the world judge as it will.

## April 19

Last evening to dinner with Gladys Yang, an Englishwoman who has spent half her life in China, and her husband, Hsien Liu Yang, both in their seventies. His student years were spent in Britain long ago. He has translated the *Odyssey* into Chinese. "It was easier than into English," he said in response to my congratulatory amazement. She, like him an old campaigner in what often seems the interminable internecine cultural wars of the Chinese, has done a fine job as editor and translator into English of five novellas by Chinese women, a volume I have been immensely enjoying. Her limpid language conveys the quiet precision of Chinese imagery without making it "charming." The new Panda line of paperbacks are her babies, and she has seen to it that they are also well printed and on good paper. The line of books is one more attempt to show a contemporary Chinese face to the world.

Their apartment is on the ground floor of a building that stands behind the Foreign Languages Institute, separated from it by a large earthern courtyard within which stands yet another rectangular wall, topped with broken glass to protect some house inside. Chinese boxes are not about to vanish, apparently.

"Welcome. Come and make yourselves comfortable in this dismal apartment," Hsien said. The room, in fact, had windows that face a brick wall; in the narrow space between them a half-dozen improbable tulips in flower grew out of the cinder-gray earth. "They all said you couldn't raise tulips where there is so little light, but of course tulips don't need much light," said Gladys tiredly.

We'd brought them a bottle of whiskey, which he served up straight, a happy treat for them both, apparently. I can't vouch for the color of the walls anymore, but as I write a day later I think they were a kind of dark mustard color; the furniture was lined up against them as though for a conference, and was interrupted by old black rectangular wooden chests of classic Chinese design.

Hsien has what one always supposed is the Chinese patrician face—long lids that deeply hide the eyes, the mouth very slow to change expression—and delicate hands that move gently as fishes' fins through water. Inevitably, Inge and Gladys became involved in a two-way conversation, and Hsien and I sat apart with the bottle between us.

"In some important respects China today is the equivalent of the 1400s in Europe," he responded to my remark that China seemed in many ways about to enter the 1920s. China was his despair and his love and, of course, the center of the world. He had recently been with a cultural exchange group in the United States, just at the time when Reagan decided to turn the tennis player into a political refugee, thus triggering the angry Chinese withdrawal of their cultural delegations. "I was in Los Angeles for two days," he said in a level voice, "and had to get back on the plane and come home."

His indignation was only as powerful as his restraint, and the delicate color of laughter accompanying his words alone revealed it. "Los Angeles?" he asked, as he prepared to answer my question. "How I liked Los Angeles? Well, let me see . . . it wasn't too bad."

"Don't lie," Gladys interrupted from across the room—I hadn't thought she was listening. "He hated it, despised it, as he does American culture in general."

Then, trying to think of something positive, he said, "Disneyland . . ." and failed to continue. He gave the impression of a scholar stunned by the sheer brutality of American pop culture, the way it grinds up musical sounds, words, colors, dancing bodies, bits of cloth, and pats them all into a hamburger with ketchup.

Gladys was imprisoned for a long time during the Cultural Revolution, foreigners having been focal points of the officially whipped-up paranoia. Now she spoke with a grim laughter as she sipped at her shot glass of whiskey. Her face was pale as paper, her hair white, and her hopes for China and the world blanched out, too, I suspected, excepting for some bits of beauty still to be found in good writing. "My guard one day said, 'You'd better not complain. How'd you like to be kept in an American jail? Be thankful.' And I said, 'I'd *much* prefer an American jail.' And he said, 'You prefer a fascist jail to a socialist jail?' And I said, 'I prefer to have some human rights. Here I have none!'" The level, angry laugh came then; she is a tall, thin woman with her black silk Chinese jacket fastened to the chin. Where is hope?

I complimented her on her preface to the Panda paperback of novellas by women. "It's one of the few such prefaces that do not try to pretend that the contents are master-works."

"Oh, how tiresome, all that *advertising* . . ."

"I really got a clear notion of what stage the writing had arrived at . . ."

"Yes. It is good, it is all right. It will be better. They are coming out and looking around for reality now. It is going to be good." In her determination not to overpraise, one saw the long, overpraising past.

"It was a pleasure to read something one could believe."

"That was the idea, exactly."

Hsien had good things to say for an interview of mine in *Chinese Encounters* with an old American friend of theirs whose blithe defense— in 1978—of China's all but nonexistent legal system I hadn't stomached. The man had not even conceded a need for lawyers, so beneficent did he find China's classless system.

"But I read that they are training thousands of lawyers now," I said.

"They have to. We are in hundreds of joint enterprises with foreign companies. Somebody has to know how to draw up contracts."

"Property breeds lawyers," I said, forbearing to add a belief that unfortunately property now seemed the only thing palpable enough to demand the respect of governments, and perhaps was the generating clout against encroachments on the spiritual protections for speech, assembly, and so on. It might turn out that without the right to possess we are not sure we really have the right to speak and to be.

A fine dinner of meat and fish and blackened eggs at their round dining-room table. They seemed so determined to sustain a level of brutal candor that the air filled with their taunting of old censorious ghosts, and one couldn't help sensing remorse for truths they had suppressed lest they disserve the great cause. They must surely have disagreed with some things in my book, but returned more than once to compliment its straightforwardness.

Hsien speared a flake of fish. "What I am doing now? Well, let me see." His expression remained imperturbably ironic. "I attend meetings called to decide who should be advanced to which post and be given what reward. I am doing bureaucracy, is what I am doing."

"I hope," Gladys said quite suddenly, "that they will let the public see your play."

"But why wouldn't they?"

A cryptic shrug.

"Please tell me. Ying Ruocheng is pressuring them to sell half the tickets at the box-office window."

"Well, that's good." But she is full of skepticism.

"I don't understand."

"They won't publicize it," she said with what sounded like assurance. "You have to do lots of publicity here to rouse them."

"But why won't they, after they went to all the trouble to get me here?"

She shrugged, silent. I could only wonder if she was referring to a sector of the Party that is still powerful enough to shut off the production's accessibility to the public. Was she expressing her general experience with isolationists, who would die fighting off the New China? Had she had terrible fights trying to publish living stories that confronted reality instead of the Chinese advertising that has so often passed as literature?

We agreed to see them again—she would invite several writers next time, and I was all for that, especially a couple of the women authors whose works are in her anthology.

Hsien walked us across the courtyard. It was dusk now. He gripped my arm as we passed into the long, low-arched corridor of the Institute toward the doorway to the street. With sunlight gone it was very dark in here. He whispered—in effect: They will try to prevent a success. . . . The shock of it has kept me from remembering his actual words. He was deeply concerned, almost totally in doubt that I would be allowed to show *Death of a Salesman* to the Chinese people. When we emerged outside on the wide street, there was exuberance again, loud goodbyes and warm handshakes. The street was filled with people shopping in the night at pushcarts; it seemed as if two thousand of them were swarming around, densely blocking our car, talking, talking, under the yellowish, poverty-dimmed streetlight.

"I can't say 'walrus.' It won't mean anything in Chinese, so I've translated it as 'a barrel of oil,' which gives the image," Ying Ruocheng explains. We are working on his soliloquy again, standing on the extreme forestage while Linda sits mending stockings behind him in the kitchen. The energy of the production is still too general, too *demonstrative*. I want him to work even more on creating a privacy of mind now. I ask him to feel a much deeper anguish about his appearance: who does not look in the mirror and hate his face, his body, from time to time? It is our prison, I tell him.

"You are looking into a mirror. You are alone. You are only imagining Linda, she isn't really here."

"Yes. Okay, that's good." He now stands still, looking out at the audience. "I'm fat. I'm very—foolish to look at, Linda. I didn't tell you, but Christmas time I happened to be calling on F. H. Stewarts, and a salesman I know . . . I heard him say something about—walrus. And I—I cracked him right across the face. I won't take that. I simply will not take that. . . ." He is better, more private, but still has to work against trying to put it over; he must let the audience come to him in his privacy, but something is swelling in him now, becoming more mysterious, I think.

I return to the soliloquy to try to deepen it even more. Somehow we get onto the subject of bound feet. I had heard that the Manchu conquerors had introduced this horrifying practice, and Ying Ruocheng instantly denies it. "We were the ones who opposed it, not introduced it!" His theory is that the Emperor adored a concubine who had extremely small feet, and that this started a fad which spread through the court and out into the country. The arch was broken and the foot held clamped by bandages, which could become gangrenous, but the smell itself was aphrodisiac. Materialists have ascribed the practice to the male exploitation of women, who were kept at home as helpless prisoners, but it also would have made them nearly useless as workers. I opt for Ying's explanation, especially after noting how nearly slavishly the Chinese so recently followed Mao in all things.

Biff has such an emotional fluency in his scene in Willy's Boston hotel room — when he describes how he caused his teacher, Birnbaum, to hate him by getting caught imitating his lisp and cross-eyed look — that I have to wonder again about the nature of our cultural differences. He *leans* on his performance here with the kind of complete confidence that an actor can have only when the image of the character is coterminal with his own. Maybe Chinese high-school kids do these same imitations (although Biff says they don't dare), or perhaps they dream of doing them. And his transforming himself from a bitter man in his thirties to this nineteen-year-old athlete a few moments later is magical. He practically dances and skips upstage when obeying Willy's command to go down and tell the hotel clerk to check him out — his ability to switch on that specific kind of nineteen-year-old energy! And it is always exactly the same performance, no matter how many times he rehearses. They rarely lose anything they have incorporated into a performance, something I attribute to a basically rational approach to acting: they are creating their roles to appease not some hidden God of the Authentic but the audience. However, this can also lead to shallowness.

I believe Ying Ruocheng has found far more in Willy than even he bargained for as translator of the play. I have the feeling that he started out doing a job of work and it has now taken over his life. And of course it amuses and intrigues him that "the message is hard to define in this play." It is a real adventure to be playing someone who is not good and for whom one still expects sympathy.

## April 20

In the evening we return to visit Hsien Liu and Gladys Yang, and their two guests, the cartoonist Hua Jünwu and Zhang Jie, whose extremely popular novella Gladys has anthologized and which has been made into a hit movie. Zhang is a rather tense woman in her late thirties, a divorcée with a young daughter at home. Her novel is in the first person and tells of the narrator's mother, who lived out the anguish of a love affair with a married man, the mere shards of whose life were all she was given to share. She has become dissatisfied with the book and wishes it were different now. She seems both proud of its success and unable or unwilling to be pushed forward by it into the limelight. We met a year or so ago in Los Angeles, where she was part of a group of visiting Chinese writers. She hated American food. I ask now, "Did you see in the States any clue to a possible future for this country?"

She reacts sharply. "Not at all, there is nothing in the States that applies to China. We are different. We are going to make our own path . . ." I think she mistook my question for some self-congratulatory smugness, as though we Americans held the future.

We talk at random, with Zhang Jie gradually losing interest in the awkwardness of translated conversation and ending up chatting comfortably with the cartoonist in Chinese. He is a very handsome man in his late forties who is noted for his hard-hitting drawings on social issues. He enjoyed my book *Chinese Encounters,* but wryly admits he was somewhat nervous about what I would write about him after tonight. He isn't kidding; his remarks are unrelentingly cautious and short.

He has been in New York on a visit but hates traveling and is not going to make much comment about New York, either. But I catch his absence of enthusiasm for the city. It is all reminiscent of France. French intellectuals used to line up, doubtless still do, for and against any and all American things, and I sense this happening in China. No country can enjoy living in another's shadow—and for a time, that is how it is bound to appear to them.

Knowing she has been divorced—she is the first Chinese I have met who has been—I draw the conversation with Zhang Jie to that painful subject. Divorce in China is extremely difficult to get. "Courts are trying to prevent middle-class people from breaking up, since they are so vital to the economy"—the first reference to such a class I have heard here. She speaks very factually, and if she seems defensive I suppose it is out of pride. I make it clear that the American divorce rate hovers around fifty percent of the marriages, and this seems to ease matters for the moment. She writes much the way she sits—intensely erect, staring into the murk for a clue to the truth. I like her, but she is difficult.

The cartoonist tends to sit back and smile, out of it. But suddenly he offers a fact. "It is very difficult to get a divorce but artists break up frequently. In fact, this is getting worse and worse among us. Sometimes it seems nobody is staying together."

"Sounds like New York."

Gladys, in this second of our visits in two days, wants to correct an idea of mine that there is far more candor in the press nowadays than four or five years ago. "There is, but it has its limits, too, you know. That infanticide scandal would never have come out, though, one has to admit that. But there is still a taboo on reporting the carryings-on of the highest officials and their children."

Hsien has been quietly sipping his drink and refilling mine—straight whiskey. Inge and Gladys pair off, as Zhang and the cartoonist do, and now Hsien and I.

He seems to want to round out my Chinese education, for which I am eager. Knowing about China is like eating peanuts: the more you get the more you want. "China," he explains, "is really far less like Europe than like Byzantium. The load of bureaucracy and the frame of mind have less in common with the West, even though we provided the West with so much at a certain vital moment of her history. It is Byzantium. Byzantium is the closer analogy in our social systems and our attitudes toward life. But we have already lasted far longer than the Byzantine Empire."

"And the American model? What relevance does it have for you?"

"Not much, you are far too lax." He speaks with deliberate professorial irony, enjoying the chance to veto China's ever becoming Western. His eyes are barely slits now. "We have been cut off, and that is destructive, but we cannot follow the chaotic American route. China needs stricter forms, it is our nature." No isolationist, for many years he edited *Foreign Literature,* which poked open the door to the world, within the allowable limits.

Listening to him, watching him, I don't know why I have the sense of a spirit despoiled by too much political interference, by having to do too much tacking to the changing winds, too much that he does not love to do. It is the same with many other intellectuals here, and there is no blame to it, not at all. They are a humiliated little tribe in this sea of men, but at least they are not defending their humiliations anymore, not even justifying them as something that was necessary to a larger historical enterprise. They are unlike the Russians in this—far, far more outspoken and genuine in their desire to understand what Maoism meant to their country.

The three dualogues swiftly merge in one line crossing the dark carpet when *Death of a Salesman*'s probable fate comes up.

"You should try to get us as many tickets as possible," Gladys warns from across the room, "so that the audience won't be totally restricted."

Again this cryptic warning. The room has gone silent, and this underlines the seriousness of the threat that the Party, I presume, will limit ticket distribution to the absolutely faithful. And I recall Ying's persistent hints that I ought not beg off being interviewed, so as to get as much publicity as possible and that way guarantee access to the people for the show.

"The play will have a big impact," Gladys continues, "if people can get to see it. Especially the young."

All of which leads us to the critics in China.

"There are none," Zhang says, with no indication of sarcasm.

"No critics?"

"None. It is not at all like America."

"What happens when a book is published, then?"

"Someone may write about it."

"Not a critic?"

"No, anyone with a name . . . a name based on anything."

"And is it completely a political review?"

"Almost always—they search out the 'message.' There is no interest in the form or style, at least not in any critical sense."

"And does this have an effect on sales?"

"Oh yes. If they condemn it, it usually sells out the same day."

"People disbelieve the press?"

"On art, totally."

"Then I should pray for negative reviews."

Hsien puts in, "We have never had a tradition of criticism."

"Ying Ruocheng has told me. Even before Liberation?"

"Yes. We had no Sainte-Beuves, not even a Voltaire. There was never a critical profession in China."

I can only ascribe this to my image of Chinese order, a triangle with power flowing down from the narrow top, not up from the broad bottom. In short, if a work is published at all, its authority is not to be severely questioned. Unless there is a crisis, of course, and a play or poem can be used as a focus for a whole mass movement.

I am high by now, and before I can think about it I am directing a question at Zhang. "I am wondering whether, since the Cultural Revolution has been understood as a disaster for China, there is any tendency to reconsider the belief that man under Marxism controls his history for the first time. What I am getting at is whether the tragic view of life, which I detect in your novel, is likely to displace the official optimism as a permissible way of thinking about the human condition."

Gladys, strictly neutral, poker-faced, translates; the cartoonist, leaning far back in his chair, stares at me as though I had dropped in through the ceiling; and Zhang keeps glancing toward me and away.

There is simply no attempt at an answer. Perhaps I haven't been understood. Perhaps the time hasn't arrived to begin facing the consequences of the past decades. The other day, we visited a very old European lady who, like Gladys, had spent a lifetime in China and had been harshly persecuted. That woman had answered a similar question quite candidly. I had speculated whether Mao had known by the end that he was leaving China in a calamitous state. "He always knew he had failed," she said quite simply. She had loved Mao enough to have broken up her own marriage to a Chinese scientist who could not bear the leader's philosophy. "He wasn't merely a leader, he was a poet, a real one; he played China like a line of dialogue, a poetic stanza; he improvised and sometimes it sounded marvelous and other times the music dropped right out of it. Of course he knew. He was a genius and he knew that China was still China, and he was dying and, irony of ironies, leaving it all in the hands of that stupid, dreadful woman of his."

## *April 21*

I am becoming more conscious of our observers, who sit in a silent row behind me as we rehearse or run through. Their ages run from the late twenties, men and women, to the sixties. But since they are all dressed in almost exactly the same uniform it is impossible to guess their rank or importance, if any. I know that some journalists who have power have been in to watch rehearsals. I have never been so aware of the leveling effect of the uniform; but it is not that everyone is equal, rather it is that no one stands out—not at all the same thing. And it reminds me of the Salem colony: one woman was accused of trafficking with the Devil, the evidence of her individualistic *attitude* being a red sash she had taken to wearing around her waist. The desire to exceed, let alone succeed, is enough to warrant suspicion of traitorous thoughts in an egalitarian society. But at the same time I find it lovely that the actors feel perfectly free to advise or criticize one another, and this, I imagine, is part of the same social psychology of equality.

Ying Ruocheng is showing no sign of fear of the production's being blockaded by the Party, but he has not yet got a promise that they won't sell more than half of the tickets to organizations. But I don't believe this is a political ploy. It is simply good old Broadway opportunism. If they can sell out a house in one fell swoop, why bother selling tickets one at a time?

One of the women looking on at the run-through last night asked Ying Ruocheng if the main issue of the play was the inheritance of Willy's insurance money by the elder son—primogeniture. She is an academic and had read somewhere that primogeniture was a great issue in the West. This is why the earth wobbles a bit as it circles the sun.

It is always quite wonderful to hear "Hebbatza Feel!" from Ying's mouth and to think that I have immortalized Ebbets Field in this way. And who was Mr. Ebbets? The stadium itself is long since gone, along with probably ninety percent of the fans who ever saw a Dodger game in it.

I am wondering if I have been spending more time with Hap and Biff than the others, and if it is because they seem somehow more American, although they speak no English. We seem to be laughing together all the time.

This morning's paper tells of a woman who smothered her infant daughter some time ago but had supervisory rank, and so she was not turned in for fear of reprisals. But at least the paper is reporting this now.

We are approaching May and in our rides around town it is gratifying to see the early budding on lilac, sophora, willow, plum, peach, and linden. The earth wants us to feel at home; every one of those trees and shrubs is growing around our house in Connecticut.

I am afraid that Ying is acting too much of the frustration and anger and not his extraordinary love for Biff, and through him his drive for a touch of immortality. Willy really wants to live forever and will sacrifice everything for that. In the penultimate scene, his epiphany—"He loves me"—should be not only a surprising discovery but on top of it the resurrected knowledge of his union with Biff, his seed and hope. It gives him the value he needs in order to sacrifice himself. Such a moment can't be reached with mere deliberation. How can Ying be freed for it? I wonder. He can make it, I am sure of it.

## April 22

I always arrive within a minute or two of our time to start rehearsal and find the whole cast assembled behind a row of tables facing the mock-up of the set. A few minutes of chat with Ying and we begin work. But as our opening approaches I detect an unacknowledged heightening of tension in Ying and realize all over again that, having been the main force behind the decision to select this play and me as its director, he has a great deal riding on our success, far more than I do. For me, whatever the result, it has been a worthwhile experience to have worked for two months in China rather than to see it as a tourist again. And now that Reagan has, in the Chinese view, insulted Deng, we may well find that this wonderful production is closed down before it ever opens.

This is Ying's report this morning: a few of the Chinese journalists who had seen the play at the "press run-through" a few nights ago are apparently withholding writing about it for fear of going out on a limb and finding themselves publicizing an event just as it is condemned by the government. Others, however, are proceeding to write and presumably will publish their stories. One, in *Beijing Daily,* has already appeared and when I walk in I find Ying at the Lomans' kitchen table reading it. He thinks it quite good, particularly in its making no reference to monopoly capitalism; this, of course, would tend to derail any discussion of what he thinks are the innovations the play can offer the Chinese. Already we are hearing people expressing great surprise at the acting in this production, which, to Ying's satisfaction, is seen as a departure from the "pointing" of the traditional style.

There is also a chance to discuss the inevitable—critics and criticism—for a few minutes before setting to work this morning. It seems strange that a country that has produced so much in the arts should not also have a critical tradition, let alone a profession of criticism. Maybe the absence of critics left the way open for art! But Ying misses good criticism, as anyone who deserves the praise of his peers would, and does not wish to be lumped with inferior artists. His idea is that the protracted existence of feudalism, along with the remarkably early unification of this vast country under a single emperor, created the familiar triangular structure of power with its narrow ruling apex. "Strictly speaking, there never really was an exchange of ideas in the European or even Russian sense, simply a situation where life consisted of finding ways to carry out the Emperor's wishes. And even after one of the peasant rebellions, the new Emperor simply reinstituted exactly the same system, called back the same scholars, and proceeded as usual." He has criticized such reviewing as there is in modern China for its sycophancy, the reviewers being friends of the artists involved. I would only add my own notion, that every sponsored action, be it a new apartment complex, a sewing machine, or a play, since it cannot appear without the Party's fiat, cannot be criticized without implicating high Party people—and this is the basic inhibition. But if what he says is the case, the situation goes a long way back into Chinese history. Still, he is not despairing and thinks as far as *Salesman* is concerned the inhibited journalists will only be a small minority. We shall see.

Yesterday, an American wire-service reporter reminded me in a phone interview that at my first press conference on arriving I had stated I was not going to ask the actors to try to imitate Americans, something I have forgotten was even a problem. By now they simply are the Lomans-as-Chinese-looking-people. This places them in some country of the mind, I suppose, certainly not in any earthly geography. I must remember to ask Chinese what they feel about this. I have simply lost all such identification. If I still keep seeing Lee Cobb behind Ying, it is not because he was American but because he will always be the ultimate

Willy to me. I also saw him behind George C. Scott, Paul Muni, and whomever else I have seen in the part.

Nevertheless, there are moments when the women especially—I should say solely—stand out as eminently Chinese and nothing else. This morning is really the first time I take the two young women, Miss Forsythe (pronounced by her "Fausit") and Letta, through their scene in the restaurant with Happy and Biff. Round-faced Miss Fausit, superbly confident now that she is sure she is not playing a prostitute, which I was right in sensing would frighten her, brings Letta back into the place after having left to call her on the phone. Letta, twenty, is a petite thing with delicate hands sporting black open-net gloves—what an idea!—and from the tip of each finger an exciting little knotted tail sticks out. She has the voice of the highest violin tone, faintly reverberating, and the sloe-eyed reserve that speaks of total innocence and an invulnerable depravity at the same moment. When she learns that the distraught Willy, who on her entrance is hearing his voices, is the father of the two young men she and her friend are to go out with tonight, she delightedly exclaims, "Isn't he cute?" and a moment later, "I think it's sweet to bring your daddy along!" Her nonjudgmental joy seems a measure of how far the Lomans have departed from life's primordial sensual order and how doomed they are to their unhappiness. She speaks, and is merely the world. It is beyond me to imagine, in any case, how to begin to internationalize her Chinese-ness. Finally, in an interval when she and Miss Fausit have no lines but must occupy themselves while the Lomans finish their argument a few feet distant, this Letta looks at herself in the mirror of her compact, holding it almost at arm's length away from her face, while with infinite delicacy, within range of her reflection, handling a long-stemmed red tulip in her black-net fingers. And she invented the whole picture—which I must claim the sense to have accepted without alteration.

I can find little more to add to the production in the way of interpretation of the play, and so we try to track story and character through small segments in deeper detail. There is still a certain pale generalness for me in Ying's rendering of his story of Dave Singleman, the legendary salesman who'd "go up to his room, y'understand, put on his green velvet slippers—I'll never forget—and pick up his phone and call the buyers, and without ever leaving his room, at the age of eighty-four, he made his living. . . ."

Miss Forsythe.

Letta, in costume, with red tulip.

Ying has "understood" the speech, of course, but it still seems an entirely intellectual kind of recollection despite our previous attempts to find its emotional life. He himself was not put at risk in the way he spoke it; rather he stood safely apart from it. But Willy knows this history with his stomach, and deep down it brings anxiety and an awakened romanticism.

We sit quietly, trying to penetrate the problem, I wondering if I have forgotten that Ying's references are still thoroughly Chinese despite his sophistication and experience in America and Europe, his "modernism."

"Isn't there anything in your past that resembles this? Willy is not altogether romanticizing the past here, you know. Remember, these men actually referred to themselves as knights of the road. . . ."

This time something strikes him in the feudal idea of knighthood. "I think we did have something analogous in China. A hundred years ago there were certain armed men whose job was to escort goods wagons across China to protect them from bandits. A sort of outrider. And they were away from their homes for months and months at a time and had a certain mythology about themselves, a camaraderie all their own that set them apart. Then the railroads came and they weren't needed anymore, and a lot of them took to drink or ended up performing kung fu, feats of strength and daring, at local fairs for a few coppers. Give me a minute, I'd like to try it again."

Our Howard takes his position once more at the wire recorder, and Ying sits down facing him, hat in hand. "You don't understand this. When I was a boy—eighteen, nineteen—I was already on the road. And there was a question in my mind as to whether selling had a future for me. Because in those days I had a yearning to go to Alaska. See, there were three gold strikes in one month in Alaska, and I felt like going out. Just for the ride, you might say."

HOWARD: Don't say.

WILLY: Oh, yeah, my father lived many years in Alaska. He was an adventurous man. We've got quite a little streak of self-reliance in our family. . . .

Ying becomes different, internalized, recollecting in some alarm, as though what was passing away was also taking him with it into oblivion. When he is finished—it is the first time this has happened—he has been fired and humiliated and sits in silence, slumping in the chair not only as "Willy" but as Ying Ruocheng. One wants to rush to help him, not admire his slumping technique.

"What is it?" I ask.

It takes a moment for him to speak. "My God—what am I going to tell Linda!" It is a new realization. The scene has entered him, borne toward him by his image from Chinese history. I have the feeling that he no longer feels himself above Willy, perhaps because he has truly felt a certain nobility in his suffering in that instant.

I am taking another Saturday off, in part because I cannot keep giving the actors new feelings when my own are worn down with repetition, and partly to leave them alone with their own Chinese reality for a day. I have become more aware that a certain overelaboration has crept into some of the smaller roles that comes very close to plain overacting in any language. The problem is harder here because they have a support in their tradition for what they know quite well is showboating, an attempt to draw the audience into admiring how strenuously they are having to "act." But Biff and Willy are also getting overloud at times—in the restaurant scene and in the showdown in the ultimate kitchen confrontation. So I was glad, in a way, at the end of the Friday night run-through, as I was going to the door to get into the car for the railroad station, to hear from Ying that he felt empty in the final scene, where he should in fact be most full of feeling and even a kind of knowledge. He had seemed the same to me, simply standing there in the kitchen like a wounded bull awaiting the next blow. But his asking for help is a very good sign, and I will have a day to think about how to fill him up.

## April 24

I have never been able to sleep in a vehicle, car, train, or plane, and the sleeper from Beijing to Datong was no exception, although it is a well-run, clean train (with the natural exception of the powerful ammoniac typhoon in the toilet). The train resembles the Soviet type and is quite comfortable, but all socialist structures I have ever encountered have toilets stemming from a single model engineered by the Orthodox Church in Tsarist Russia to ensure that man never be allowed to forget the corruption of the flesh.

In that sleepless night I sought, and think I have found, what has been lacking in this production. Whether I can find a way to instill it is another story, but it is clear to me that under the press of technical problems, especially having to frame my direction in rather broad, easily translatable terms, the central drive of the play, which is not technical but spiritual, has been allowed to recede. As I told them on our first rehearsal day, it is a play about love, the love of father for son and son for father; this is the thread that I have allowed to be submerged or at times severed by anger, resentment on the part of Willy and sometimes Biff. I am anxious to begin as soon as Monday comes.

Little Swallow, our diminutive Chinese guide, is sweet and dear and quite capable, but knowing as she does that Inge is perfectly able to do all my interpreting as rapidly as needed, she lets her mind wander, and sleeps a lot, besides. But she has seen a run-through of the play, and Inge at some point hinted to me that she had certain reservations about the acting, so at the first opportunity I must ask her now what they were.

In the four-place compartment with us was an Inner Mongolian young man with a gold incisor and a fat kilo plastic bag of tea. "I love tea and cigarettes," he announced as soon as we were settled, with which he happily sprinkled some tea in each of our cups. It was indeed delicious. The cigarettes we could have done without, but his evident happiness with our presence, with China, his factory job, the train, his family, the weather, would have pleased God. With Inge and Little Swallow out of the compartment for a moment to wash up for the night, he pointed up at Inge's bunk and asked, *"Ti?"* I nodded that she was indeed my wife, and this pleased him, too, and he snuggled down into his bed, which he also obviously adored, and blinking once or twice across the tea table to me, smiled and instantly fell fast asleep.

The famous grottoes an hour's drive from the coal and textile town of Datong are a kind of celestial theatre carved into the sandstone mountain in the mid-fifth century. Vaulted idol-houses, actually, where immense Buddhas sit, one of them four or so stories in height, surrounded with dancing attendants, saints, women servants, and guardians—all carved into the walls of the place in a single integral piece directly out of the rock within the room itself, rather than brought from outside. The guardians interested me most since they were overacting. These giants, ten feet high, with brazen armor strapped around billows of chest, ham-fisted mitts gripping thick weapons, teeth bared, and eyes popping with ferocious ill-will, had succeeded in scaring away predators until now, when the tourists have arrived to mock them. The guardians are opera and extroverted, while the Buddhas are attempting poetic realism, making the audience come to them in their inwardness, their tender relaxation. I must find a way to breed this inner stillness in the acting of my play and to ward off the example of the guardians.

After our single perfect day and an overnight stay at the hotel, described in the guidebook as "very bad," which in fact was about the best we have stayed at in China, we returned on the afternoon train to Beijing on Sunday. Then, with long daylight hours before us, it was time to ask Little Swallow what in the acting in the play had troubled her. She thought everyone was very good, although now and then too loud, excepting the actor playing Happy. "He seems very nervous, playing such a part," she said in her perky English.

"Nervous? Why do you think so?" In fact, Happy is one of the most experienced of the cast and a very sure performer who could hold up a collapsing set and deliver his lines without anybody realizing an emergency was on.

"He just does. It must be very difficult to act that character," Little Swallow went on, combing out her pigtails and looking around for her eyeglasses, a perpetual quest that always ended in the same place, her red zippered shoulder bag.

"Are we talking about the character now or the actor?" I asked, sensing the old demon of Chinese puritanism clearing his throat in the wings.

She tried to deny it was the character who was making *her* nervous, but finally conceded. "He takes so many women and tells so many lies!" she protested.

"But aren't there such people in life?"

She was flustered and giggled and did not know what to say. "But he lies so *much!*" She could not go on, and I dropped the questioning. To watch her it was quite as though she had never heard of people in real life who could lie like Happy, despite the story of her family. Her father, a general in the army, had been arrested during the Cultural Revolution, falsely accused of "opposing Chairman Mao's thought," and sent to jail for five years, where he died of cancer, his family forbidden to visit him. So it could not have been lying that was so disturbingly novel, but

Happy's attractive personality shining through his immoral character. Such ambiguity has no place in the art Little Swallow has ever experienced. And I am thrown back again to a question. America, too, had her innocence once, in the time before the "modern" era when grammar was taught through the homilies of civic virtue in McGuffey's reader, and the Horatio Alger stories pitted good people against bad and reinforced the monochrome virtues of thrift, forgoing, and hard work. How will they approach its dire prospect of human ambiguity? Or will it seem at all applicable to China?

## April 25

Back in Beijing and eager to come to grips with the powers that I am quite sure are ready to explode and are still under wraps in the production. At seven-thirty in the morning stretching my legs in a walk down the sunny *hutong* around the hotel, I hear wafting from a window the haunting melody of "Red River Valley" sung in Chinese by a quite lyrical and delicate soprano. I have no idea why this gives me an optimistic lift, and I recall that Little Swallow at one point in our train trip had handed me a piece of paper with some lyrics she had written on them and asked if I knew the melodies. So I sang "Surrey with the Fringe on Top" for her, and "You Are My Sunshine," and "On Top of Old Smokey." She loved best "You Are My Sunshine"—which may help explain why Happy made her so nervous.

I had all but forgotten that we had agreed to give Ying's understudy a chance to show me what he could do with Willy. It is important, because Ying will be playing for only a month; then he must leave for Italy to pick up a television prize for his performance in *Marco Polo*. If the play is a hit, this actor will probably be taking over the part, at least for some of the time into the future.

 He starts with the opening scene in the bedroom with Linda. A taller and stouter man than Ying, his eyes, mouth, and nose formed close together, his lips pursed, he seems to have a small, querulous face in a large head, but five minutes into the role and he is nothing less than incredible. Every least move, turn, bend—nearly the very same gestures that over these weeks Ying and I have worked into the role seem to belong to him, quite as though it was he who had been rehearsing all that time.

He does the memory scene with the boys, a very rapid dialogue, without a hitch, with all the inner expansions and contractions—the role's breathing—faultlessly. I had noticed him jotting down notes of everything I told Ying but it never dawned on me that he had such talent, too. His scene with Howard, the young boss who ends up firing Willy after he has come in to ask to be transferred off the road, is perhaps the best-structured performance of the scene I have observed since Lee Cobb's, a nearly visible crumbling, yet so inevitable, so unthought-out.

Watching him leaves me absolutely convinced of what I must do with Ying and Biff—the love at the center of their lives must now move into the performances as the main theme. Is it too late for this? I can only try. I begin by making a short but purposely undiplomatic speech "to everyone" but really directed to the Waiter in the restaurant, Bernard, Howard, and in different ways to Ying and Biff. I had left after Friday evening's run-through a bit shocked by what the Waiter and Howard and to a lesser degree Bernard had injected into their performances— "Acting!"—and I had fired off some shots directly at the Waiter's performance just before rushing to make the train.

"I started to say before I left on Friday," I begin, "that there was overacting in that run-through. Why is it bad? Because it is senseless. The Waiter behaves as though everything Happy says to him is perfectly hilarious, but it really isn't that funny. You are acting the result, and so you don't need an audience. You're the actor *and* the audience—you say something slightly witty and die laughing yourself. What is left for them to do but disbelieve in the reality you claim to be creating? I know you have a tradition of this sort of thing, but leave it for some other play. In this play you are true to reality." And so on. They understand exactly and there are some weak smiles all around. "So you see?—I have caught you in the act-ing." Ying, genius that he is, can transliterate this quasi-pun and it breaks them up. But the main work lies ahead. And we begin, Biff, Ying, and I, to discover the dialectics of the love between them through the last third of Act Two. But before long we are interrupted. The wiggers have arrived.

But this is not quite accurate. Rather, they have sprung out of the cracks in the floor—three sallow, small, middle-aged women with expressions of infinite seriousness, plus the tall, burly man whose own short gray hair I had had them reluctantly copy for Ying's wig. I am in deep conversation with Ying and Biff, musing about love, when from behind me I hear the spirited chirping and highly charged humming of actors pampering themselves. Suddenly, the whole cast, people I have come to know and love over six weeks, are weirdly unidentifiable not only as individuals but as humans. Nylon is sprouting out of every head as they crowd together before the two full-length mirrors, in wig heaven after six weeks in the desert of reality. They have suddenly become like Russians with noses—give a Russian actor a new nose and he will give you any character in the book.

Even worse, they are all glancing at me, hopefully awaiting my approval of these sprouts of spun chemicals flying out of their scalps, quite as though the reality we have been working so hard to achieve were not destroyed in their appearance. There is no way around it. They want to imitate Americans, to play-act people they are not, when what I want is exactly who and what they really are. I am aware, of course, that this crop of wigs is more subdued than the first offerings, a wiggers' plot to slide past me to second base without my catching on—there are, at least, no outright platinum blondes this time. But Uncle Ben, the high-rolling drifter from the diamond mines exemplifying the rugged West, has a mauve piece as coiffed and sharply waved as any Flatbush beauty-parlor trainee would be struck from the rolls for having inflicted on a customer. I explain to the wiggers—who naturally are busy, morosely complimenting the actors on their transformations—that Uncle Ben cuts down whole Alaskan forests, digs up endless diamond mines, rushes about making billions of dollars—he wouldn't have *time* for such a haircut.

One of the lady wiggers whispers to the other, and I ask Ying what that's all about.

"They think maybe they cut it too short, she says."

"Get me Walt Whitman," I ask of Ying. "You ever see pictures of Walt Whitman? But without the beard. You ever see a Civil War general's picture?" Dear Ying—he tries to think, but I see we have two cultures now, for he has no such memories. In any case, they now understand that Ben's hair has to be longer and less kempt.

I turn my back to the next patient and when I look around again there is Uncle Ben ruggedly rewigged, and perfect! The wiggers offer me proud grins, seeing my pleased surprise, and now produce Letta for my inspection. She is the face of China under a chestnut mass of wavy hair piled high in front to match Dorothy Lamour, Loretta Young, and Hedy

Uncle Ben and Letta trying on Western-style wigs.

Lamarr all together, including the long sweep of curls over the shoulders. Gone is China; in comes Hollywood as remorselessly as an oil slick. And the dear girl, who has spent whole days selecting this creation—the same one who had the exquisite taste to slip on the net gloves and hold the single tulip—awaits my inevitable approval.

I flounder about for my diplomacy and give up; it is simply one man against four wiggers, that much is clear, and they are going to fight me down to the wire.

"This girl does not need a wig at all," I am forced to say yet once more. "Please, now, take it off and let us see her own hair."

The actress shows no emotion—after six thousand years you learn how not to—and slips off her beloved wig. I fluff up her own hair, praise her beauty, and pass on to the next problem, which is that they are once again discussing wigs for Happy, Biff, and Bernard, three young men with wonderfully dense black hair of their own. And yet again I find myself having to ask what purpose there could possibly be in wigging these fellows? But of course I understand perfectly well that if you know how to make wigs you are duty bound to wig every head in sight, regardless.

"But maybe they could give Biff a haircut?" Ying insinuates. He is still unsure about this entire question, philosophically on treacherous ground. Originally accepting my theory—that we are playing this play in a region of the imagination and not in any actual country—he seems unsure now whether the audience is going to be able to understand and accept this.

To my eye, of course, wigs and whiteface place the play in a region of the mind, too, and in addition disfigure the human physiognomy. I do not say so, but supposing they were blacks: would they want to paint their faces white? Or should whites—as they used to do in our South—put on blackface? But I see that at the present juncture in their history, this may be one of those conventions whose rationale has dried up and disappeared and must simply be pushed over the cliff. There really is no way to convince them excepting to play it straight and prove that the audience is willing and able to follow right along. "Biff does not need a haircut," I am now saying. "Why should he have a haircut?"

"They think maybe a butch." Ying apologizes for the wiggers, who stand in a covey, waiting and hoping.

"He is very close to a butch right now—" But before I can go on, Biff, who is in dread he will be disfigured for months to come, offers to comb his hair immediately so that it will look much closer cut. I dispatch him at once to wherever he must go to have that done. Within five minutes he is back, his hair combed down, looking perfectly butch. But then or now I do not understand what it is that moves them so to change hair— even Biff's mere haircombing seemed to gratify everyone, and I am left to wonder whether there is some lingering subliminal belief that the stage just has to be a place of magical, poetic nobility that is somehow debased when it attempts to imitate life at all. I believe, in fact, that were they not convinced that *Salesman* is already in itself a transubstantiation of reality rather than a naturalistic report I would run into even more resistance to their appearing on stage as they really are.

The quickest and easiest one to convince turns out to be Linda, who has been crowned with a wig indistinguishable from her very own hair! It is now bordering on the incomprehensible. The wigger's excuse is that for her scenes in the past she must wear, as indeed I had instructed her, a youngish-looking hairpiece with a bow fixed on it. But this slight strand can be instantly attached to her own hair as well as to a wig, and so the wig is quickly discarded and Linda herself is relieved. This woman is turning out to be not only Willy's "foundation and support" but mine.

All of which has left us with one fine wig for Uncle Ben, others for Willy, Howard, and Charley—Howard to make him younger, Charley for a touch of age. I have not done too badly, so I thank the wiggers profusely and make my short speech once more about our not trying to imitate Americans. Of course they are all standing there with the unused hair hanging from their hands, like a band of Indians after a scalping raid, nodding profusely and doubtless in total agreement among themselves that the whole production is now doomed. A Chinese play without wigs—you might as well send on the actors without clothes!

## *April 26*

This afternoon to the offices of *Foreign Theatre* magazine to discuss with editors, authors, and a few academics—perhaps twenty people in all. There is always great and I think genuine warmth at these klatches, and in this case really profound peanut brittle, which my dentist, I knew, would appreciate. Once again, the building is in the Dungeon Style, but one gets used to its depressing shadows. I am asked to lead off with a question or whatever else I wish to say.

I have given the matter of a speech not one instant's thought, but what comes out of my mouth does not at all surprise me. My main point: "By and large almost all the plays of the West that you admire were written in moods of dissidence. Yet of your own writers you demand support rather than questioning of the way life goes. In effect, you condemn your future to importation of foreign works of importance. The artist is a dissident—there is no way around this, apparently. You respect O'Neill but in the 1920s, his best period, he turned a harsh face to the national economic boom, seeing through its optimism to question and condemn its deepest aspirations." And so on.

There is, I believe, uneasiness. To hell with it, why not say what they all know and maybe reinforce the liberals among them? But no one lets on where he stands, no nods, no facial agreement, nothing. "You seem trained to demand one thing and one thing only of a work—its 'message.' But don't we know by now that the 'message' of a work is only of value to it if, like a sail, it spreads out and manages to catch the winds of life? This message mongering is a deformation, a reductionism fatal to art. What do your own lives 'mean'? Can you put that in a sentence? Then how can you make the same demand of a work of art that tries to interpret not only one life but many, indeed a whole nation's life?"

Opposite me sits a gentleman in his late sixties, whose eyes have been playing upon mine, and who just might be looking agreeably pleased—it is impossible to really tell. He is a big, broad man, a Hans Christian Andersen expert and novelist whose name, Professor Ye, all the literate know. "The messages of Hans Christian Andersen," he says with cool assurance and a flicker of a smile, "have long since vanished into accepted bromides. They are totally unremarkable and in many instances always were. But his wit, his ironies, his art are immortal."

Just as I am getting the feeling that he and I are in an uncounted majority around the table, another professor, a specialist in American literature, about Ye's age and size, takes an extraordinarily deep breath and, seemingly without breathing again, speaks for at least eight minutes. His eyes are weary, his patience interminable, but his philosophy has not quite yet ceased to rule this nation of a billion, although its end is possible to theorize as being close. "Chinese conditions are not comparable to other countries'. Our people are interested not in what you call truths but in survival, and literature must help them survive. We are living too close to the edge to afford mistakes, and literature must not push us over into the abyss." In other words, a Wise Party must control print, although he forbears saying it that way.

"There is no point in my talking about suppression as a problem," I rebut. "But I will only say that it must be clear to you, after the past twenty years in China, that you cannot rely wholly on politics for your safety. Life, in short, is a tragic business and will continue to be no matter how official viewpoints try to fool around with the rules. So it would seem to be better policy to ask ultimate questions, if you can, than to be smacked in the back of head by them every few years, as you have been.

"Humanity lives trapped, milling about in a dark room, trying to find where the door is to the outside; but the political rules—as they always do—prohibit opening certain doors, so art is the license to try any door at all. Of course it is important what a work is trying to say, but not all-important. We could fill a big book on what Shakespeare's messages were, but a bigger book on whether those, indeed, were really his messages. Yet he will never die. Let art live, is my message."

And an hour's worth more, during which I come to believe that mine is in fact the majority view, and if I can't prove it I know there is a wide debate going on in China on Marxism versus Humanism, or Marxism as a Humanist philosophy—is man to be molded to fit a system, or is he the center around which the system must be formed?

As we leave I do not think I am any more discouraged than after similar engagements in the United States. These things are not settled where there is no power around the table, but editors and academics do often bring on the furniture and props with which the new reality plays itself out.

The play has been losing a minute or two in length with each run-through. With nobody especially rushing, this means the rhythms are quicker, more alive, less deliberate. Ying is no longer worrying about its being too long.

They have brought in the refrigerator that will actually be used on the set, replacing the cardboard box that they covered with a sheet of white paper. The new prop is a remarkably accurate 1940s job, and I wonder how they found one. It turns out to be papier-mâché, modeled on an old *Collier's* magazine ad. Even the hinges are papier-mâché, look chromed and actually work—so that Willy can take out his glass of milk.

When I inspect it and rave over it, the young man and woman from the Prop Department look on, unable to accept my verbal medals with more than the faintest, most austere little grins.

"A man can't go out the way he came in, Ben, a man has got to add up to something. . . . Why? Does it take more guts to stand here the rest of my life ringing up a zero?" In a short break in our work on this last Willy-Ben scene, Ying recalls that Buddhism has man coming into the world naked and going out naked. Taoism goes further toward a nihilistic negation of effort itself. Willy's credo here is Confucian, which teaches accomplishment in this world and the bequeathing of its rewards to one's children. The inheritance is a central idea in Chinese psychology, which lays great emphasis on continuity itself. And the inheritance is the materialization of continuity. Thus, by a long circle through the East we arrive at Willy's thrust toward immortality, his awareness that he has been writing his name on a cake of ice on a hot July day . . . in Brooklyn.

We work—I think well—on filling him up in his last fight with Biff. Gradually I am supplanting the anger with the anguish of a forsaken lover—Biff is about to leave him forever. But he is still a step or two away from it—anger for an actor is a sword, easily picked up; love is a balloon that has to be cautiously embraced or it pops out of his arms ridiculously.

We are now eleven days to opening.

We are now eleven days to opening.

Once more we are talking about the filthiness of money in both Chinese and Western thought, and I repeat that in Freud it is "like shit." Mrs. Shen, my interpreter at the moment, turns to Inge and asks, "What is shit?" Inge explains, "Like in the toilet." "Ah!" But Shen is not at all embarrassed; it seems a reasonable proposition to her.

Ying tells the story of the scholar for whom all money was unclean, whose wife, in order to cure him of this phobia, set coins all over the house and especially in a circle around their bed. But he commanded her to clear a path so he could go to sleep.

"I was in a film with Anthony Quinn and Burt Lancaster, who both got rich on it. My money, except for five percent, went to the government." Ying laughs, and I believe his lack of interest in money is genuine. I tell him that the last artist I knew whose money had gone to his government—

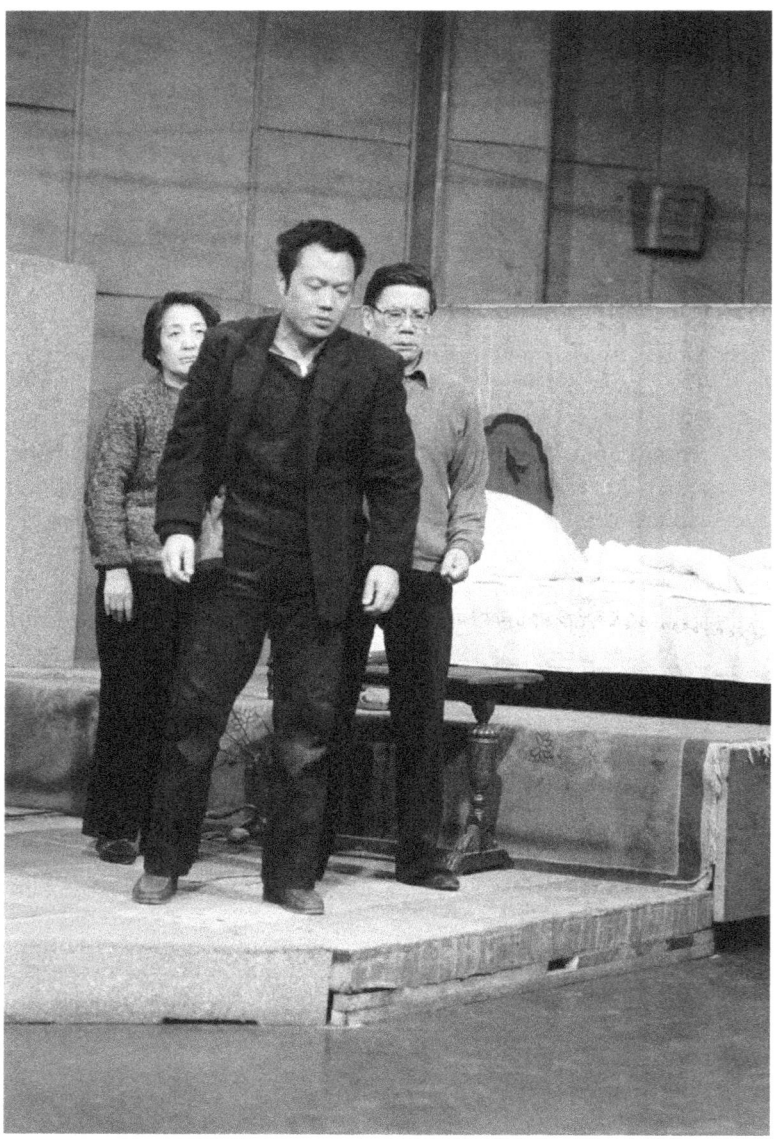

Rehearsal scenes.

Rehearsal scenes (continued).

but in his case entirely—was the Israeli novelist Amos Oz, who lives on a kibbutz. I never sensed much conflict about this in Oz either. But I wonder aloud how long Chinese airplane captains would continue uncomplainingly accepting their 150 yuan a month if they knew that foreign pilots are making eighty to a hundred grand a year. Ying does not think this will be all that big a problem.

Again, I am having to kill off Biff's sentimentality in the scene with Linda in Act One—"All right, pal, all right. It's all settled now.... I'll stay, and I swear to you, I'll apply myself." This must evoke some archetypal Chinese dramatic situation—the sainted mother and the repentant son—for he has to steel himself against batting his eyes and giving us a look of high and noble resolve. But he doesn't succeed, and so I have to break in again. "You shouldn't have any emotion at all here. Except maybe that your trip back to the ranch is being interrupted." He grins, gets the point, and goes back to repeat the scene with far more manly dignity. His bad habits are like a hangnail, very difficult to bite off. But he is very good.

There is no black netting in Beijing for Linda's mourning veil. Anyway, the color of mourning in China is white. For weddings, red. But no one doubts the audience will find it easy to inject white emotions into a black veil. If it can be found.

Ying, as our opening approaches, seems to be playing his scenes with the Woman even more chastely.

## *April 27*

The Woman, Liu Jun, had us to lunch at her "dormitory" this afternoon. I had envisaged some kind of sleeping area in a school, but it is merely an apartment on the ground floor of a large apartment house. She kept referring to it as being "in the country," but it was in a newish suburb, fifteen minutes by car from the center of Beijing, whose streets are muddy and the landscaping still raw. Her husband is an actor, a member of the People's Art Theatre, an immensely happy fellow who is a fanatic fish-raiser. But they turn out to be small ornamental fish in tanks. She had talked of his "raising fish in the country," and I had had visions of ponds full of trout and bass.

The apartment is mud-colored but very clean, and they spent most of our lunch cooking and serving up nine or ten courses. As I have learned by now, in common with every subsidized state theatre I know of, the problem here is that out of some one hundred and fifty actors, not too many are first-class talents or of a useful age any longer. But Liu Jun and her husband are both very excited by China's new vitality and have much hope for, among other things, a larger and better apartment. They feel, I think, that they are alive at the beginnings of some great new age that they want nothing to abort.

But fish are also political—it appears that during the Cultural Revolution he had had to bear the sight of his tanks being smashed up. Keeping fish was one of the Four Bad Habits, along with keeping birds, growing flowers, plus one more that I didn't quite catch—probably cats. ("The Four Bad Habits" sounds as much like a nursery-school slogan in Chinese as it does in English.) But nowadays one sees people, especially middle-aged or older men, taking their birds for walks, and of course there are once again birdcages hanging out of windows. Many groups of card-playing men squat on their tiny chairs on the sidewalks with their beloved bird-cages next to them. Years ago—and possibly now, too—they used to take their fish for walks, but we haven't seen any.

On one of our strolls through a market beside Back Lake, near our quarters, we came on a man selling birds who had one for sale, about the size of a lark, that he claimed spoke and whistled. Beside this cage was another one, covered. I asked what he had in there, and uncovering it for me, he displayed a rather miserable, startled specimen with neck feathers missing and a generally depressed air, of whom he said, "That's this one's teacher."

Liu Jun and her husband, after a couple of decades of marriage, are deeply attached—in love, I think. Their son is away, studying cookery and English, and his lack of any acting talent pleases them, the art being too difficult and especially too unrewarding, although the boy has some regrets, since Chinese girls are fascinated by actors.

This is a sunny day and there is a view of a tree out the window, but the building, like all in China, is dismally lit, and the plumbing and finish of the crudest. But there is a toilet. I am reminded of a worker at our hotel who keeps fish, too, but he has some ten tanks, and asked me not to tell anyone, as other workers resent him for such a display. I gorge myself with some of the best *jaowdze*—spicy dumplings—I have ever tasted, plus fish and shrimp and too much else. Liu Jun looks quite beautiful in her own home, a happy but thoughtful woman. "The production will open the eyes of theatre people about what can be done by breaking through the unities of time and place." Imagine! They have no question that the play will have a wide audience and a long run, speaking as though these observations were too obvious. I have not yet had this from anyone; was the general silence a matter of etiquette? Praise is touchy here.

They are clearly survivors, and again one is thrown back to postwar Europe, excepting that here they were fighting each other. Our Biff and Happy represent, they claim, a generation of actors in the thirties, in short supply due to the Cultural Revolution's destruction of the theatre. The "intellectual," it occurs to me now in this packed apartment, is still a kind of persecuted minority; I sense in Liu Jun and her husband a tentativeness, a residue of humiliations and fear.

"We are constantly being surprised by what a good eye you have," Liu Jun says, and laughs. "We can't get away with anything, even a misread line." I attribute this again to Ying Ruocheng's incredible translation. The play is now running a mere two minutes longer than it does in English, something not possible even in French or German.

In this relaxed and intimate atmosphere of their home, it seems a good time to ask Liu Jun and her husband about the Chinese fascination with wigs. Naturally, I expect some arcane, deeply historic explanation. "It's just that we all love to play. It's fun putting on different wigs, changing yourself, maybe even your fate, for a few hours. It's just dress-up, like children do. The talking theatre usually has no glamour, so any chance you can get to add color is grabbed at."

Here for the first time we hear the phrase "Stinky Number Nines," used to describe intellectuals under Jiang Qing's regime. There were ten gradations of value in the various occupations of the people, with the peasant at the top and at the bottom some vile creatures like the cleaners of outhouses. One notch above them were the Stinky Number Nines. Both our hosts laugh right out of their bellies at it now. They obviously didn't a few years ago, though. Many young neophyte workers get more money than actors or teachers, when bonuses are added in, and this is mentioned as a smiling reminder that the equality of the intellectual has not yet arrived—by a fairly long shot. In fact, they sound like blacks or Jews sometimes, with their impatient patience at the absurdities of their social inferiority.

On breaking up after the evening session, the "assistant director"—actually a super-stage manager in our terms—hurried into the rehearsal hall from the front of the theatre, his face charged with excitement, and with hushed voice announced, "They're lining up at the box office!" There are tentative signs of joy all around, and this moves me to ask Ying once again if the theatre is really going to let the public in, as he had hoped. He reassures me, but I have the feeling he is still not really certain of this himself. The box-office activity results from a single ad in the *Beijing Daily* about half a miserly inch deep.

I have been handed a particularly stupid paragraph from the latest *Newsweek* referring to "the particularly appreciative audience" here for *Salesman*—i.e., an anti-American one—and how it will find it hard to appreciate the "masterpiece," since "there isn't a salesman the length or breadth of China." Another piece of American snobbery that calls itself reporting. Two things whose smell is unmistakable: shit and cultural snobbery.

We have been working more, Ying and I, on his scene with Ben at the end when he openly discusses his suicide with him. "A suicide in China," Ying recalls now, "is enticed by a spirit belonging to a person who committed suicide before, the Soul-Snarer. This spirit cannot be reborn in human form unless he helps another to kill himself, through which he earns a new life on earth." This, however, was merely interesting, and I could not see how it would help Ying to make his self-destruction more real for himself. But having said this, Ying remembered something else, something far more useful. "Actually, you know—when a suicide looks through his noose he sees the most beautiful landscape, a serene place of long vistas and pools of water and lovely trees, and he is going toward that." He has been trying to break out of a kind of slumping attitude at the end, which is totally wrong. Willy is indeed going toward something through his dying, a meaningful sacrifice, the ultimate irony, and he is filled, not emptied of feeling. This vision through the noose seems to have helped Ying to justify this for himself as a valid process over and beyond its being called for by the play—and by me.

I recall a piece of business Lee Cobb invented and ask Ying to try it. He is seated, talking to Bernard-the-lawyer, trying to inflate Biff's career

The director assesses the costumes.

with nearly no conviction; Bernard offers him a cigarette from an open solid-gold case but instead of taking a cigarette he absentmindedly takes the case and continues, "Well, Bill Oliver—very big sporting-goods man—he wants Biff very badly. Called him in from the West. Long distance, carte blanche, special deliveries. . . ." And as he turns the gold case over in his hand, it silently embodies Bernard's success and his son's failure, and he then simply hands it back to Bernard. It seems so easy, but it is terribly hard to "not-see" something one is looking at, and to "not-think" what one is thinking, for the whole action is being done without the least deliberation, yet before our eyes. Ying tried it, then chucked his head with the awareness of how profound an action it really could be, and how difficult. I think it was Lee's masterstroke, a little thing that shone forth his greatness.

Biff's taking a violent fall time after time when Ben "strikes" his forehead alarmed me until he explained how he learned to do this. In the army he belonged to a unit that fired antitank weapons at very close range, which required that he leap, instantly on firing, and roll away out of danger. (Does this also imply they have no modern long-range antitank guns?)

*Before the Dragon comes rain,*
*The Tiger is announced by the wind.*

This, after Ying explains the properties of Dragon and Tiger symbolism. The Dragon, which seems like China's most widespread symbol in her architecture and painting, was probably a totem of a dominant prehistoric tribe, a version of a crocodile, perhaps, or a lizard.

## April 28

The "costume parade" this evening, and as with wig-time, this is a free-for-all with everybody trying to be inspected *first*. Thankfully, Linda's three dresses have now had their hems lifted—they had cut them to that draggy mid-calf length of the 1940s that I hated even then. And they have relented and instead of a full wig have given her a little hair-piece with a ribbon fixed on it for her long-ago scenes, and a quite marvelous sea-green, flat-brimmed, low-crowned boater with a red ribbon around it for the football game. Cute as a button. Also an apron with vertical red stripes for the old days. All of this from magazine photos and pictures we have sent them, of course. The felt of the green boater is stiff as cardboard and half an inch thick, and has been sat on somewhere down the line, but the creases won't show, I guess.

Happy has a pinkish-tan suit with large checks, really impossible west of Guangzhou but expressive here, I think. And he wears it well. Biff is disaster, however: a three-button, neon-blue suit with the edges of the jacket wandering in a wavy line, the shoulders bunched as though he were wearing it with the hanger, lapels as lumpy as crullers. This is not to be borne in *any* country, and I turn to the wan little costume woman, with her sad and much-abused look.

"This man ordinarily does not wear this suit. He puts it on especially to go to his ex-boss to borrow a large sum of money." She apparently does not get my drift. "The button-holes—why are the buttonholes not directly beneath each other in a straight line? Why are they placed an inch or more away from the edge of the jacket?" To this she has to nod that she agrees. "And this material weighs a ton—look, you can hardly bend it, and it feels like spun glass. Is there no lighter material? The play takes place in a warm time of year. . . ." She is woebegone, but looking over to Biff, I see he does not seem at all unhappy, and I recall that his own jacket fits him worse than this one. His own has its cuffs rolled up. But as a People's Liberation Army veteran he is probably used to clothes that fit like this.

Charley is perfect in a brown business suit, tall and rather suave in his gray and faintly wavy wig, my one concession to "Westernism," since it makes him look great. (Nevertheless, he did sneak it over on me.) However, all the men with brown suits have been given black shoes and everyone has identical white shirts with the same long-tab collar. On my demand, a wan assistant of the doleful designer comes rushing in from the costume closet down the hall with a dozen shirts of various patterns and colors, one more unbelievably loud than the other, and all presented to me unfolded, in a lumpy bundle that might have fallen off a truck. This quickly draws every man in the cast to take his pick, but Ying, as senior member of the company and lead in the play, gets in first and snatches a not-bad blue.

The sight of the two women whom Happy picks up in the bar reminds me of where I am. Letta, she of the lone tulip and black-mesh gloves, has been imprisoned in a rose-patterned dress with a large bow across the chest, a high-waisted bodice, and folds of material down almost to her ankles, a veritable British aunt a few months after the World War I Armistice. Miss Forsythe is at least in yellow, and if her hem could be raised and she were given perhaps a fox fur, she might excite Happy enough to make the scene possible. But Letta's look strikes fear in my heart. "My dear"—I address the now sunken costumer, whose glances barely rise off the floor—"this girl Letta is twenty years old, but this dress is for a sixty-year-old lady who is trying to hide the shape she's in." I break off in a collapse of all hope, aware again that they simply have had no contact with *any* clothing except the national uniform of jacket and ballooning trousers for more than thirty years, more than the lifetimes of most of them.

Linda now appears in her mourning gown, which for some reason has not been shortened, and I call over one of the costumer's assistants, a boy of around twenty, and instruct him to raise the hem two or three inches, folding up the excess material myself to demonstrate. Now the boy has an assistant of his own, a girl his age, who bends and takes the hem from me, and promptly lets it drop.

"Don't you pin it?"

"Oh no, we'll remember."

"Look, dears, this is serious. You will not remember unless you mark it." She giggles and the boy giggles, probably at my intensity. But behind their giggles I think I glimpse the real difficulty. "Now don't be lazy. Go right now and get some pins and pin up this hem!" She flees and he manages to blend into the moiling mob of actors until she returns and we can fix on a proper length, which is then pinned. "And you understand, don't you, that it has to be the same length all around, not like some of these dresses, up in front and down in the back." There is ample nodding. I give up. They really have no idea why it should be shorter or longer, this clothing having as much meaning for them as an Eskimo's underwear for me. I spend the next fifteen minutes snugging everybody's dresses and vests tight around their bodies, every one of them having been fitted with one size too large.

The whole exercise is as depressing as it is funny and pathetic. It has made me think once more about my recurrent impression from the gatherings of various intellectual groups to hear or honor me. There is simply no avoiding the implacable tameness and the implicit docility in

Rehearsal scenes.

Rehearsal scenes (continued).

China today. Inevitably a sinister darkness threatens one's vision of the reality at such moments, and one has to wonder whether what is variously labeled "our holocaust," "our terrible time," or simply "the lost years" is not a veritable hole torn out of their historical continuity itself by a very long reign of terror that eliminated a shocking number of people who had the brains, the courage to differ and lead with original thinking. It may seem another mere canard, but I have heard it too often not to believe it: "Even in the early 1950s, the so-called good period when the Revolution was young, I was criticized severely for my insisting that we still were obliged to continue thinking as individuals. Literally, this was incredible to a larger and larger number of perfectly good and well-meaning people. They would say that this or that problem was 'settled,' had been 'thought through and was no longer open to any question.'" This I have gotten in one or another version amounting to the same underlying idea, which comes down to a systematic destruction by the Party of the habit of thinking itself.

Of course it does not mean that thinking people do not exist here, but they are in an endless struggle against the continuous narrowing-down of the acceptable limits of speculation, whose very muscles, so to speak, seem to have atrophied in many otherwise competent people. It is comic to the point of parody to be asked yet again by a journalist or an academic or a theatre director what the "message" of my play is, but it goes so far as to make one wonder whether so many years of such terrible conformist pressure have not incapacitated them to ask any other question of a work, whether they have not been barred from thinking at all or even from receiving—or acknowledging having experienced—a work's impulses in any kind of personal and intimate way. In this context *Salesman* is a hammer to knock apart the formula, and in saying this, I see it now as they do. For Willy is indeed a social product while his autonomy as a person remains intact, and this can drive the dialecticians crazy.

The word is obviously out that it is provincial to merely ask what the message is regarding *Salesman,* however—Ying has seen to that. So one young man who read the play has taken what he thinks is a more oblique tack: "Is the fate of Willy due to his having failed to keep up-to-date with modernization in his way of doing business?"

The foolishness of the question is a significant foolishness; "modernization" is the current catchall, the "key" to China's contemporary historical necessity. It has to be applicable, therefore—if only one knew how!—to every kind of dilemma. And so when I reply that Willy's staying up-to-date could not have affected his fate, the face looking at me goes a little dumb, a little helpless. But at our first press conference, when the Chinese reporters at one point were given the floor by Ying to ask whatever they wished of us, something even more disheartening occurred.

There were some twenty of them from various newspapers and organizations, complete with pens and notebooks. Not one of them opened his mouth, and in fact they looked dumbstruck at being invited to ask questions! The moment was quickly passed over, once the silence threatened to stretch out to infinity, but everyone understood what this meant. They were there to be *told* what the press conference had decided to announce, and that was all. And to this moment, when we have been some five weeks in Beijing and have been wakened at all hours by news people from all over Europe and the United States with questions and requests for interviews, not a single Chinese reporter has asked to interview me.

Nor is it that they are hostile; on the contrary, the production and I myself are mentioned in the press with approval, and the English-language *China Daily* has predicted a "warm welcome" here. But the "modernization" of the press, at least, seems to await the future. I prefer to make the assumption—rather than to pronounce China's rising line of development an impossibility and a failure—that as foreign technology enters and as more and more Chinese return from their studies abroad, the present throttling hold on thought will inevitably relax. But perhaps it won't. All one can do now is report what seems to be true: there is an enormous amount of deadwood in this forest that is keeping fresh growth from seeing the light. If what I have learned of the operation of this theatre is in any way symptomatic of the larger society, and there is ample reason to believe that it is, the good forester is long overdue.

## *April 29*

Last night the makeup and costume parade for the official photos of the cast. Inevitably, some backsliding was attempted yet once again in the matter of playing as Chinese rather than Western-looking characters. Howard, an actor who for years played romantic leads that earned him a large following among the public, is now a balding fiftyish; I had approved a wig to make him look younger than Ying. Later, on seeing the reddish wig they had stuck on him, I ordered it darkened to some tint within the range of Chinese hair, and he reluctantly accepted the change. Now he appears for my review with heavy eyeliner to round his eyes, a nice thick base to lighten his skin, and rouge. To me it looks awful, but here cultures intervene and I beckon Ying out of the milling mob of actors to get his opinion. He takes one look and says, "It's awful." So much for culture. So back goes Howard to his dressing room to become a Chinese again.

Now Linda appears, all but unrecognizable, but thank God with her sense of humor intact. In her housewifely dressing gown and bedroom slippers, she has long Hollywood eyelashes, heavy red lipstick, coiffed hair, and the look of an escapee from the Beijing Opera. With only a little persuasion she hurries back to her dressing room, to emerge in a few minutes with short eyelashes, much less eyeliner, and fainter lipstick, and looking rather like a lady of her age and class in Brooklyn.

Being photographed in the studio that Inge has improvised on the set, under enormous old-fashioned spotlights against a black cloth background, with the actors' unprecedentedly normal human faces being registered for posterity by the camera, has brought all their doubts to the fore. "We use more makeup than this even in realistic Chinese plays," one of them remarks, "and here we are playing Americans with practically nothing on!" If it is in the nature of a small revolution for them, I am even less certain what the audience is going to make of them. Makeup is a mask here, not an emphasis of the expressiveness of the face. The stage is an artificial place where ordinary-looking people have no business. On the other hand, if layers of masking are permitted to turn the actors into symbols, in effect, rather than fully dimensional realistic people, they will be defeating their own attempts to act with, rather than against, reality. The poetry in this play arises not out of such appearances but out of the expansion of the real into many dimensions of dream, memory, and the projections forward of Willy's imagination; but without the real it won't work.

All attempts by the costumer to remake Letta's matronly dress into something enticing having failed, Inge has the brilliant idea of borrowing a dress from Jamie Horsely, our American lawyer friend, for the costumer to copy. It turns out just right—trim, shapely—and it has been bought by Jamie in a Beijing store!

Letta is content because *her* makeup is very heavy but just right for the part. And so is the Woman, Liu Jun, whose satin slip, however, she fears is too short. She curls up on the stool set up for Inge's pictures, with her white filmy scarf and dazzling makeup, and draws all the other women in the play, who stand there coaching her on how to pose sexily—which leg to lift, how to turn her shoulder—and if there is envy among them, it is undetectable. For an instant, while I watch her playfully turning herself into a sensuous magazine model, her mud-colored apartment comes and vanishes before my eyes, the view of the raw unfinished street through her windows . . .

The paper reported today that in the first three months of this year the "output value" of light industrial goods fell by thirty million yuan, of which sixteen million resulted from production of "unsalable goods." My mind, on reading this, went to Linda's dress and Biff's suit, her wild wavy hems and his buttonholes set an inch and a half from the edge of the jacket. Is this caused by the retention of the incompetent, who cannot be removed once their noses get into the "iron pot"? I shall have to have all of it ripped out and begun over again. And they have had six weeks to do these few simple costumes!

## *April 30*

Yesterday Harry Moses and his camera crew worked in and around rehearsal for Bill Moyers' half-hour show for CBS that they are putting together. I think it hurt concentration and exhausted everyone. I thank myself for having turned down the pleas of the people who did Isaac Stern's *Mao to Mozart* to film me through this adventure. I'd have been dead by now. And today the U.S. television networks are also going to film for a couple of hours. I think it important that Americans see even a few minutes of the play, if only to feel some connection with the exchanging of cultural events. Certainly the Chinese, even at this early date, are reportedly surprised by how much they share with us in the human sense as a result of Willy's emergence among them in their own language.

This morning will be our first on the set. I am praying they have lit it passably. I shall have one day only to refine the lighting, a job needing at least two or even three if it is to be done right. And I have to say a few prayers that the lone twenty-eight-year-old tape recorder that plays the music holds up. Yesterday at a conference exclusively for the Chinese press, on being asked how I liked working in this theatre, I decided to level with them and said the building was in dire need of repair and painting, the plumbing kept backing up all over the floors, the equipment was outdated by decades, and the actors were underpaid. (I did not include that, as I am sure is true, a good number on the roster are not really usable in roles of any importance.) "Perhaps," I said, "when China is rich she will begin to modernize the theatre along with the rest of the society." There were some grins, but for the most it seemed to be news that anything at all was lacking. Nobody, it seems, gets to say what he really knows and thinks, or not very often. In comparison our American outspokenness is a painful but salutary relief. Of course we are still unable to confront the depredations of brutal commercialism upon the Broadway theatre, a subject that *The New York Times,* for example, cannot find time to really investigate, scandalous though it is. The Chinese may have grown used to wading through crap to get to a urinal, but we have been benumbed by some equally disgusting stuff that is not as obvious but may do us more harm.

## *May 1*

May Day today. A near-total chaos all yesterday, between trying to light the play and at the same time satisfy the television and press people, and failing somewhat in both.

Hell is rapidly coming loose. The theatre has taken the position that the television networks must pay a fee to photograph inside. In New York this is also the case unless they keep within a minute and a half's limitation. Of course they want much more than that here. In any case, NBC refuses to pay a fee for any news event and are kept out, along with Canadian TV, which presumably also took that stand. CBS has been working inside because they did decide to pay $250. When we arrived in the car at the gate of the building's side alley, a mob of reporters was waiting. They soon sent in one of their number to ask me if the print reporters could be admitted, and I didn't see why not, there being no prohibition against them that I knew of. And so I instructed our assistant director to open the gates for them, and about a dozen promptly rushed in to sit and watch what is doubtless the most boring procedure in the theatre for those not involved in it.

Added to Bill Moyers' crew there was also the Bruce Dunning CBS network camera, plus about five Chinese cameras and some still photographers. Fellini-time had at last arrived in China. I could not turn, literally, without a flash exploding in my face. Meanwhile my heart was sinking at the prospects before the production.

The Prop Department had indeed solved a few of the mechanical problems brilliantly. The action requires Happy and Biff to lie down in their beds in the second-floor bedroom and a few minutes later appear from the wings dressed as teenagers. Then they have to exit, after their scene in Willy's memory, and reappear once again as thirty-year-olds in pajamas in the beds upstairs. In the original production, Mielziner had designed an elevator that lowered the two bed platforms, leaving the bedcovers undisturbed. The mechanism worked on a winch, was very heavy, and periodically got stuck, requiring whole fountains of improvisation to spew from Willy's mouth on the stage.

Recalling this on the plane coming over, I had sketched a hinged slab in each bed that would simply slope downward when needed, allowing the actors to slide out below, unseen. When I showed this to the designer, he showed me his solution, basically the same idea. But in construction he had refined it: the two slabs on which the actors lie under bedcovers are propped up by T's, which are pulled out of vertical positions by stagehands underneath and the actors lowered to the stage floor. Two brothers means two stagehands for this duty alone, but China has plenty of people. In New York it would mean an added nine hundred dollars a week.

I decided to "direct" for the cameras by having Biff and Happy try out the mechanism and make their costume changes to see if it could be done in the required time. The only problem was that they would have to sleep in their socks, which took too long to take off and put on, so I told them not to wear socks under their long trousers as teenagers. This instruction is immortalized on tape.

The lighting of the opening scene had terrific mood—this was to turn out to be true throughout Act One, but the mood lighting must give way to higher levels of illumination. The lighting designer did not possess sufficient lights to raise the level. We were going to have to act the play in semidarkness, a few areas lit decently, others catastrophically under-lit.

The theater possesses two follow-spots, and I ordered both turned on, although it is annoying to watch a play under moving light over a long evening. With some rewiring, a somewhat higher, barely adequate, level could be reached. We were now in trouble, I thought. As a last resort, Old Feng could take the amber filters off the basic area lights, which should raise the level, although it would harden the effect, too.

All of which underscores the poverty of the theatre and the country, but what was more surprising was the rather uncertain grasp of basic lighting techniques. It is obvious, for example, that very high contrast — white light against a dead-black background — will tire the eye over an extended period, yet the sole lighting was on the set, with nothing at all behind it. An actor exited through a door into blackness. I had some highlighting set up to relieve the blackness of the Lomans' bedroom doorway and to suggest at least that Willy will not fall five thousand feet when he walks out of it.

Inevitably, I suppose, the most difficult problem was most elegantly solved — the effect of light filtering through the leaves of two elms that once stood in front of the Loman house. As Willy begins talking to himself, addressing an empty chair in the kitchen as though he sees Biff as a boy sitting in it, time winds backward and the leaves' outlines open up on the whole set. We had never really succeeded with this in the original New York production, which was in every other respect a scenic triumph, because for some reason the leaves became a merely speckled light whose meaning was never quite clear. Here, through means invented by himself, Old Feng, sitting beside me in the dark theatre and quite obviously all tensed up, ordered the effect he had dreamed up.

It was quite fine, really gave a sense of sunlight through the branches and dense leaf structures of a great tree. I grabbed his hand and congratulated him and he quickly ordered the next cue to cover his immense relief and pleasure.

After some two uninterrupted hours in the morning session and about three and a half in the afternoon, we covered the light cues of a little better than half of Act One. I had to finish this act and in addition all of Act Two by the next day (Monday) at five, when once again we would be thrown out of the theatre so that, incredibly enough, they could dismantle the entire set, rewire all the lighting, and get ready to play *Warning Signals.* It would only be on Tuesday that I might have the theatre all day and night, which is cutting it as close to the bone as the Shuberts in their worst days. But this far I doubt even they ever went.

Nevertheless, the sky this morning was clear blue and the rainwashed air free of dust, and we cycled for three hours out to what is now the Youth Palace and was formerly Jiang Qing's personal preserve when she was running the country. It is a vast palazzo fit for an empress, with a pool and its own movie theatre, all of it surrounded by a twenty-foot-high gray brick wall with steel doors in the street entry. And she the chief leveler! Now it houses rehearsal rooms for exhibitions of children's art, scientific demonstrations, a few TV war games that children can work, and the theatre where they put on youth plays and concerts. It was crowded with young parents and their kids. Unfortunately we were trailed by a discreet but never distant Chinese TV crew with two cameras. Not much else was happening in Beijing, apparently.

It happened that a big-band recording of "Laura" was being played at high volume on the loudspeakers that cover the gardens outside—a smooth and oddly moving song that the 1940s generation in America adored, played, I thought, by Tommy Dorsey's orchestra or one very much like it. And this made me see this whole brazenly wasteful Versailles-like complex of corridors, public rooms, and sheer power-lust as Jiang Qing might well have seen it—her Hollywood dream-place come true, but on a scale not even Louis B. Mayer would have dared attempt. Here she could play the queen, this ex-Shanghai actress gone to myopia and the sags of unacknowledged age, and collect around her the choice ignoramuses of the realm, remarkable even among the sycophants of other dictators in other places for the absence among them of even educated fools. If there was a point to her direction of the nation it was to literally destroy China's mind.

Lunch this afternoon with Christopher Wren of *The New York Times* and his wife, Jacqueline. Picking us up at the Bamboo Gardens Hotel, where he had never been before, he recalled hearing that somewhere underground beneath the lovely plantings and rock sculptures, the chief of Mao's Politburo, Wang Dongxing, whose home all this was, had had a torture chamber. It occurred to Inge and me that facing the restaurant terrace there *is* an oddly placed opening carved into the rock of a small, fifteen-foot-high man-made mountain featuring small trees and plants. Thinking this might be at least a clue, the four of us crossed the central courtyard and turned into a second court, with the "mountain" in its center. Lunch was being served in the sunshine on the terrace. I went through the vaulted opening and found a cul-de-sac after a couple of yards and on the right a tremendous steel door held shut by two dogs, or clamps, around which cables and padlocks had been fixed. Facing this vault from five yards' distance I eat breakfast, lunch, and dinner on most days, and complain about the comical service—one sometimes has three pretty young girls in attendance, "helping" one another to take one's order, and all three forgetting what it was until, after a fifteen-minute wait, one of them happens to reappear from the kitchen and reacts with juvenile shock at one's presence. She then proceeds to invent an order that she reassuringly claims is almost ready. One accepts this unordered food, famished and beaten. I do not know another nationality that could get away with this, but I can't hold it against them because they're so pretty and darling and dumb. I expect to eat there tomorrow, too, facing the dark cave where I would have been dragged at night for "opposing Chairman Mao's thought," no doubt, as enunciated by the Shanghai actress.

## *May 2*

Monday morning, and one week to go before we leave. This coming Saturday night we open. I hope.

The Chinese artistry with papier-mâché continues to amaze me. After the Lomans' refrigerator, impossible to tell from porcelain, they have made two football helmets modeled after the one I brought from the States, also out of papier-mâché and painted gold—the original having been made of a smooth hard plastic that would not take paint. An eighty-year-old master of papier-mâché has supervised these constructions. He is now retired but his students did this work for us. He has made whole banquet tables complete with dishes and glasses and loaded with food, all of papier-mâché, which can be lifted in toto on one hand and carried off the stage.

He learned the technique as a young man in prerevolutionary times in order to construct funerary objects. In the case of a wealthy man, the artist would be brought to the house and be permitted to simply walk through it slowly, never taking out a tape measure, but under cover of his voluminous sleeves, pressing measuring marks onto pieces of paper with his thumbnail. He would then hurry back to his shop, construct the *entire house,* including all the rooms and important pieces of furniture, which would be set afire at the funeral. The destruction of his work finally was too painful for our expert, and it led him to the theatre, where his creations were preserved and used.

Speaking of props, the laundry basket originally provided for Linda to carry on in her appearances as a young wife was dark, heavy, had a single bowed handle, and was difficult for her to manage. I drew a picture of the common American two-handled laundry basket as it had existed at least in my youth, but, surprisingly, they had never seen one. I would have bet they were even made in China in the old days. The young man in charge of props, unbeknownst to anyone, then drove a hundred miles out into the country to a village where indeed such baskets are still sometimes used. To get there he had to drive one of the perilous motorized tricycles that go gasping around the streets here and were never intended for highway use. I had not known that his father is one of the directors of the theatre, but he told us this story at tea with Cao Yu yesterday on the terrace of the Bamboo Gardens Hotel restaurant, opposite the newly identified cave.

Cao Yu has insisted on coming up from Shanghai for the premiere of the play, despite his not having fully recovered from an operation. A tiny tiger of a man in his seventies, still charged with enthusiasm, wearing a brown French beret and carrying a cane, he is accompanied by the youngest of his six daughters, who is in her last year of medical school and looks exactly like him. Along with Lao She's *Teahouse,* his *Thunderstorm* is still the core of the theatre's repertoire; a whole company was formed around it and in fact some of its members are in my cast.

For his generation, the generation of the Revolution and the Civil War, today's China must be an open question rather than any kind of secure affirmation of former social theory. After the victory in 1949, they believed that within a maximum of ten years something called "socialism" would literally raise China not to the status of a great power—something they had no wish for—but to the level of some sort of transubstantiated inspiration for the poor of the whole world, for whom she would light the way into a stateless brotherhood of all mankind. It was a rebirth of Christian millenarianism, the Second Coming without the Christ.

I know that he fought hard to bring *Salesman* here as an opening to the modern world for Chinese actors and audiences, and now he pounds the table and insists it will run here for a very long time. I await the end of my problems, although it is pleasant to hear so much optimism. When I lead him into the mouth of the cave to show him the door he stands for a moment, nods his head, and says nothing as I repeat Wren's conjecture that this might have been the torture chamber of Mao's Politburo chief. We then proceed to climb the five steps up to the sunny terrace and our conversation. At moments like this one can only sympathize with the inability to put together in one image Mao the savior, China the light of the world, and a cave like this. It is not that paradoxes like this exist only in China, but that the scale of everything is beyond the mind's powers to embrace in a single concept.

## *May 3*

At seven this morning the phone rings, with our daughter Rebecca's clear and steady voice explaining that she and her grandmother are very well but that half the house in Connecticut has burned during the night. The neighbors are being very helpful, and she has hired a guard to stay on the place until we return. An hour later one of the teenage boys who run this hotel steps into our room and with a pleasant confidence says he would be glad to help us move. We have no idea we're to move, but apparently we are to be given a large suite to climax our last week in China instead of the two cramped rooms we have lived in until now. All kinds of good news today.

For so many years now, Chinese puritanism has been the one certain characteristic of the country, which makes it all the more strange that the dozen teenage waitresses in the restaurant, in which we are now the most durable pensioners, can be found almost any hour of the day or evening clustered around the bar, where I have yet to see a customer, chatting excitedly about hair—about waving it, washing it, cutting it, and parting it. Their order taking has now reached epic poetic levels of complete miasma. This morning I timorously ask—you never know—whether they have orange juice today, not orange soda, mind you. If so . . . But before I can give the rest of my order the waitress is off to investigate. This is known as Wait Number One and ends in about four minutes with her return with a can of the stuff but no glass. Would she bring a glass, please? Yes, of course; but we grip her by both arms before she leaves again and force upon her an order for four jam pancakes and one yogurt, and an apple if they have one handy. She then leaves to accomplish Wait Number Two. A second waitress, after five minutes, appears with two cups of coffee, for which we are grateful. She then disappears for Wait Number Three. The orange-juice can stands undisturbed. Now appears the first waitress with a glassful of orange juice, and putting it before me, she looks with astonishment at the unopened can of orange juice, but as she turns to me to ask what she is to do with this I tell her that it is all right, I do not need another glass, and demonstrate how I will drink orange juice out of the glassful she just brought, and adjure her to take away the can. As we are talking, a third waitress, doubtless having heard that we had asked for coffee, arrives with two more cups of it. Having finished the orange juice and two cups of coffee, we are served the pancakes and with a certain anticipatory dread ask if we can have yet another bit of coffee to accompany the pancakes, but suggest we don't need yet another pair of cups. I see her mystification: how can you have coffee without cups? But a third, or possibly fourth, girl enters with a pot of coffee and everyone fluffles up her hair and chats gaily as they return to the dining room from the terrace. Their imperturbable joy in living is impressive and their eagerness to help one another is striking. But it has no connection with the glum stick-to-itive puritan virtues; if anything, they are remote to orderly duty and more southern than northern in their relaxation as things simply slide down the sluice.

At the Act One run-through yesterday, the initial attempt to run the light cues and act at the same time, the Woman, Liu Jun, was very troubled that the long white chiffon scarf she has draped across her back and down her arms may cause the Chinese audience to think of mourning, and wanted to change it for a pink or red one, to which I agreed. She also wanted her black slip, in which she plays the whole role, lengthened because she was dissatisfied with her legs as the opening approached. This would look draggy and I vetoed it.

Our rehearsals have had to be canceled this morning to give Old Feng time to bring up what he calls his "reserves" of lights in order to raise the general lumin level to tolerable brightness. I have him review all the Act One cues, lighting each scene in order, and watch him enjoy playing all the parts as he mutters "Blah-blah-blah" and walks around in the set to all the main positions. He wears his usual blue smock and white-soled cotton shoes. I congratulate him on his performance, for which he grins gratefully.

In two days we shall have our first audience, and at this hour of the morning I am not sure we will have time to do more than run through the show once with costumes, makeup, and lights. Today, three and a half days before opening, is the first when I shall have the theatre all day and into the evening. But I still believe the cast is solid in the play. They could play it in the subway. Or maybe not.

In the corner of practically every Beijing courtyard there is a pile of old used bricks, neatly stacked. Occasionally there is even quite a pile in front of a house, and I asked the cast the other day, as we sat down to discuss my notes on one of their performances, what these bricks signified. Biff said they had been lifted, in effect, from one or another of the construction projects springing up all over town; when a man had accumulated enough he might build an additional room or repair a falling wall. With a grin that burst into his boyish laughter he added, "I just finished a new room myself!"

"Then you know what it feels like—Willy saying Biff had been bringing home all kinds of lumber from where they're building the apartment house."

"It's one of the biggest occupations in Beijing!" he yelled, and everyone roared, and another "Americanism" hit the dust.

We have been having talks from time to time about father-child relations in China—I am still trying to lock in the actors' feelings about this conflict, which is so central to the play. I know, for one thing, that it is only in the final fight in the kitchen that Biff, in Ying's translation, is using the intimate personal pronoun. Only then, as he desperately tries to reach his father, can he address him this intimately! Yet, in terms of his acting behavior, he is of course under my direction and plays it quite as an American would, with the same violence and anger. Yet that formality had to remain until the last moment or it would lack credibility for Chinese.

This brought up the "Twenty-six Filial Acts," a onetime code about which the cast now laughs, that in properly run families would govern father-son relations. For example, the young son should warm up his father's icy bed before he crawls into it in winter evenings. One good son is particularly commended for having lain down on the ice so as to melt it enough to draw a glass of water for his dad. The great writer Lao

She ground all this to pulp for its hypocrisy, but one has to wonder what remains of it in the psyche.

There is now a full-fledged battle going on between NBC, and to a lesser extent Canadian TV, and the management of the Capital Theatre over their refusal to pay a fee to film parts of the play. CBS, having paid, filmed again yesterday while I worked at reviving a few of the acting details Willy and Biff have lost as a result of our layoff for two days. The Chinese have now apparently decided to change tack on the NBC-TV issue and "leave the decision up to Mr. Miller"—which is just dandy, now that I need every minute of rehearsal time through the remaining days before opening. The problem is that apart from refusing the fee, NBC also wants its own separate session with the actors, which is precisely what I said in the first press conference I had no time to provide; I had said that all the cameras would have to work on the same day with an equal shot at the material. But only CBS showed up prepared to go to work.

Last night Uncle Ben entered his first scene carrying a marvelous Gladstone bag of a style never seen on earth before. It turned out to be papier-mâché but looks like good brown leather that has traveled from Africa to Alaska and back a few times. However, some of the actors think it looks like the kind of bag "rat-poison salesmen" used to carry, but there is a lack of unanimity on this.

I have put "Jack Benny" back in Howard's enthusiastic speech about the virtues of his wire recorder. I had changed it early in rehearsals to "Bob Hope" (Boba Hopa), but later recalled how on a plane to Los Angeles sometime in the 1950s I looked up from my magazine to find Jack Benny bending over to introduce himself. He and his wife were traveling with George Burns and Gracie Allen, he said, and he just wanted to tell me that he had seen *Salesman* a few nights after its opening with Lee Cobb, and when he heard his name mentioned twice in Howard's speech, "I realized that now I was immortal!" It suddenly seemed wrong to take him out even though his name means nothing here, while the Chinese know Boba Hopa from his television program shot here. So now it is "Jacka Benny-ah" whom you can hear in the middle of the night if your maid has turned on the machine to record his program while you were out.

Jack Benny reminds me of vaudeville, and vaudeville of a bad Chinese actors' habit of throwing in little "uh's" and "ah's" when they should be listening in silence. This is to keep things sounding active and alive and sometimes has to be scratched because it breaks up their partners' speeches in a senseless fashion. Most of the time it is harmless and satisfies them that they *seem* to be paying attention.

## *May 4*

Coming down to the wire now, and after six weeks of rehearsal when it all seemed to cohere, the damned primitiveness of their lighting equipment has stopped it all cold. We are literally using their last light, and it is really not enough. The whole area behind the set is pitch-dark and only by stretching the imagination beyond breaking is it believable that any scene is happening during daylight, such as the opening of Act Two, as well as the scenes in the past that should be redolent with optimistic light.

Old Feng is exhausted trying to patch it all together. I have come to realize that it is not merely their reluctance to voice any reservations or criticisms before foreigners; I very much doubt that they do it before their own leaders. This play is being put before the public with what comes down to two technical rehearsals, one of which had to be taken up largely with revising the lighting scheme that had been previously prepared for it. This was either too dismally underlit, or lit brightly in the centers of scenes with violent fallings-off at the peripheries.

I am afraid I have been trying to make up for their customary reticence by openly telling anyone who would listen that the theatre technically simply does not exist. A Mr. Wang stopped by to say hello yesterday with Mme. Zhou (Joe), our friend and liaison with the Theatre Association, the sponsors on the Chinese side; Wang is just leaving for Washington to take up his post as Cultural Counselor to their Embassy there. I figured he might be of some importance in the hierarchy and for fifteen minutes held him a little less than spellbound with a lecture on what they had to do if they were seriously thinking of creating a world-class theatre here. He seemed to take it in, but it could also have been his way of staying awake, you never know. Joe seemed to feel backed up by what I was laying on her, but I have more hope in her as someone who will pass on my attitudes.

So this morning I run through Act Two again, basically to rehearse light cues for the electrical crew, and in the evening we have a complete run-through with lights and costumes. We have an audience the following evening, God help them.

I am still astonished by the tremendous interest in this production on the part of the press and the foreign political community. There is a rush on the box office, too, or so I am told. It is surely a mark of China's isolation and secrecy that the staging of a play — any play — should seem so epoch-making. We bused the whole cast and crew over to the American Embassy for a reception in my honor and there must have been a hundred members of the diplomatic corps milling around in the rectangular courtyard of the modern-style glassy building. We had only an hour for this and would miss dinner, so the cast and I were busy spearing the canapés as the butlers floated them by. Present were the ambassadors of Great Britain, West Germany, Ireland, Sri Lanka, and a number of others I failed to catch. Two of the Americans present, a soft-speaking Texan and his wife, expressed their delight in meeting me here in Hong Kong!

Inge and I are both trying not to think about our house having burned. When I told the news to Ying Ruocheng's wife, Wu Sheliang, and mentioned all our best books being destroyed, she said she understood. "It's just what happened to us in the Cultural Revolution."

At this morning's lighting run-through about half the cues either were late, never came on, or when they did were strangely darker than we had all agreed on yesterday. I felt an anger rising in me, it was so consistently wrong. When the end came I started after Old Feng, who looked at me in surprise. "But it is the morning now!" he explained.

"What's that got to do with it!"

"The Beijing voltage drops during the day because the factories are working. It will all be brighter this evening."

I sat down again, but ran off a four-page list of his failures, chief of which is to provide daylight in any scene of the play. "But that is the nature of the set being so open," he excused himself. The truth, which slowly emerged, is that he misconceived the lighting to indicate practically every scene as being a part of Willy's fantasies, and fantasy is always moodily lit. He now understands, he says, and will provide sunlight when required. The first scene of Act Two, after all, cannot be mistaken for a fantasy when Willy is full of energy and plans to convince Howard to give him a New York job. But it is lighted as though it took place at midnight. "He's not a night worker, Feng," I finished by saying, and to this he did not reply except to promise daylight again.

I suddenly recalled, as I watched Biff sitting on his suitcase in Willy's Boston hotel room, that the character in the original production had worn a raincoat over his athletic sweater, and that it was a strangely concrete sort of detail that showed he had traveled up from New York. Also that it was raining out, another touch of reality in Boston. So I had the costume man summoned, and Ying Ruocheng asked him for a raincoat for Biff. The fellow looked a little doubtful and asked what kind of raincoat, and I said any Western type would be all right but tan would be a good color.

The prop man happened to be standing on the stage staring at something on the floor and looking like Buster Keaton. He has an unsmiling, terribly serious, knitted expression that is also oddly remote and sleepy. In his sixties, he pads about, looking underneath anything that has space beneath it — for what, no one seems to know. Overhearing our raincoat discussion he blinked his eyes and looked down at the group of us scattered in the orchestra seats and said, "Why not get him a PLA raincoat? They're the best, you know." That Biff Loman wearing a commonly recognized People's Liberation Army-issue raincoat in Boston might strike an original note never entered his mind, and Ying, with his unbreakable patience and sympathy for these people, kept from laughing and simply changed the subject.

The stage apron on which we play several vital scenes consists of various lengths of black-painted boards that have obviously been pieced together for lack of regular lengths of lumber. Some boards are resting on nothing but goodwill and give when stepped on, and besides they are all rough-sawn and splintery. I complained to the set designer, who, I thought, felt I was being a bit deluxe in this, but the day after Happy tripped and Ying's understudy put his whole lower leg through an open space, a crew appeared and laid down fiber-covered panels, but they are about one sixteenth of an inch thick and while they offer a smooth surface it still goes up and down under the weight of the actors. Linda has now fallen over an iron weight left on the floor behind the set, where it is always totally dark, just as I had tripped over it ten minutes earlier. Apparently people are expected to look after their own safety.

To begin the scene in the kitchen following the return of Happy and Biff from their night on the town after the restaurant scene, Happy is supposed to part the curtain to the living room and start in, but back out on seeing Linda sitting within. In yesterday's rehearsal we had taken so long discussing the lights that when Happy finally got to act and opened the curtain he leaped back, startled, and then began laughing hysterically. Linda eventually emerged, holding her head and also laughing: she had been waiting so long she had fallen sound asleep back there, and when Happy opened the curtain she had nearly fallen off her chair.

As head of the theatre, Cao Yu has among other perquisites a car and driver permanently at his disposal and a large, airy apartment in a new building on one of the newly created boulevards of the outer, more modern city. He was victimized during the Cultural Revolution when his library was confiscated and never returned to him, but not long ago the fine marble-topped desk he had worked on for years was given back. The Red Guards had moved out all his valuables and kept them for nearly a decade in a warehouse where there are still tens of thousands of "bundles" whose owners are dead or dispersed. It is generally conceded that the Guards were on the whole honest young idealists, but a considerable number pocketed some of the proceeds of their depredations.

At lunch today in his apartment, Cao Yu, ebullient and with a tendency to shout enthusiastically in what seem excessive appreciations of whatever comes up, took out an album from his bookcase and showed us a letter of several pages, beautifully written in a calligraphy even I could appreciate, from his old friend Huang Yongyü, the famous painter. The gist, as Cao Yu translated it character by character, was: "My dearest and oldest friend, as I love China so I love you and must therefore tell you the truth. As an artist and writer, you were an ocean once, and now you have become a trickling brook. When will you cover our pages with grandeur again? Everything you have written since 1942 is of no truth, no beauty, no use. What has our country done to your priceless talent, and what has she done to deserve to lose it?"

This can only be a rough and debased rendering from memory of a compactly composed and devastating critique of the writer who was reading it with intense emotion to Ying Ruocheng and his wife, Inge and me, and his two youngest daughters. I was sitting close beside him on a small wicker sofa, with Ying Ruocheng on his other side translating the eight horizontal rows of strongly inked characters on succeeding pages, each of which pounded another nail into the coffin of his dead art. Once the loving salutation was past and the dirge over his expired talent had begun, I thought for a second it was to be a joke, some piece of Chinese wit whose cruelty at the last moment would be rounded out by a gracefully ironic turn to bring all back into an encouraging if monitory picture. But it never let up to the end. What could have been in Cao Yu's heart not only to have respectfully, if not lovingly, mounted these pages in a special album but to have read them to us?

Huang Yongyü had been our guest in Connecticut two years before, and he told in the letter to Cao how he had just returned from the woods, riding behind me in the trailer of my tractor along with a load of firewood I had cut, and how the day before he had spent a short time at a rehearsal of a new play I was directing. So the letter began with a contrast between what he considered my energy and free creativity and Cao Yu's having agreed to be an official—hence a servant—of the regime, thus trading his talent for perquisites. From this I take it that one impulse for Cao Yu's reading the letter was a desire to praise me convincingly. But as he is one of the main sponsors of the production of *Salesman* here I did not need this further proof of his estimate of me. There was more.

His two youngest adoring daughters nodded as each character was read of this painful criticism of their father—nodding in recognition of the validity of each barbed point the letter was so poetically but cuttingly making. But without any apparent emotion—at least no embarrassment or feeling of anguish for his sake. What could one make of this apparent welcoming of such a condemnation of their father's whole life? It was astonishing, and continued remorselessly with Ying's intelligent English that never for an instant deflected or even acknowledged the content of what he was reading.

All this time, Cao Yu, whose own English is rusty but usable, attempted to accompany Ying, occasionally suffering his younger friend's correcting his inaccurate translation but pounding along beside him anyway, damning phrase after damning phrase. When it was finished, the small man pushed a finger into the album and shouted, "The truth! This is the work of a real friend! Absolutely true!" And he looked at me from only inches away, a storm of feeling in his eyes, and a ferocity, too.

I still cannot fully take this in. Is it possible that after so many years, decades, of being edged farther and farther away from simply writing what he knew to be true, Cao was now trying to rescue his real life at any cost—even painfully shedding the false skin with which he had pretended to be the same color and pattern as everyone else—in the only way left to him: in reading the loving condemnation by a friend of his worst, forced work? The letter clearly isolated his best work as having been done before the Liberation and the Party's hand began weighing on his own. Through my embarrassment, my regard for him soared.

A little while later he would not let us leave without taking us through his rooms to show the carved rosewood bed his second wife, twenty years his junior, whom he married some years after the death of his first, had brought as her dowry. And then in his study he showed his newly returned marble-topped desk. "I finally got it back, but the Red Guards took all my books, and I will never see those again."

This little tour seemed, consciously or not, related to his reading the letter to us. For the Cultural Revolution, indeed the entire Revolution itself, had to inflict certain costs to pay for its gains, and one of these was the constant suspicion, if not outright contempt and violent persecution, of intellectuals. Their humiliation has a left a mark upon writers and artists that will not soon disappear. Even now reports appear of engineers—they are classed among intellectuals—leaving China in frustration at having been so boxed in by factory management as to make their valuable contribution to production unavailable or useless. In the West it is usually forgotten that China's was a peasant revolution and Mao was a peasant. To their mentality intellectual activity is at best an adornment in comparison with the true creativity of food production. The other side of the coin, of course, is that China traditionally created a class of intellectuals whose sole function was to pass the imperial examinations, after which they were not obliged to do anything whatever for the remainder of their lives. The sheer uselessness of these people is symbolized by the fact that one of the most vital elements in the exams was a test of their abilities at composing standardized lyrics. Intellectual activity is not real work to a great many people still. Perhaps the American anti-intellectual tradition—or parallel Russian resentment—is not altogether out of place here. But in no country has this feeling been carried into political persecution on such a vast scale and over so much time.

Inevitably, then, in China—and to almost the same degree in Russia—there is an obsessional quality to their worship of intellectual integrity. I can never raise the questions surrounding the Cultural Revolution without sensing a mixture of shame and the implication of guilt. Nothing of consequence has yet been written about this latest and most complex of Chinese catastrophes, and the explanation is always the same: it still seems unresolvable in its ambiguities, more time will have to pass before it can be approached. But it often seems that the generation that experienced it was, or feels it was, somehow implicated in it—a movement that began in a sweep of idealism against crude bureaucratic socialism, and degenerated into outright anarchy controlled at the top by a mafia of ignoramuses who had captured the Party itself. Worst of all, it is impossible to stare for very long at Mao himself and his role in it without going blind. It is too horrible—China's savior and very possibly her ruin.

## *The first preview*

The Capital Theatre is very large, about thirteen hundred seats, more than in any but the very biggest in New York, but acoustics are quite good. About halfway up the orchestra is a double-width transverse aisle in which I have a seat with Shen beside me in case I need interpreting. At seven-fifteen the seats are filling up fast for the seven-thirty curtain, a nonpaying audience—theatre employees and friends—who seem mostly young people under twenty-five. Some have even brought their small children. The noise level hovers between that of a large lecture audience in the States before the speaker's entrance and that of a high-school basketball audience before the teams trot out. A joyfully energetic banging of seats as at least half the more than thousand present decide to rise and change places with the other half. (On later investigation of the violence of the seat-banging sound, I determine that the rubber buffers underneath are completely worn off the steel stops, so that the horrendous sound is metal on metal, like shots from a .22 pistol.) I sense something wild about the audience, something untamed, avid, and, for want of a better word, uncultivated. Already babies are being taken out—to the toilets, I presume. We might as well be at the circus or a lecture demonstration on child care. But unlike the common situation five years ago in Chinese theatres, there is absolutely no spitting. My mind, however, wanders back to the American Cultural Attaché's telling me that this audience in China is "unsophisticated." Are we lost?

Once the theatre is in darkness there is a noticeable lowering of noise. Without a curtain, the set has been on display from the time the audience entered the theatre, so that when the lights come on again the spectators are used to the openness of the stylized Loman house, and now they are fairly quiet, excepting for the ceaseless conversational, oceanic hum that in China is the equivalent of silence. Naturally some people, no more than two hundred, are still exchanging seats.

Now Willy enters the swath of blue nightlight across the forestage, carrying his legendary valises, putting them down, entering his house, to be greeted by the "Willy!" of his just-awakened wife. Roughly a hundred other people now decide to return to the seats they had earlier exchanged, and some are inevitably left over to wander up and down the aisles. Willy and Linda launch into their carefully rehearsed, beautifully modulated scene in which Willy's mental condition is first broached, his delusory belief that he has been driving all day in a car he has not owned in twenty years. This rather subtly rendered information seems to unloose some hidden exuberance in the audience, which suddenly regains its vocal powers after the short rest of the previous moments.

Directly in front of me a young man sits slumped in his seat combing his hair with a nearly ferocious vigor. Once again seats are banging all around and there seems to have arisen a subject of conversation so common to all present that the sound of it is evenly spread over the entire auditorium. The young man in front of me is now changing his part from right to left, but oddly enough with his eyes still fastened to the stage. Beside me a relaxed young couple are discussing something at pretty much the same vocal level they would use in their own living rooms. Yet on closer observation they do not seem to be turning away from the stage despite their continuing their discussion.

All this I will soon look back upon as riveted silence compared to what happens when Willy, following Biff and Happy's scene up in their bedroom, emerges into the empty kitchen and starts talking to Biff across the kitchen table, Biff being invisible. At this moment the two actors are being lowered through their beds to the stage floor and a telltale movement of their bedclothes has been spotted. A medium roar has developed through which Ying is happily talking to an empty kitchen chair in which he sees, in his mind's eye, his beloved young son. Now he follows Biff with his gaze, and stands, steps out across the wall-line of the house into an explosion of sunshine on the forestage, and in a moment both boys, who had been thirty-year-old men up in the bedroom, spring out from the proscenium as teenagers carrying a football and a punching bag. The house rises in a roar.

Shen is shouting into my ear, "They are trying to figure out if these are the same actors, or if you have found actors who are twins, or what happened!" And she, too, is delighted as she looks rapidly around—"Yes! They are amazed how they got down from the beds!"—as triumphantly as if our sly mechanical system had worked instead of failing utterly to create an illusion of the past coming to life in Willy's mind and, we hope, in the audience's, too.

The entire auditorium is half standing now, arms are waving, people are laughing insanely, at the same time pointing and jabbing each other. A number of young children are being rushed out to the toilets.

There wafts across my mind the thought, which I abruptly expunge, that for this I have given nearly two months of hard work. Yet I can also not deny that there is nothing like boredom in the house. It is more like a total, irretrievable absence of comprehension. There is not and never can be a unity of mankind, and so on.

By the intermission I can hardly suppress my anger not only at the Chinese audience but at my own presumption. I walk down the dark and dismal corridor into which the dressing rooms open, the foul smell of the toilet once again powerful in my nostrils—in the past weeks of near-victory it had not seemed to smell so bad—and sit down beside Ying Ruocheng's dressing table. Charley, Biff, and Happy are watching me for a reaction but I haven't the strength to dissimulate.

"You people are made of iron to be able to play in front of a mob like this, I really must give you credit," I say in my bitterness.

"Why!" Ying laughs. "They're really not all that noisy. And nobody's coughing. That would mean they're bored, and there's nothing like that out there." I search his eyes but he seems to mean what he is saying.

There is more cold comfort of this sort from the others, and I return unwillingly to my seat. Reviewing Act One, I have to admit that the audience, in some way beyond my powers to comprehend, has apparently followed the play—Zhu Lin, working her long speeches with the two boys in the kitchen scene where she reveals Willy's suicidal tries, has clapped a dead silence on the house. And they laughed in the card-game scene at the right points. It was their astonishment at the appearance of Hap and Biff as kids after they had just seen them as adults that set them off in what to me seemed a chaos of noise and inattention. As one who is no more partial to reality than the next man, I decide to face the possibility that the play may be penetrating that mob, but how is beyond me.

It seems to me that apart from Linda's Act One success in silencing even this audience, the next time they are really tamed is in Willy's confrontation with Howard. Are they sensing a "message" looming and, with it, a familiar territory? Perhaps, but on Howard's exit, Willy summons up his dead brother Ben, whose appearance does create a hum of comment, but far less than in Act One. They seem to have absorbed the form at last.

At the end, marked only by a slow fade to blackout, followed by the raising of the houselights, the whole audience abruptly leaps to its feet, with a slamming of the damned seats, and applauds. At the same time people are dashing out of the theatre at high speed to catch the last buses of the night.

Backstage, Ying and the company are amazingly charged with a look of success. For a Chinese audience such applause is extremely rare—the great majority remaining to clap their hands and risk losing the last bus is a real tribute, they say.

There was relaxation enough only next day to discuss the preview with the cast, most of them of course long experienced with this audience. Only then did Ying drop the fact that the audience was largely made up of the workers who supply the theatre's canteen with vegetables and meat, people who never see plays, most of them with little education. Under the circumstances they were thought to have been captivated. The theatre had given them tickets to be sure to get the best cuts, the freshest chickens, and a minimum of spoiled onions in the future.

But the most astonishing element of all for them, which never occurred to me, was the absence of makeup on actors playing foreigners. According to Charley and Biff, many viewers had said that for the first time "it made us feel like *them,*" meaning Westerners. If this turns out to be the case for the audiences in the future, it alone will justify the production of *Salesman* here, at least for me. It can really open the world repertory to China, not merely as a curiosity, but as an experience in which they can participate, and one that would do much to penetrate their isolation as a culture, a major accomplishment whose resonances can roll out in many surprising directions.

For me the preview still remains ambiguous. The one real gratification is that the company kept its concentration absolutely solid, never broadening the performance in order to flag down the attention of the audience. I feel now that however long *Salesman* runs, it will not betray the performance we have worked so long to forge.

## The second preview

As Ying predicted, this second audience is of a different order, made up as it is of editors, authors, artists, and academic people, as well as theatre lovers who managed to snare tickets. But all seats are unpaid, since we are still calling the performances rehearsals. As in the States, no audience reaction is "real" unless the seats are bought. Those who pay make the best audiences, they say.

Cao Yu decided to see this performance, as well as the opening tomorrow night. Once again I am reminded of how much is riding on our success for him and Ying and others who share their views. For a man in his seventies who had major surgery only a few weeks ago, he does very well indeed, considering that earlier in the day he officiated at a three-hour banquet luncheon for the cast, along with some ten or twelve Americans, friends of Inge's and mine who decided to make this occasion the time for their first visit to China. They will all be at the premiere tomorrow night.

This second preview audience, while not silent as we know silence in the West, is nevertheless clearly attentive and deeply moved. But the problem remains of slipping the boys down from their beds without the bedclothes moving and tipping the audience that something weird is going on up there. I see suddenly that the white bedclothes moving even slightly against the black background attract the eye and can simply be covered with dark blankets.

# 'DEATH OF A SALESMAN' IN BEIJING

Willy Loman.

The Requiem scene.

Old Feng has at last lit the show with a decent balance between mood and visibility of actors' faces, and when I shake his hand and congratulate him, he looks immensely pleased, gives me a middle-range grin, and says, "I had to—it was my duty."

I wonder why Ying stumbled over his words at one point in his last scene with Ben, when he is discussing his suicide. He tells me that there are two different words for death; one refers to it as mere death; the other includes respect for a parent as well. He had inadvertently slipped into the first usage and then realized his mistake and stumbled.

The spirits are high and everybody is talking his head off. It's just like a promising hit anywhere—loosens the tongues backstage. Charley tells me that at the end of a show during Jiang Qing's reign they would have a stagehand carry an enormous red flag on a long pole across the stage, guaranteeing that the audience would stand up and applaud!

The assistant director admits now that when he first read the play he could not understand it at all or how it could work, certainly not with a Chinese audience. It wasn't until he came on the scene toward the end of Act One when Linda reveals Willy's suicide attempts that he got interested, turned back to the beginning, and started over again. As he tells me this, I can see in the faces of the other actors that it was the same for them. What doubts they must all have had when I first arrived!—and I never noticed.

I am still ashamed that at a run-through three nights ago I stood up and stopped the play after a few minutes into the first Linda–Willy scene, when a photographer simply strolled down to the edge of the stage and started shooting flash pictures. What was odd then was that neither Shen, who was sitting next to me in the orchestra, nor Ying, on the stage, volunteered to translate my angry commands to the photographer to sit down. Finally, Ying talked to the man, who turned to me with a surprise that incensed me even further, and then sat down. I asked Ying to start the show again. This morning it simply came to me that he is, in fact, our own theatre photographer, a sweet little mild man who cooperates in everything. So I found him and apologized, but as I approached him to do so, he retracted as though he was going to be bawled out again.

In any case, there is really no more I can do and I feel it is time to go. I find in myself a not-surprising absence of any terrific anxiety or even desire: now that my powers are used up I could just as well be somewhere else. What will come of it all is beyond me to influence from now on.

## May 7, the opening

It is impossible to sleep past six, so when I get up I go through my notes for anything I may have forgotten to say to the cast before we "open." In fact, it is only nominally an opening, since whatever reviews there are will come out over the next weeks rather than tomorrow morning. I find more notes on both previews than I even recall making—as one's function vanishes, one's notes proliferate.

Miss Forsythe keeps stroking the head of the fox furpiece slung over her shoulder, and looking lovingly into its little glass eyes. I had called for a furpiece in order to distract from the propriety of her dress and now she is turning the scraggly thing into a pet. But I suppose she means it as a come-on. Maybe it works on the audience that way?

In the second preview there was suddenly a break in the music preceding the restaurant scene, and I knew immediately that this was the dreaded breakdown of the tape recorder. This would mean that Willy would not be given the cues of the phone operator in the Standish Arms presaging his final scene with the Woman in Boston, or the wild music that forces him to his feet in the hectic dialogue with both sons. But after a lapse, the sound came back and kept working through the rest of the show. I learned later that in the darkness backstage the sound man had spliced a new connection for a broken input plug. Heroic cool.

Odd laughs that I still do not quite understand: on Willy's response to Bernard's advice to "walk away" if you don't succeed—"But if you can't walk away?"—why do they laugh? Is it a recognition of fate's heavy hand?

With Charley, who keeps offering him a job, Willy angrily says, "I've got a job." Charley answers, "What kind of a job is a job without pay?" for he has been loaning Willy money for months now. They laugh with what I feel to be a certain cruelty here. Likewise when Charley gets fed up with his saying, "I named him, I named him Howard"—his boss who has just fired him—and cracks, "You named him Howard, but you can't sell that!" A big laugh.

And when Willy accepts Charley's loan with "I'm keeping strict accounts," another big laugh, but beneath its cruelty I sense a comprehension of Willy's character, a recognition. Which I suppose means they share these embarrassing weaknesses?

Late in the morning a visit in our suite from Professor Ye, the gentleman who spoke up in agreement with me at the klatch in the Foreign Languages Institute, who has written on Hans Christian Andersen as well as his own novels. He spent World War II in London working for the Nationalist Government and returned with the Revolution and remained. He is a handsome, soft-spoken man in his sixties, and mournfully loving toward "this terribly old-fashioned country." A novel he wrote in the 1940s which was long out of print has been reissued and is the big hit book now, obviously pleasing him greatly, especially because it is the discovery of the young. It is without ideology.

He believes a battle with the conservatives is still going on but there will be no returning to the old revolutionary rigidities if only because the current policy is raising incomes, especially in the country, where all but ten percent of Chinese live. Surprisingly, he insists there is no censorship now—within the very broad boundaries of the necessary support of, or nonopposition to, "socialism." It is not, however, a matter of an anticensorship policy or commitment but that "there is no one anymore, not since Mao died, who has the prestige to issue a directive that could stop a book or play." Of course there are choices being made as to what to publish, just as there are everywhere, "but the heavy hand of the government is motionless now." I take this to mean that there is no censorship *in effect,* but not necessarily *in principle.* Even so, if true, this in itself is an enormous step.

*Salesman,* he thinks, will revolutionize the theatre and spill over into other arts "not only because it so free in the formal sense but so moving," and this is said without the least doubt, quite as though I must surely have never had any myself. The cultural mismatches—there being no salesmen here, the more formal child–parent relations, and so forth—are mere details of exotic behavior and won't stop the audience from reaching into the play.

I wonder, again, about Mao—had he been aware that he had failed in his last two or three years?

"Oh, far longer than that. He had never found the right path, it was all a series of staggering sorties into the unknown, and the Cultural Revolution was merely the last of them." But he is not ready to come down with a final judgment on the Cultural Revolution, in which he, too, suffered very much, and he seems typical in this. "It is terribly complicated, a rope of good and evil impossible to unravel as yet."

As we part he offers a gift of a print, a rather sentimental drawing of a cat—quite untraditionally composed, it seems to me. And I am left to wonder if, like the rest of us, Chinese are on very uncertain grounds of taste once they leave behind their own native traditions. Inge returns as he is about to leave and he is so animated, suddenly, talking to her in Chinese! I think it is less the fact that he is relieved of having to speak English, which he does with perfect fluency, than that it simply gladdens his heart to know that a foreigner has loved his language enough to have learned it so well. My offer to secure two tickets for the play leaves him speechless, and as he is thanking me I wonder all over again why it should be, as it evidently is, so impossible for a man like him to buy a pair.

In the afternoon I go to Ying Ruocheng and Wu Sheliang's house to sit together one more time. As well to give me a chance to do something that there has not been time for—I have been wanting to take down some samples of the imagery he has used in his translation of the play that differed from the original. And while Inge and Wu Sheliang sit together on one side of the cool, book-lined living room that faces their little courtyard, Ying tries to remember some of his images.

I have never had this kind of relationship with an actor—primarily, I think, because Ying is also a scholar and approaches concepts passionately; thus he can draw feeling from ideas as well as from sheer psychological experience. I have never really seen myself as a director, probably because actors can ordinarily use only one impulse at a time rather than the clusters that life offers at any one moment. I have to warn myself against overcomplicating matters, something that can lead an actor to a hard intellectualized rendering rather than a felt performance. In this production, forced to find the central lines of motion by the sheer difficulties of translation, I have inadvertently undergone a kind of exercise that has kept me stimulated and sensitized to a play I wrote more than three decades ago. Ying Ruocheng has been my rock, a man of double consciousness, Eastern and Western, literary and show business. And he has managed to contain his actor's necessary selfishness through all our trials. I am happy to be in his house now with nothing to do but enjoy the delightful absence of necessity. We are merely going to talk about images.

In the opening scene of Act Two Willy is full of optimism and promises to talk to his boss, Howard, about giving him a New York job. "I'll put it to him straight and simple. He'll just have to take me off the road."

The translation is a four-character image: "Open door see mountain," or, in other words, a direct confrontation. Ying explains, "There is a famous line by a Tang Dynasty poet saying, 'End of the mountain, end of the river, so one feels the road should end there; however, with the shade from the willow and brightness from the flowers the road meanders and goes on.' This, of course, is the opposite image. But for Willy there can be no more meandering—he will open the door and face the mountain right in front of the door."

I ask about the play's own store of time-worn clichés, like "Business is business"—a phrase without any meaning in Chinese, it now turns out. "I made it, in effect, 'Kin is kin, money is money,'" says Ying. This resonates destructively upon Willy's repeated "I named him. I named him Howard"—his attempt to transcend the money relationship with his employer.

This reminds me of "Blood is thicker than water," which in turn reminds Ying that it is precisely the phrase used to describe Taiwan's separation from China, where indeed Chinese kin are separated from each other by a body of water.

Referring to his dead brother Ben, Willy says, "That man was a genius, that man was success incarnate!" I know that this bit of Lomanesque hyperbole has intrigued Ying Ruocheng from our first rehearsals. "In Chinese this is a very dense image, and a pun," he explains. "Genius in Chinese is conveyed by a double symbol—Heaven-Talent, *Tian-Cai*. *Tian* written one way can mean talent or another way it can mean money—money in a rather abstract way, not the coin or bill, more like 'wealth.' So the word *far-tian*, which we use all the time in this play, means 'get rich' but also 'success.' Hong Kong people eat a water plant that looks like hair that is called '*far-tian*'—they eat it for luck. For thousands of years somebody is said to have '*far-tien*-ed'—either become a big official or a landlord or some way struck it big (like 'lucked-out').

"Now 'incarnate' I translate as 'heaven-sent,' so it embraces the gift, like a talent that comes from off the earth, combining with money and success and the power to prevail—all of this packed together in one image. So . . . *tian-cai* is a slightly ludicrous punning on 'heaven,' 'success,' and 'making a buck.' And the audience laughed lightly at this last night—they caught it."

"In other words," I concluded, "to exaggerate slightly, it's like being blessed by heaven with the power and the talent to collect second mortgages."

Through our laughter we both acknowledge our mutual attempt to find the common ground beneath both our cultures. If Chinese has a more pictorial imagery it is nevertheless expressing like human situations far down below. (And this, as we both realize, makes the success of the production of far more importance than merely a theatrical success.)

Which leads to Ying's telling how he experienced American culture for the first time, years ago. "Superficially, everything is opposite between American and Chinese ways. Like we have soup at the end of the meal and you at the beginning; and the first time I had a haircut in the United States, I was amazed that they washed my hair before they cut it. Here we wash it afterward. But there are great similarities, and for me the main reason is the immense size of both countries; when a country is so large it tends to break down narrow-mindedness because people have experience with all kinds of other people, unlike in very small countries. America is very young, but people have been endlessly moving around in it, and China—at least for the last twenty-five hundred years—has been a unified state; but it is a mistake to think that China was created by a single tribe, it melded a large number of intermingling peoples. You've been to Datong, the great cave sculptures by the Meo Dynasty, who were entirely nomadic. There are dozens of other examples of very high cultures being worked into the Chinese culture. So that you don't get that provincial outlook, the narrow-minded thing."

"China was really a melting pot."

"Oh, very definitely, and in many ways like the American one. Last time I was in California—"

"Incidentally, California's going to have an Hispanic majority soon, you know—"

"I'm not surprised. Almost all the workers in the hotel were Hispanic, with a thin layer of Chinese above them, and the customers were all white." And he added, "And Japanese, of course."

My next image—"I won't take the rap for this"—he has translated, "I won't carry this blackened cooking pot on my back." And he calls across the room to Wu Sheliang, "What is the origin of that 'black cooking pot'?" She has no idea either, except that the soot blackens the clothes of the carrier.

I wondered if Chinese actually "saw" a man with a cooking pot when they used this common phrase, or the actual picture of any common metaphor.

"Not at all," Ying says. "Any more than you actually see a little mouse when you say 'quiet as a mouse,' or the vision of a hill when somebody is 'going downhill' in his career."

"It is only consciously poetic to foreigners."

"In any language, I should think."

As he is parting from Willy at the end of the scene in Charley's office, Bernard tries to cheer him up with "Goodbye, Willy, and don't worry about it. You know, 'If at first you don't succeed . . .'"

WILLY: Yes, I believe in that.

BERNARD: But sometimes, Willy, it's better for a man just to walk away.

WILLY: Walk away?

BERNARD: That's right.

WILLY: But if you can't walk away?

How had he translated the last line? In our two previews the audiences had laughed, inappropriately it would seem.

Ying grinned. "Literally, 'walk away' doesn't mean anything in Chinese. So Bernard is saying, 'It's good to be able to pick things up but also to be able to put things down.' And Willy answers, 'Suppose I can't put them down?' He is implying he can only pick things up, and by that time the audience, I think, has identified themselves with Willy as a man who picks up all sorts of things without being able to put them down. And that's funny."

With our rehearsals past now and the play all but finally launched and a well-prepared cast of actors relaxing all over the town, it is time to relish some of the fruits of work—the power that the play obviously exercised over the second audience.

"That first audience was the worst you are going to get in China. First of all they don't pay, and on top of that they have no idea what theatre is, anyway—they're the people who provision our canteen."

"They think it's a place where you bring meat and vegetables."

"Right!" He laughs. "And then there's also our messengers. Most of our people, including myself, of course, have no telephones, so we need messengers. And to buy them the best Japanese motorbikes, to have an adequate supply of gasoline, to have a place to fix them up—you have to keep all those people happy. Then various clubs and universities, factories, are in a position to order five hundred, a thousand tickets at a time—these people are not really interested in art, it's their job, that's all, to get tickets. The second audience, as far as we're concerned, was perfect. But of course with our noisy seats you have the feeling that they've all left just because four or five have gotten up to go to the johns. But last night with those curtain calls I was surprised and I thought, Nobody left! Chinese are quick to leave a performance, you know, and that kind of applause at the end is very rare."

I had wanted to visit an ordinary Beijing bar and had never had time to. So now we walked a couple of blocks to a clean, long, whitewashed room where beer, brandy, wine, tea, and pastries are sold. It is privately owned, one of many in town these days. Service was quick. A few tables distant, four Mongolian-looking men were sitting at a table loaded with empty beer and brandy bottles. One of them kept saluting us and silently offering a drink, a blinded smile on his face. But I had the feeling he was constrained by some unseen hand of good order in the place that kept him from getting up and coming over to us. Ying had two brandies and I one—delicious, and costing about twenty cents a shot. The atmosphere reminded me of *Teahouse,* Lao She's play, in which Ying played the Procurer. The teahouse, a metaphor for China in the half century before the Liberation of 1949, is a collecting depot for Chinese characters, mostly men who are quietly searching out ways of surviving the violent disintegration of society. According to Ying Ruocheng, the original version began with the characters gathering in the teahouse, but the play then became a polemic around the issue of the constitutional question. The actors, Ying among them, persuaded Lao She to drop the politics and concentrate on the fates of the richly drawn characters. It is as famous now as *Gone with the Wind* in America, and played endless times every season.

I have decided to wear a shirt and tie and a blue blazer tonight to reassert my real identity as a Westerner. I don't know exactly why. Except that after two months of daily wear my bush jacket's buttons have all dropped off and it is filthy. I suppose I know in advance that the play is a success if only because all the waiters want their pictures taken with me, and we were waited on for breakfast this morning by no less than a young man and five young women. They showed me my picture in the paper, about the size of a postage stamp and unrecognizable, but they all want it autographed. Apparently the papers approve of the play, but it would not be necessary—the publicity itself is the important thing, the media recognition alone. So much for the decade of leveling of the Cultural Revolution.

In the theatre three quarters of an hour before curtain time Harry Moses, producer of the Bill Moyers television show built around this production, tells me that they interviewed people coming out of the performance last night and were floored by "how profoundly they understood the play." I am far less surprised than I would have been a few weeks ago, but glad to hear it nevertheless. The closing shot on the program, he says, will be a close-up of a young Chinese who speaks some English, saying something about China being full of Willys, dreamers of the dream. What is so weird about all this, of course, is that in 1949 the play cut right across the presumptions of the new "American Century" that Henry Luce, for one, had proclaimed. With the exception of Willy Loman, America was a complete success. Now he apparently represents America somehow, or at least for some people. It reminds me that Ambassador Hummel, on our second day here, when he hosted a lunch for us at the Embassy, gave me some advice about how to handle what then seemed the inevitable politicization of the Chinese reaction to the play—that it simply proved capitalism's inhumanity and decay. "Don't pay any attention to it; nobody does. The play is a portrayal of tragic elements in American society. So what?" It may, in fact, turn out to be better for us to admit our suffering than to show the world our bathrooms and ceaseless success. But I think it will be some time before its effects on Chinese opinions of America can be rightly read.

When I visit the dressing rooms, where they are getting into makeup, the behavior of the actors reminds me again of the replication of human life that a production represents. The actor begins in helpless dependency, gradually grows up to feel strength, often rebels against director/author, and finally in maturity faces the world as though he had invented himself. Where once they loved me like a parent, now they can't help overdoing gestures of affection to their onetime leader, for whom they have no real need anymore. The hairdo's the thing now, the eyebrow, the necktie, the fingernail, and the teeth. Now I am rather in the position of a beloved aunt who taught them as children to play the piano; they are overjoyed to see me, and to see me go.

Exactly as it should be. Their obvious confidence throws my thoughts across the vast sea we have traveled since those first days when we seemed unknowable to one another and lay as privately as ships in the water, signaling across our decks with the grossest general concepts, anything finer being impossible to decipher. I visit from room to room to wish them luck and get out of their way as quickly as possible. We are, I think, as close as we would be in sloppy American friendships, but a certain formality here is never erased and tends to give our mutual affection more promise of lasting. Happy—our first one, who fell ill—hands me a gift, a piece of blue silk with his calligraphy of thanks and best wishes; and from Biff, that Mongol horseman, I have a little statuette of a reclining Buddha with a comfortable round belly and a benign, amused smile. Jabbing a finger at him Biff repeats his special name, "Mi-la," sounding enough like "Miller" to rouse Charley and Ying, who share this dressing room, to warm laughter that in reality celebrates our having committed an act of love in this production.

I find I am not worried about Ying anymore and sit for a moment to watch him gluing on his eyebrows. He has been wearing his Willy Loman suit for days to break it in, a nice gray with a lighter gray pinstripe, made for him by the last remaining Beijing tailor capable of making a good Western suit, a man in his eighties. He had had only enough cloth left to make this last suit and would not snip off an inch swatch for me to see to okay; the whole yardage had to be brought to me to inspect. Ying Ruocheng has ceased to feel he is empty in the final confrontation scene with Biff, for the same reason none of us feels empty when love is in us. Willy is a lover forsaken and seeking a lost state of grace, and the great lift of the play is his discovery, in the unlikeliest moment of threats and conflict, that he is loved by his boy, his heart of hearts. In fact, I don't worry about any of them now because by one means or another they have all learned to become the different but related notes of a love song.

Sitting and watching Ying making up I feel his ownership of the role, his security in its convolutions. Willy, it has been said a thousand times, is so American because he so wants love; but why then has this Chinese actor responded so quickly to the same profile of fear and longing? I sensed in the beginning that Ying had felt a certain superiority to Willy; as though to say, "I understand Loman but I am not to be mistaken for him." But when he gave up his own invulnerability he began to acknowledge his affinities with the character and in the bargain transcended himself. The actor or artist who can't bear to lose himself will never win.

To the women's dressing room, where Linda is making up, hardly able to listen to me at all, as who can blame her when this role is such a departure for her and her public? She has a gift for me and for Inge, her special friend. And the Woman and Miss Fausit and Letta—all of them ambient with a happiness that must derive from comments they have read or heard. But nobody tells me anything, I am deaf in the midst of this symphony, all I can read is the absence of fear in their eyes. And they doubtless think it bad form to report comments to me, the man who is beyond all that. Our first Happy stops me in the hall carrying his five-month-old son, introduces me to his young wife, and I can't ward off the absurdity of the thought, terrible in its difficult simplicity in that dim corridor—God is love and so is art, and in this is its universality for mankind.

Alone again, halting in the corridor, knowing that just about now in the front of the house the audience must be starting to file in, along with our dozen or so American friends and the American Ambassador, as well as other ambassadors and high officials, I am amazed all over again by how magnified this project's importance has become, far beyond its being a play or an artwork. It is now a test of some kind; but of what, precisely? The incommunicability of the Chinese? If I can't claim to know my actors, I know them as well or as little as I would an American cast. I can no longer call up the notion of Chinese mysteriousness. Their language is outrageously different and most of their conditions, but they themselves? Can it be they seem so apart and often so difficult because both they and we drag our chains into the room when we sit down together: they, their mix of inferiority before the successful Westerner (and Japanese) and their resentment toward their own feelings; and we, our condescension, which as often as not takes the form of Chinese-worship? If nothing else, I have treated them as equals, but it was easy in this art, where you are only your talent, your insight, your grace on the stage, nothing less or more. So the relationships of the two cultures are purified, oddly enough, shorn down to the core of humanity in us all. We do not meet defensively in the theatre, quite the opposite—here we have to search each other out. If I fail to understand them or they me, we have a mutual catastrophe. Thus we dispense with culture, hammer away at the opacity of our languages, strive to penetrate rather than justify ourselves or defend the long past. Indeed, our whole objective has been to unearth our common images and analogous—if superficially different—histories. If they are making the Lomans intimately comprehensible to their fellow Chinese it is because they have found the Lomans in themselves. This was why I did not want to wig the play, making it an exotic experience rather than a personal one for them; the people were not to sit in the theatre admiring or "distancing" themselves from a bizarre set of humanlike figures from some exotic Brooklyn, but to absorb the play as closely as possible as a life experience that would enlarge their experience of the world. The job of culture, I have always thought, is not to further fortify people against contamination by other cultures but to mediate between them from the heart's common ground.

Our assistant director (who could not understand the play until he realized Willy was contemplating suicide) now finds me in the corridor to bring me to my seat. He no longer asks me, he tells me, with Shen's excited translation, that I am to sit where the spotlight can hit me at the end, because I am to join the actors on the stage—it is the custom. And with peremptory command he leads me down the corridor by the arm.

Louis Auchincloss is sitting in front of me, the most cheerful fine novelist I have ever met, his recent book miming Saint-Simon still fresh in mind. Beyond him and his wife are Milton Gordon, a sad-faced, soft-hearted, tough-minded, rich businessman, then Geraldine Stutz, who runs the women's department store Bendel's but spends more time with the New York State Council on the Arts, and Theodore White and his wife smack in the center of the house, and the Davisons. He is a banker in New York and has a nice tendency to modest laughter. They all have copies of the play open on their laps, and their excited glances at the audience remind me that one's first contact with a mass of Chinese like this is an exciting, almost shockingly mysterious circumstance. Their American faces are full of a naive happiness and perhaps some pride.

Just on the other side of Inge in our row are Ambassador Hummel and his wife. I am sure he has had to think twice about coming tonight, the Chinese having broken cultural relations with us over the tennis player, something he obviously regrets and, I think, wisely spreads the blame for. I can't help recalling that in the early 1950s, about two years after *Salesman* appeared, the State Department denied me a passport to travel to Europe for the opening of *The Crucible* in Belgium. Tonight a play of mine is our sole cultural contact with China and one for which the Department is doubtless grateful. The thought makes me happy for the power of art.

The light dims over the set, the mournful flute is heard—gratefully heard, I should say, given the condition of the tape recorder—and for the first time we have a Western-type silence in the theatre.

Inevitably, I suppose, I find myself more intrigued by what the Americans are making of the play than the Chinese, who by this performance I am sure will be captured by it. My throwing blankets over the boys' sheets has solved the problem of their being noticed as they descend out of their beds, and with this distraction eliminated the Chinese no longer break into loud astonishments at the reappearance of the two actors as teenagers, merely exclaiming in delight at the transformation and quieting at once to hear the dialogue.

The Americans are avidly following from their English texts, but Auchincloss relaxes me with his chuckles and laughter and obvious delight in the proceedings, his head turning back and forth as at a tennis match.

I will never see this production again, and so I let it seep into myself, all tension gone, part of the audience at last. The play's endless variety, Willy's unexpectedness, his autonomous freedom are my joy, and my mind goes back to the ten-by-twelve box I wrote it in in Connecticut thirty-six years ago; all I can really remember is my laughter then. That, and stepping out the door exhausted at the end of a day and looking up at the night sky and saying, "Talk to me, Willy, what should I say?" He seemed to be in the woods, watching me through the leaves, standing there in his pleated trousers, felt hat, with the valises in the weeds.

Watching the performances. I can sense how effective the actors are, but at the same time I know how much more color and spontaneity they will gradually bring into their roles as the weeks go by. The art of acting is the mastery of a contradiction: its object is to place the actor in "the now," the moment, but at the same time he has to be planning his next move, building his climaxes with modulations of voice and emotional intensity. By virtue of training and temperament the Chinese actor creates feeling by acknowledging his debt to his objectifying techniques. He does not "throw himself into the part" but builds a performance by pieces of knowledge, as it were, of story, character, and specific circumstances. He doesn't start with frenzy but hopes to end with it. But of course it doesn't always come and one sometimes would like more carelessness, invitations to the sublime accident. It is not easier to calculate oneself into a frenzy than to leap into it, and if the actors in general tend to err on the side of calculation, I suspect that given enough performances they will come around to the spontaneity that finally justifies everything.

But whatever my own reaction, the audience's is passionate. At the end they would never stop applauding. Nobody left. When he was taking his bows, I thought I saw a tremendously serious victory in the look on Ying Ruocheng's face. The gamble had paid off, the Chinese audience had understood *Salesman* and was showing its pride in the company. The

Opening night.

row of Americans were cheering, Milton Gordon's eyes were still red and wet, Ambassador Hummel was pounding his palms together, and I thought Chinese and Americans alike were trying to assure each other of the durability of both countries' affection. The spotlight sweeping the theatre found me, and I brought Inge with me to the stage where we stood beside little Cao Yu, whose victory was solemnly written on his face, and Ying and Linda and the others. A mass of white lilies was hoisted onto the stage before us as at an opera. A menace of television cameras faced us from the audience.

The Hummels appeared at the roaring party a three-flight climb up—a surprise, since they were ever so slightly disinvited due to the strained relations, but I was glad that they came and, after a few minutes, left; Hummel was not cool, despite his reputation as an imperturbable man, but grabbed my hand and yelled, "It comes over in Chinese!" and we were both glad it had all worked so well. America will be needing this country as an enrichment to our culture one day just as China needs us now. I suppose the most gratified as an American was Teddy White. He had spent the most dramatic years of his life as a *Time* correspondent in the China of revolution and war, but returning last year, so I have heard, he was shocked at his old friends' remorselessly dressing him down for the U.S. policy that would treat Taiwan as a separate country despite Nixon's and Carter's pledges to the contrary. Tonight once again he could be the prideful American he wanted to be.

As the final token of its poverty the theatre had a mess of slightly dried-out little ham sandwiches on the table, but they were an American note that I appreciated even if they were not easy to get down. Now Inge had to take pictures of every actor in the company, plus our depressed Costume Department ladies, and the old doorman, and Buster Keaton, our prop man, who always looks underneath chairs and furniture in search of God knows what. Cao Yu made a long speech, I made a short one, others felt they had to do likewise, and the hundred or so people present paid not the slightest attention, such was the great joy abounding.

At last, near midnight, time to go. As we shook hands and kissed and yelled into one another's laughing faces, Biff started a cheer, takeoff of Willy's final Act One speech from his bed, when he recalls the cheers from the stands for "Loman, Loman, Loman!" This one was "Mee-la, Mee-la, Mee-la!" And the only Chinese word I could dredge up to respond with was *laila*—as when Willy, boasting to his young sons that unlike other salesmen who have to sit waiting for hours to see a buyer he simply walks in, calls out "Willy Loman *laila!*"—"Willy Loman is here!"—and he goes right through. I yelled, "Arthur Miller *laila!*" and the party ended, laughing.

We had checked our bags through and were waiting for our flight to be called. Suddenly, an old bus drove up to the large plate-glass window of the airport lounge through which I was staring, and there was Ying Ruocheng beside the driver, behind him the whole company. Again the handshaking and the photographing and the laughter, but this time there was something more than levity and joyful leave-taking in the air. Ying especially seemed rather solemn, even troubled. Could there have been something unpleasant in the press? Or was he merely moved to have to see us go after so intense a collaboration over the months? Or was I reading too much trouble and sadness into his look? There was no time to ask. We moved through the passport control and waited for the officer to stamp and turn pages; the twenty or so people of the Beijing People's Art Theatre remained on the other side of the barrier, waving, smiling, refusing to turn their backs until we were gone out of sight. The passports back in our hands, I whispered to Inge not to linger, and I could not do more than glance once again at the company and hurry away.

At some point in our milling around for our last farewells, for what reason I have no idea, I felt a kind of despair; maybe it was a fear that when all was said and done I could not know what I suppose I had come here to find out—what my play really sounded like to the Chinese, and what in their heart of hearts these actors had made of it. In a word, the old opacity of "China" was once again descending over my vision. I know the audiences laugh in just about the same places as we do in the West, and I have seen many of them weeping for Willy, so maybe my questions don't matter. It is possible that I ought to heed my own advice, given when Chinese would ask in what place the play was happening, since they were not permitted to make up like Westerners: namely, that it all happens in some country of the mind where people with Chinese faces and straight black hair speak and behave as though they were in another civilization. So I will try to console myself with our having met and together created a kind of house, and a family, and a struggle to live, on the plain of imagination where indeed it is possible to share everything we have come to be.